Advance Praise for

Heal the Ocean

In *Heal the Ocean*, ecologist Rod Fujita shares
invaluable knowledge — that of the scientist who serves society
by sitting through endless, sometimes contentious, meetings
to resolve complicated choices between the interests
of the natural system and human needs. That he
shares his well-informed, personal experience in
such a readable book is a gift to us all.

— Jean-Michel Cousteau, President, Ocean Futures Society

Dr. Rod Fujita, one of the nation's foremost leaders
in marine conservation, has shown an exceptional ability to
anticipate and help avert emerging threats to the ocean
environment. *Heal the Ocean*, with its eloquent
outlook on the problems at hand and the remedies that
can make a difference, is a timely reminder that
we need to act now.

— Fred Krupp, President, Environmental Defense

A challenging but hopeful book: serious problems,
plausible approaches to solving them.

— Michael Oppenheimer, Ph.D, Milbank Professor of
Geosciences and International Affairs, Princeton University

Every effort being made to reverse the tide of ocean abuse
is an act of honor for mankind. Books like this are an
important part of this process. At Heal the Ocean™ we hope
that many readers will join the writer of this book,
and us, to take up the good fight to have the Ocean
respected as it should be respected.

— Hillary Hauser, Executive Director, Heal the Ocean

Heal the Ocean is a profound summary of the reasons
we need a new ocean conservation ethic to protect this great
resource for future generations.

— Leon E. Panetta, Chairman, Pew Oceans Commission

Rod Fujita has worked in and around oceans issues for
a long time and he brings a big-picture, level-headed voice.
Heal the Ocean wields the most important weapon we
have for overcoming the world's problems: hope.

— Carl Safina, author of *Eye of the Albatross:
Visions of Hope and Survival.*

A provocative and eloquent plea for the use of "ecolacy" in
addition to literacy and numeracy in forming our policies aimed
at healing the oceans. Fujita's case studies focus on
what has been done and, by extrapolation, what can
be done by citizens and community organizations to build
constituencies for activism in order to restore
one of the planet's greatest assets.

— Dennis J. Aigner, Dean, Donald Bren School of
Environmental Science & Management, University of
California, Santa Barbara

Heal *the* Ocean

SOLUTIONS FOR SAVING OUR SEAS

ROD FUJITA

Forword by Peter Benchley

NEW SOCIETY PUBLISHERS

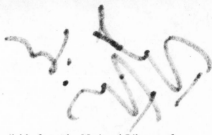

Cataloguing in Publication Data:
A catalog record for this publication is available from the National Library of Canada.

Cover design John Nedwidek. Cover photo: Photodisc.

Printed in Canada.
Second printing April 2005.

New Society Publishers acknowledges the support of the Government of Canada through the Book Publishing Industry Development Program (BPIDP) for our publishing activities.

Paperback ISBN: 0-86571-500-9

Inquiries regarding requests to reprint all or part of *Heal the Ocean* should be addressed to New Society Publishers at the address below.

To order directly from the publishers, please call toll-free (North America) 1-800-567-6772, or order online at www.newsociety.com

Any other inquiries can be directed by mail to:

New Society Publishers
P.O. Box 189, Gabriola Island, BC V0R 1X0, Canada
1-800-567-6772

New Society Publishers' mission is to publish books that contribute in fundamental ways to building an ecologically sustainable and just society, and to do so with the least possible impact on the environment, in a manner that models this vision. We are committed to doing this not just through education, but through action. We are acting on our commitment to the world's remaining ancient forests by phasing out our paper supply from ancient forests worldwide. This book is one step toward ending global deforestation and climate change. It is printed on acid-free paper that is **100% old growth forest-free** (100% post-consumer recycled), processed chlorine free, and printed with vegetable-based, low-VOC inks. For further information, or to browse our full list of books and purchase securely, visit our website at: www.newsociety.com

New Society Publishers   www.newsociety.com

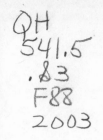
TABLE OF CONTENTS

DEDICATION

To Joyce, with love and gratitude

ACKNOWLEDGMENTS

I am grateful to my wife, Joyce Selkow, for her love and moral support. She read drafts and added her creativity and intelligence to the book. My daughter Eliana's enthusiasm for all sea creatures inspires me and gives me hope. I thank my parents, Kenji and Maruka Fujita, for encouraging me to pursue my passions.

I salute the Pew Fellows in Marine Conservation Program for their support of my efforts to research and write this book, and for creating a true fellowship for people dedicated to saving the ocean. The David and Lucile Packard Foundation has consistently supported my work for years, making possible many of the success stories I recount here. I am grateful to my excellent colleagues at Environmental Defense, especially Richard Charter, Johanna Thomas, Christina Avildsen, and Jenny Chu, all of whom shouldered extra work to make it possible for me to focus on research and writing. It is a pleasure and honor to work closely with brilliant and effective advocates for the ocean at many other organizations, as well. They are the steady upwelling of the ocean conservation movement, fertilizing and supporting it with their ideas and energy. I thank Paul Dayton and his colleagues at the Scripps Institution of Oceanography, and the staff of the Marine Biological Laboratory in Woods Hole for hosting me during two wonderful summers of reading, thinking, and writing. Numerous other individuals and foundations have contributed to my work as well, but more importantly, they have contributed to the ocean conservation movement, and I am deeply grateful to them all. This movement, composed of countless citizens who have been energized and moved to action, is the real hope for the ocean.

PREFACE

I remember the morning so well. I had gone to the beach for my daily swim in the ocean off my favorite Santa Barbara beach, and as I waded out through the surf I was surrounded by oil as well as other gunk. The sight made me stop in my tracks. I was determined to swim anyway, so I parted the gunk with my hands and went under, a quick dip, and then I got out in a hurry.

On this day, over fifteen years ago, I thought, what if this becomes the everyday state of the ocean? How would I feel if I could not go regularly into the sea, because of the persistent, obnoxious pollutants we insist on pouring into it? Into the sea that has so faithfully fed the souls of so many people, provided reefs to explore and waves to ride?

Ten years later, when the beaches started to close from unsafe levels of bacteria, I became angry. Having been a reporter for the Santa Barbara *News-Press* for a number of years in the 1980s, I had covered many subjects about the ocean, and had investigated sewage disposal at sea. Now, with the beaches closed, I started calling everyone — local, regional, and state pollution and health officials scientists, doctors, and surfers. I spoke to people who had experienced health problems as a result of being in the ocean.

What I found out I resulted in a 23-page manuscript that the *News-Press* ran in its entirety as a Sunday editorial.

I was totally unprepared for what happened: radio commentators started to read the editorial in its entirety over the air. People called in to the stations, weeping, and I received many calls at home from people offering me money to *please do something about this terrible situation!* Then there was a public demonstration on the Santa Barbara County administration building.

As a result, Heal the Ocean™ was born. It is a Santa Barbara non-profit organization whose total focus is on wastewater infrastructure — sewage disposal at sea, leaking sewer pipes, improperly placed septic systems.

Six years after our formation, we are glad for progress. Septic systems are being abandoned by beachfront homeowners, sewer pipes are being checked and double-checked, groundwater is being mapped and tested, and the whole practice of using the ocean to dilute human waste is being scrutinized. Changes are being made.

In *Heal the Ocean*, Rod Fujita examines other aspects of improper use of the ocean, together with positive aspects of doing something about such misuse. This book is an important contribution to the list of serious efforts being made to remedy the ocean's ills.

I have thought about the public outcry many times since my editorial appeared in the Santa Barbara *News-Press*, and I have come to believe that ocean pollution hurts humans on a very primitive level. Mankind came from the sea, and our circulatory systems are a complicated version of those belonging to our primitive one-celled ancestors, whose circulatory fluid was seawater. Our air, weather — our very ability to live on Earth — is because of the sea. The Sea is Us, and to defile the Sea is to defile ourselves.

Therefore, every effort being made to reverse the tide of ocean abuse is an act of honor for mankind. Books like this are an important part of this process. At Heal the Ocean™ we hope that many readers will join Rod Fujita, and us, to take up the good fight to have the Ocean respected as it should be respected.

— HILLARY HAUSER, EXECUTIVE DIRECTOR
HEAL THE OCEAN
SANTA BARBARA, CALIFORNIA

FOREWORD

In the thirty years since *Jaws* was published, my perceptions about the sea — and the creatures in it — have changed radically. Back then, I (like most people) still believed that the sea was invulnerable and eternal, capable of recovering from anything we did to it, guaranteed by nature to be an infinite resource and a bottomless dump. How wrong we were. By now, we have come to understand that the sea, which covers more than 70 percent of our planet and makes life on Earth possible, is not invulnerable and is, in fact, very fragile. We can destroy the oceans and the life in them, and if we humans don't change our ways soon — very soon — we will do so.

In *Heal the Ocean*, Rod Fujita offers a lively look at ocean habitats and creatures, with a harrowing description of the dangers posed by things such as pollution and overfishing. But unlike other books on the ocean, Fujita focuses on clever and workable solutions, in the tradition of the organization he has worked for since 1988, Environmental Defense (formerly, the Environmental Defense Fund). I've followed my own urge to understand and protect the ocean by becoming a national spokesman for Environmental Defense because I believe in its mission to find the ways that work.

Though it may seem strange or unlikely that the vast and powerful ocean needs our help in any way, looks can be deceiving. Under that perfectly reflective surface lies all manner of danger — much more to sea life than to humankind. The power balance has changed. While the sea still claims human life (fishing is one of the most dangerous occupations in the world), humans have managed to remove 90 percent of the ocean's large fishes, such as cod, tuna, and swordfish, since the dawn of the industrial age — a mere blink in the life of the ancient ocean. Fujita analyzes the causes of this remarkable impact and provides solutions that are proven to work — if only they were adopted on a far larger scale.

Humans have not only caused the collapse of ocean ecosystems by removing astoundingly large amounts of fish, we may also be altering the very circulation of the ocean by changing the concentration of certain gases, such as carbon dioxide, in the atmosphere. This may sound like fiction, but it's not. Global warming is a fact, and the ocean is already showing symptoms of it — in rising sea levels, melting ice, and colorful coral reefs turning white and dying. Fujita shows ways to slow or stop global warming before it is too late and also warns against efforts in the works to provide a quick fix by dumping excess carbon dioxide into the ocean.

Heal the Ocean is filled with good ideas but is also grounded in the reality that it will take much more than just good ideas to save the ocean. Fujita describes successful efforts to create marine reserves, safe havens in the ocean where fishing and other extractive activities are banned, and shows how the ranks of ocean activists can swell to create the political will needed for meaningful change. Success will require a lot of perspiration and some inspiration as well.

Read *Heal the Ocean*, go to the beach or out on a boat, breathe deeply, and take action.

— Peter Benchley
June 2003

1

TURNING THE TIDE:
An Introduction

The ocean is alive. The waves change shape constantly, mesmerizing us with their infinite variations on a theme. The sound of the surf is soothing background music for contemplation. The vast panorama and the roar of breaking waves inspire awe and expansive thoughts.

Changes in perspective offer glimpses of the ocean's nature. At night, the waves sometimes glow with the light of tiny organisms excited by the surf. I leave bioluminescent swirls behind as I swim through warm water in the darkness. Bouncing along in a boat, I am moved by the sight of a pod of dolphins, or of young humpback whales leaping out of the water. But the ocean hides most of its treasures below its mirrored surface.

Putting on a mask and snorkel can induce a startling revelation. Life is everywhere. Clouds of small silvery fishes part as I approach. Tiny damselfish fiercely chase me away from their carefully tended gardens. Elegant sea fans wave in the surge. With the aid of an air tank, I can take the time to return the inquisitive stares of cuttlefish and swim with graceful eagle rays. I meditate on the sound of my breath and the bubbles I leave, and become aware of a school of big tarpon fish cruising by, their beautiful scales gleaming in the sunlight. I have come to know barracudas as individuals, guarding their territories merely by glaring at me.

The ocean seems too immense, its life too vibrant, to be affected by tiny humans and their industries. But scientific papers and data from around the world offer other perspectives. They show that humans have in fact decimated enormous herds of sea cows, sea otters, and sea turtles. The great oyster beds of the Chesapeake and other estuaries have been reduced to pale, sickly vestiges of their former glory.[1] Mind-boggling numbers of fish have been removed from the ocean and as a result, global fish catches are declining, and several major fisheries have collapsed altogether. Some ocean species are already on the verge of extinction — and we have only just begun to explore the ocean's biological diversity.

Beyond all these losses of a precious natural heritage, we have done even worse by the ocean. No living system can function properly without all of its essential components. This is easy to understand in terms of an individual — but it applies also to whole ecosystems. Sea turtles eat seagrasses, and so killing off the sea turtles has contributed to the decline of seagrass meadows which are the productive rangelands of the ocean. Hunting southern sea otters to near extinction and killing off lobsters and fish has allowed purple sea urchin populations to explode in the absence of their natural predators. The grazing urchins have then reduced majestic forests of kelps up to 100 feet (about 30 meters) tall to rubble — bare rock covered with hordes of urchins. The excessive harvest of oysters over the decades appears to have interfered with the ability of estuaries like the Chesapeake to cleanse themselves — the oysters were once capable of filtering the entire volume of the bay every three days, but no more.[2]

These are not isolated examples. Because everything is connected, most of our actions have indirect and unintended effects. How can driving a car or using electricity affect the ocean? The burning of coal and oil to propel cars and power our society releases carbon dioxide and other gases that have warmed the world significantly over the last century. As the seas heat up in response to global warming, intensely colorful coral reefs are bleaching, turning a deathly white and starving to death. In 1998, coral reefs suffered their most severe bout of bleaching, associated with unusually warm waters. The great systems of ocean life that we depend on, and are part of, are collapsing — silently, below the waves.

Nearly a decade before, some cautioned that reefs would die in just this way if global warming proceeded. Yet few actions were taken to reduce emissions of carbon dioxide and other gases that cause global warming. Almost a hundred years ago — long before recent headlines announcing that "fish stocks are crashing" — people had sounded a warning.[3] Could the collapse of several major fisheries have been prevented with earlier and more powerful intervention? Why do we so often find ourselves dealing with environmental crises instead of preventing problems or resolving them early in their evolution? How can we break this cycle of denial and inertia followed by crisis, and instead, take action early? Why are we not protecting the sea that we love?

Powerful forces are arrayed against ocean conservation. Precautionary behavior in advance of a crisis is difficult to motivate. Factors contributing to inertia include strong vested interests in the status quo (both economic and ideological) and flawed socioeconomic analyses that omit many of the true costs of business. A double standard prevails. Economic activities are allowed to begin and continue, and are even encouraged, despite little understanding of their ecological or health impacts. But extensive evidence is often required before conservation measures can be implemented. Scientific uncertainty about the exact causes of environmental problems is often used as an excuse to justify failure to prevent, reduce, or eliminate threats to the environment. These forces have led to areas devastated by pollution, the dispersion of persistent pollutants throughout the environment, global warming, and many other problems that have degraded all kinds of living systems — including human societies. The same forces have created serious problems in the ocean — one of our

great global commons, the cradle of life, and the engine of ecological processes that sustain the planet.

To break the cycle of denial followed by crisis we need to
examine and correct the thoughts, perceptions, attitudes, and
behavioral patterns that reinforce the status quo. Because the
threats to the ocean result from human activity, the key to
addressing those threats is to understand ourselves and how to
change others. Part of the problem lies in how we think about
technology and the environment. The psychologist George
Howard identified "killer thoughts for a world with limits."
These thoughts include the notions that consumption will produce happiness, that we don't need to worry about the future,
that it's okay for profits from industry to accrue to individuals
while the costs of pollution from industry are borne by communities, that ecological threats are innocent until proven guilty, and
that we can solve environmental problems with technical innovations, including problems created by technology.[4]

To counter these cognitive tendencies, we need a new way of
thinking about ourselves and nature. We need to develop "ecolacy" to complement the essential modern survival skills of literacy
and numeracy. Ecolacy is the eminent ecologist Garret Hardin's
term[5] for the prudent practice of asking "and what then?" of any
technological innovation or economic activity. Ecolacy is part of
the wisdom we need to go along with our enormous power to
alter the planet. It will help us anticipate the effects of new technologies or practices, replacing unquestioning acceptance with a
reasonable weighing of pros and cons, costs and benefits.

To be useful, the analysis of the costs and benefits of any
important decision must reflect reality. Accurate assumptions and
full sets of facts are obviously essential for making a good decision, but are sometimes difficult to come by. Costs such as losses
in fishing revenue or the price of pollution control equipment
can be estimated in terms of dollars. But the less tangible (but no
less important) benefits of passing on a natural legacy, of protecting a beautiful place, or even of keeping the water and air
clean are not as easy to add up. Too often, policy makers rely on

flawed analyses of conservation measures such as pollution control, restrictions on fishing, and habitat protection — analyses that emphasize the costs to industry without properly accounting for the benefits of conservation. This is like thinking about buying a house knowing only the price and all of its problems, but remaining ignorant of the beautiful views, comfortable living space, and excellent garden that it offers. To make prudent decisions and avoid crises, we need improved analyses of the full range of both costs and benefits.

To avoid crisis, we need to think about current trends and the future. Strategic thinking about how scientific, economic, and technological trends may affect the ocean in the future helps us identify threats early. Foreseeing threats may allow us to intervene before large investments of time, energy, money, and ego are made, rendering corrective action more difficult. So, too, will new policies that embody the principles of "do no harm" and precaution. Such policies will reduce the incidence of intractable environmental problems and crises.

But a new way of thinking won't break the cycle of denial and crisis by itself. Even better policies and more comprehensive analyses will not be enough. Behavioral psychology informs us that incentives need to change as well.[6] Institutions and policies aimed at protecting the ocean can thrive only if people get behind them and support them. Consequently, such policies and institutions should provide constant reinforcement and incentives for people. Economic incentives — such as tax breaks for solar power or steep penalties for pollution — can reinforce precautionary behavior and spur technical innovation. Building community around the protection of a special place on land or under the sea can help meet our deep-seated need to relate to one another. At a more profound level, environmental actions can flow from the realization that all of nature is interdependent — ourselves included. Economic incentives, efforts to build community around environmental protection, and a new ocean ethic based on interdependence can reduce the risk of dangerous ecological and economic surprises, as well as inspire acts of healing and restoration.

To create a world in which we not only do no harm but also act to restore nature, we will need to find ways to create a large and active constituency for ocean protection. Conservation efforts at all scales from the local to the global are hampered by a lack of political will. A redoubled effort is needed to spread awareness of the ocean's nature and the serious threats the ocean faces. The Internet and mass media are useful indeed for quickly reaching large numbers of people, but I believe we also need to encourage discourse in community centers, in chambers of commerce, at book clubs, and even in hair salons and the supermarket to generate the sustained activism that will be needed to heal the ocean. As Benjamin Barber argues in his book, *Jihad vs. McWorld*,[7] a re-invigorated civil society full of educated, informed, and empowered citizens is needed to counterbalance big government, a powerful private sector, and special interest groups. Citizens and civic organizations skilled in ecolacy can help direct economic activity and the use of technology to serve the public good, promoting a range of interests and values including ocean conservation.

In this book, I will provide an overview of the nature of ocean environments, briefly describing some aspects of the natural history of the coastal zone, nearshore waters, coral reefs, the continental shelf, the open ocean, and the deep sea. I will go out on a limb and make predictions about what some of the next big ocean conservation issues might be, then lay out potential ways to address these issues early on. I will describe effective techniques for building constituencies for ocean conservation and relate success stories to inspire effective activism to protect the ocean and help create a new ocean ethic.

This book is not intended to be all-inclusive. The focus is on issues that I have been working on over the past 25 years, including climate change, ecological restoration, fisheries, and pollution. The predictions of emerging issues are based on my understanding of current trends and likely developments. I hope they are proved wrong, and that this book will have helped to turn adverse trends around in order to heal the ocean.

2

THE COASTAL ZONE:
From the Mountains to
the Sea

The Nature of the San Francisco
Bay-delta-river System

Everything ends up in the ocean eventually. Snow falling on the high peaks of the Sierra Nevada mountains in California melts in the spring, resulting in surging streams and swollen rivers rushing to the delta and estuary, where fresh water mixes with ocean water moving inland. The plume of water enriched by forests, grasslands, floodplains, and wetlands sometimes extends 20 miles or more offshore, strongly influencing the nature of coastal waters and their inhabitants. Protecting the ocean's headwaters in coastal mountains and rivers will be essential for healing the ocean.

I was raised in California, and have spent many happy days hiking along the sunny banks and swimming in the cold pools of high mountain streams that rushed down to meet the Sacramento River. I knew that the Sacramento River dominates the northern half of the great Central Valley of California and meets up with the San Joaquin River to form the delta, eventually spilling into San Francisco Bay and out under the Golden Gate Bridge. But I only began to really appreciate the true aspirations of the Sacramento River while flying over it after the flood of 1997.

Soon after the rains had stopped, I boarded a light plane, joining a small group of scientists led by the irrepressible Phil Williams. For years, Phil and his merry crew of avant-garde engineers and hydrologists have been educating environmentalists, scientists, policy makers, and anyone else who will listen about the virtues of something they call "physis" — restoring the natural processes that created and maintained rivers so as to allow them to heal themselves — after the Greek word for natural self-healing. Our goal on this day in 1997 was to inspect the flood damage and to try to glean some lessons about restoring rivers.

Flying over the swollen river, we could see clearly how it was re-claiming its curves, meandering over the landscape in a pattern modulated by the terrain and the flow of water. The flooded river washed right over the levees and dams that confine it in a strait-jacket most of the time. We could see the old oxbows carved by the river — curves that had folded back on themselves, waiting for water to bring life once again. It was a beautiful and awful sight — the great floodplains covered once again by water and whole towns cowering behind lines of sand bags that seemed pathetically inadequate against the mighty river.

I could easily picture the endless tule marshes abounding with huge herds of elk described by early naturalists, and the sinuous curves of the river lined with great cottonwood trees and other vegetation alive with an enormous variety of animals. Tangled roots and fallen trees created a wealth of habitats, including riffles, small pools, and quiet eddies where young salmon could safely spend the winter. In these refuges, the salmon could fatten up for the long drift to the estuary, where they would undergo their amazing transformation from freshwater fish to long-distance ocean wanderers.

In one of his many entertaining lectures, Phil compared the seasonal flood cycle of a river to the beat of a human heart. In seeking our "manifest destiny," we strove to reduce the strength and variation of the river's heartbeat to meet our needs, and in so doing, reduced it to a machine needing our constant intervention to keep running. We humans seem generally to favor stability over variability, monocultures over diverse crops growing together, straight and predictable rivers over wild and uncontrolled rivers. Only now are we realizing that variation is the living heart of natural ecosystems that keeps the ecological goods and services flowing. Reducing that variation to maximize economic efficiency and otherwise serve our short-term needs is like caging a wild animal and wondering why it becomes listless and unhealthy.

The Perilous Journey of Salmon

While nature tends to operate in cycles (like the water cycle and the cycling of nutrients in the soil through plants and animals and back to the soil), our preoccupation with taming nature and accumulating wealth has led us to create one-way processes. We convert natural resources into products that are sold for money and dump wastes into the environmental commons. Profits accrue to individuals; costs in the form of pollution and environmental degradation are borne by society and living ecosystems. Only now are we fully appreciating the consequences of this logic, which failed to ask "and what then?" often enough and persistently enough. That's the problem with logic — it seems beautiful and effective until something happens that you haven't anticipated. Another beautiful theory slain by an ugly fact, as the saying goes among scientists. Most technological innovations bring benefits and transfer wealth from nature to society — and also result in adverse impacts to both nature and society, some anticipated, some not.

The imperative to tame nature arose out of a need for self-preservation on a wild and dangerous frontier, but the need for survival turned into the need for wealth, and our withdrawals from nature were not balanced by sufficient deposits. We constructed dams to protect croplands from floods, allowing farms and orchards to spread throughout the fertile bottomlands and delta of the Sacramento River. We built levees to keep the river out of towns and farms. We reduced flows in the winter and spring (when they would naturally be high) to prevent floods, and increased them in the summer (when flows would naturally be low) to irrigate thirsty crops like rice and cotton.

Of course, the ecosystems and ecological processes that had become attuned to the natural cycles and variation that had driven evolution in the region had a hard time adapting to this topsy-turvy world. The enormous runs of salmon that had sustained First Nations both spiritually and physically, and which had also supported valuable commercial and sport fisheries, declined rapidly. The high elevation watersheds where salmon once spawned have probably declined in productivity, too. Recent studies have shown that salmon bring large amounts of energy and nutrients collected during several years at sea to these watersheds — after spawning, their decomposing carcasses nourish their own young and many other creatures. Dams eventually severed the connections between the mountains and the mainstem rivers, cutting off more than 90 percent of salmon spawning grounds and completely altering the flows to which salmon had become exquisitely adapted. These dams and levees stopped the two-way, pulsating flow of organisms, nutrients, water, and sediments that forms the very physical and biological heart of the ecosystem.

Especially hard hit were the winter run and spring run chinook (or king) salmon. The winter run chinook lived in the cold, clear mountain streams above where Shasta Dam now sits, thriving in cool spring water percolating up through rocks fractured by ancient volcanoes. Shasta Dam blocked the winter run from nearly all of its spawning habitat — this was one boulder that even the fittest salmon could not jump. The population was put on life-support, and hung on in a controlled flow of cold water from the dam and in captive breeding programs. The winter run not only had to deal with the loss of almost all of its natural spawning habitat, it had to run a gauntlet that included the ocean fishery (where it mixed with the abundant hatchery-raised fall run chinook, getting hooked occasionally by accident) and various man-made obstacles on its long journey home from the sea to spawn.

A salmon has a tough life even without our intervention — drifting down into the estuary, transforming into a saltwater fish, and then having to swim upstream over long distances. Salmon have had to survive periods of poor ocean productivity, drought, fires, floods, and even earthquakes and volcanic explosions. Perhaps that is why there are so many different kinds of salmon — there were four distinct salmon runs in the Sacramento and San Joaquin river systems alone. A diverse portfolio is a good hedge against risk. When we made its life harder still by blocking its way with dams and sucking up young fish in our pumps, it is little wonder that the winter run population declined steadily. In 1995, only 189 individual winter run chinook returned to the base of Shasta Dam to spawn. If this last cohort (a group of fish born in the same year) had not survived, that might well have been the end of the winter run's long evolutionary history.

The spring run chinook is one of the endurance champions of the animal world, leaping over boulders and swimming powerfully up streams to spawn at very high elevations. The dams cut off much of its habitat, and so like the winter run, it has also been listed under the Endangered Species Act. The fall run chinook has been able to continue spawning below the dams, helped along by hatcheries, so much so that enormous runs of hatchery-raised salmon now sustain the fishery.

While the maintenance of the salmon fishery is a noble goal, I think hatcheries are a poor substitute for natural streams and watersheds, the loss of which they are intended to mitigate. Hatcheries cost a lot to build, maintain, and operate; one wonders whether the economic returns from the fishery justify these costs. Although there is a lot to be said for the non-market values of keeping salmon fishermen in business and for keeping salmon anglers happy, the ecological impacts of hatcheries are also of concern. Aggressive hatchery-raised fish stray into natural spawning areas, where they have been likened to a motorcycle gang invading a tea party, interrupting the timeless and elegant mating rituals of the native fish with their thrashing about. If successful in spawning, the genes of hatchery fish could harm the genetic makeup of wild salmon. Millions of hatchery fish may compete with wild fish for food in the rivers, estuary, and ocean. Although wild fish are probably more competent predators, and may be better able to avoid predators themselves, the sheer number of hatchery fish may give them the upper hand. There is also evidence that they spread disease to wild fish.

The flawed logic of taming nature resulted in a huge agro-economy that greatly enriched California and the nation as a whole with food, money, and the farm culture. But it also brought on endangered salmon, the decline of the salmon fishery, the loss of bird populations that once "darkened the skies," and ironically, the loss of some of the farmland that all of this engineering made possible. The fertile peat soils of the delta, "reclaimed" from the tule marsh with extensive levees and pumps, is rapidly disappearing into thin air. The delicate peat soils oxidize when exposed to air, so that now the farms are far below sea level, with the tides held back by fragile levees.

A Second Chance for Salmon

Careful analysis of the full range of costs and benefits associated with dams will no doubt show that many of the thousands of dams scattered throughout the country are not worth the trouble. Dams need to be maintained, and have limited lifetimes. Silt builds up behind them, reducing space in the reservoirs. Multiple water diversions (pipes and pumps for moving water from rivers into canals or irrigation ditches) can be integrated into fewer pipes and pumps, necessitating fewer diversion dams. The restorative effects of removing dams and levees, if done correctly, can seem almost miraculous — every monkey-wrencher's dream. Released from the grip of these structures, natural processes (such as flooding and the movement of sediment) take over once again. Life responds rapidly. Vegetation starts to colonize and stabilize the river bank and soon fish begin to hide, rest, and feed among the roots and pieces of wood that have fallen into the stream. Aquatic insects chop up the fallen leaves, launching an invisible food web of small invertebrates and bacteria. A diverse community of animals comes to the new riparian forest, to enjoy the cool temperatures, shelter, and food there. Ranchers whose grandparents had never seen trees along their creeks and who had become accustomed to losing ground every year to erosion marvel at how rapidly everything changes when the levees come down and the cows are kept out of the streams.

Most of the dams were constructed to control floods and store water. Remarkably, about half of all the water flowing down from California watersheds into the delta of the Sacramento and San Joaquin rivers is diverted for farm and urban use.[1] On a monthly average basis, these diversions have reached as high as 90 percent during spring months — a critical time for young salmon migrating toward the sea, when they need the extra push from high flows to help them along their journey. New economic incentives for water conservation, combined with markets and money to keep more water in rivers, will be needed. Right now, farmers get water cheap, heavily subsidized by tax dollars spent to create and maintain the vast infrastructure of dams, levees, pumps, and canals that supply the irrigation districts. The water users of the Central Valley Project, for example, have, over 50 years, repaid only about five percent of the project's capital cost — and continue to receive water at a fraction of its market value.[2] Today, the guiding policy for water in the arid west is still "use it or lose it" — a policy more appropriate for taming the wilderness than for living sustainably with nature. Clearly, water policy must change to "use it efficiently and profit from saving water."

CALFED, a partnership of federal and California state government agencies, has launched an Environmental Water Account which buys water from willing sellers and banks or stores it for release when fish and wildlife need it most, or to compensate water users for water released at critical times. The account is intended to increase the agencies' ability to respond quickly to changes in the distribution or migration patterns of fish and wildlife. To date, these water acquisitions have been short-term, though CALFED hopes to secure long-term supplies of water for streams, rivers, and wetlands through its Environmental Water Program. Interest is growing among nongovernmental organizations (NGOs) such as Environmental Defense in the creation of a substantial water trust which could acquire water for tributaries in need, complementing the land trusts that have protected so much valuable wild land.

The Return of Physis

After reviewing the scientific literature on ecological restoration, I concluded that Phil Williams' concept of physis, or allowing nature to heal itself, made more sense than trying to engineer our way out of the problems that were created by engineering the river to suit our purposes. After innumerable lectures, seminars, workshops, field trips, meetings, and airplane rides, the followers of physis have largely succeeded in transforming the paradigm guiding one of the largest and most expensive ecological restoration efforts in the world. The focus of these efforts has changed from a search for engineering solutions to protect individual endangered species to the restoration of natural processes that will protect whole communities of species, including the ones that we know nothing about at present.

Constant pressure from Environmental Defense, the Bay Institute, progressive fishing groups, and others helped to influence how state and federal funds were spent. For example, dams have been removed from Butte Creek (a major tributary of the Sacramento), greatly increasing flows and the return of salmon. To be sure, there will still be plenty of engineering required to allow the continued extraction of water from the system — the Sacramento and San Joaquin Rivers supply most of the water for California's huge agricultural economy and for a considerable number of urban and suburban dwellers as well. But the intention of most of this new engineering is to reduce the ecological impact of diverting water with sophisticated screens that keep fish out of pumps, new techniques to accelerate the filling in of highly subsided farmland in the delta, biological pest control, and many other techniques. We can only hope that the natural processes that created the rivers, delta, and estuary remain sufficiently intact that — once we back off — they can sustain themselves, drawing on the remaining wildlands and natural stretches for seeds, animals, sediments, and nutrients.

One can still get a glimpse of the past along the Cosumnes River, one of the last rivers in California without a large dam on it. Big, graceful trees lean over the shady river, whose waters swirl in complex patterns around roots and old logs. Land trusts, with the support of CALFED and private foundations, have acquired large tracts of land adjacent to the river and are bulldozing some of the levees to allow the river to return to its meandering ways. Cottonwoods and oaks are being planted to accelerate the restoration of the verdant riparian forest (forests that border rivers) that is key to maintaining biodiversity in this region. CALFED, land trusts, and other agencies are acquiring more lands near rivers, moving people out of harm's way and letting the rivers flood naturally, so that the riparian forests can restore themselves (though often requiring some help). Allowing the rivers to flood will also allow the floodbasins and floodplains to function once again as sources of nutrients and feeding grounds for young fish. State and federal agencies have even bought some of the delta islands which have subsided farmland within their boundaries, in an attempt to restore them to the shallow-water habitats and marshland that once nurtured a vast array of birds and native fishes, including the endangered delta smelt.

Meanwhile, environmental groups like Environmental Defense, The Bay Institute, and the Natural Resources Defense Council helped create the governance structure and accountability mechanisms that will manage this grand experiment in restoration (or more accurately, rehabilitation). These non-governmental organizations monitor the complex operations of the maze of canals, sluice gates, and pumps that suck water out of the rivers and delta and transfer it to farmland and urban areas, trying to ensure that not too many fish are killed in the process. They are also constantly pushing for increased water efficiency, above-the-board accounting for water and money, and the use of more water to support natural ecosystems. The NGOs are inventing new ways to protect wildlands and wildlife, such as the safe-harbor agreements pioneered by Environmental Defense, in which landowners actually create habitat for endangered species on their land (instead of actively trying to exterminate them for fear of inflexible regulations) in exchange for the peace of mind that one gets from knowing that the government isn't going to require you to do anything else. Environmental groups are also trying to get the federal government to purchase water to put back into the environment, because fish need water more than anything else.

In general, more water means more fish in the tributaries, main-stem rivers, delta, San Francisco Bay, and beyond. The winter run chinook survived its close brush with extinction in 1995 due to a fortuitous combination of rainfall, sophisticated fish screens on pumps, intricate pump and dam operations, and careful fishery management, with environmental and fishing groups holding resource management agencies accountable for their actions. The winter run population is growing, and in recent years an average of 1,800 fish per year have returned from the ocean to spawn, up from only 189 in 1995. The winter run is still in a fairly precarious situation, though: in 2000, only 1,312 fish made their way up the river.

In keeping with physis, a bold plan to remove several dams in the beautiful canyon of Battle Creek (a tributary to the Sacramento River) got a boost in the form of a grant from CALFED. The David and Lucile Packard Foundation kicked in money for adaptive management — the wise practice of learning through action and changing course if necessary. The removal of the dams is expected to open up some 40 miles of prime salmon and steelhead habitat, suitable for the winter run because it is fed by cool springs at a constant temperature. To bring the spring run back, small dams are being removed, more diversion pumps are being screened to keep fish out of them, fisheries are being controlled, and many other measures are being taken.

Even the wetlands are making a comeback, after almost all had been dredged and filled to make way for industrial parks, highways, and airports. Government officials recently announced the purchase of evaporating ponds in the south end of San Francisco Bay (where the Cargill Corporation used to make salt) in order to turn them back into wetlands — for a price of $100 million, plus about $35 million for planning, management, and permitting.[3] The successful restoration of wetlands can be difficult, but the deal illustrates the value that we now place on wetlands, and shows that we recognize how important they are to the proper functioning of the whole system and to our own aesthetic sense.

Nature Restored

Snow melting in the high peaks of the Sierra Nevada rushes down steep mountain slopes in the spring, forming clear, cold streams. The water moves sediment — ranging from pebbles to boulders, depending on the flow — depositing them wherever the water slows down. Gravel beds, perfect for salmon spawning, are laid down. As the fast-flowing streams cut through the softer sediments of the foothills, the water picks up finer sediments that can stay suspended. Native fishes and young salmon shelter in the quiet eddies that form behind large logs that have fallen into the water, and amongst the roots and niches of a living river bank. The water becomes murkier and richer as the tributaries join the slowly meandering mainstem rivers, the Sacramento and the San Joaquin. Sediments are deposited in the shallow waters of the delta where vast tule marshes lay down peat in their race to keep up with the rising sea. Ocean water mingles with the river water, creating a rich and turbulent zone that moves back and forth with the tide and depending on how much fresh water the rivers deliver. Young fish and invertebrates move into the sinuous channels of the wetlands that embrace the estuary, hiding from predators and feeding on the rich wetland food web. Juvenile salmon transform themselves into sleek ocean-going fish and wander the ocean for three or four years before returning to the mountain streams of their birth, to spawn the next generation and to nourish their young and the streams with nutrients gained during their years at sea, to complete the cycle. This is physis.

Sewage in the Sea

The beauty of the coastal zone draws people of all kinds in great numbers. As of 1998, more than half the U.S. population was crowded into just 17 percent of the land area in the lower 48 states that constitutes the coastal counties.[4] Rapid urbanization and suburbanization have claimed wetlands, wildlands, and increasingly, even farmland. The waste products of all these people include both point and nonpoint source pollution. Point source pollution flows from easily identifiable pipes or smokestacks that can be readily regulated. Nonpoint source pollution is just a shorthand term for the miscellaneous pollutants that run off streets, parking lots, lawns, and farms into rivers, estuaries, and coastal waters.

Since the 1970s, great progress has been made toward cleaning up point source pollution. But remarkably, the U.S. Environmental Protection Agency granted an exemption to Orange County in affluent Southern California allowing them to release partially treated sewage into the ocean — some 240 million gallons (1.1 billion liters) per day. Millions of dollars worth of studies into the impact of this torrent of sewage proved inconclusive; one study suggested that the sewage was not moving back to shore, while others contradicted this. The search for the cause of contaminated ocean waters and beach closures in Huntington Beach was complicated by the fact that this stretch of ocean also receives a considerable amount of suburban runoff. While this runoff almost certainly contributes to the fouling of coastal waters, all that sewage cannot be a good thing. The closure of beaches — once famous for surfing, sun-bathing, and the whole California beach culture — due to contamination with human waste has served as a wake-up call, at least for those who were still in denial. Recently, years of fierce debate and strong activism by local environmentalists culminated in a narrow vote by the county commission to accept responsibility for treating all of the county's sewage.

Diffuse Pollution

The federal Clean Water Act (and lots of successful activism and lawsuits) has dramatically reduced industrial discharges and the amount of raw sewage entering rivers, estuaries, and the ocean. But nonpoint source pollution remains a large problem.

We know how to reduce nonpoint source pollution, the largest threat to water quality in the United States. But we need policies that encourage people and institutions to implement tried and true methods, and to invent even more effective solutions that are tailored to specific situations. There is no "one size fits all" solution. Farmers and industrialists often resist attempts to force them to comply with "best management practices" (BMPs) designed to reduce pollution by scientists and bureaucrats who live and work far away. These BMPs don't always work in every situation, and furthermore, some plants or farms within a particular watershed may have very cost-effective means to reduce their pollution, while others may find it very costly to reduce pollution even by a relatively small amount.

In these cases, it may make more sense for the government to set an enforceable cap on total pollution coming into the river from the whole watershed and to let people and markets determine the best ways to meet that cap. The cap can shrink over time if the goal is to reduce pollution. Citizen monitoring groups working with agency scientists can trace pollution to their sources using sophisticated tools such as maps coupled with computer models of the flow of ground and surface water. Using this information, agencies can require each source to cut a certain amount of pollution — and then allow people to cut deals with one another to reduce costs, while meeting the overall goal of pollution reduction. Policies like this are "hard on the goals" (stringent, no-compromise performance standards) but "soft on the people" (allowing flexible responses to the challenge of meeting the standards).

Conventional wisdom has held that nonpoint source pollution from farms is an intractable problem. Most agricultural pollution is exempt from direct regulation under the Clean Water Act.[5] Moreover, the prospect of requiring thousands of independent farms to reduce their pollution proved daunting because it was thought that costs would be high, that farmers would not comply with onerous requirements, that compliance (or lack thereof) would be difficult to monitor, and that there were simply too many farms to regulate individually. As a result, farmers have generally been asked to voluntarily use BMPs. Agricultural pollution has emerged as the leading cause of water pollution in the U.S.

The conventional wisdom was challenged and overcome in California's San Joaquin River Valley. Nonpoint source pollution from farms in the valley had drawn particular scrutiny, in part because the build up of selenium in Kesterson Reservoir killed and deformed baby birds in the 1980s. Federal and state agencies had been frustrated in their attempts to reduce selenium discharges from farms — after eight years of voluntary efforts, pollution had not diminished. While farmers were willing to adopt the BMPs, they were concerned about the high costs that might be associated with meeting the water quality standards which environmentalists were insisting upon. These concerns were stalling progress. Despite general skepticism at the time, Environmental Defense scientist Terry Young and her colleagues proposed in 1994 that the agencies set a cap (known as a performance standard) on the amount of selenium that could enter waterways, and then allow farmers to choose different ways to reduce selenium runoff, tailored to their individual farms. Agencies would monitor compliance with the overall cap, with little discretion to alter the cap or allow large violations. If the cap were to be exceeded, all discharges would be banned, effectively putting an end to farming. After tough negotiations, the farmers agreed to this approach. In addition to choosing a variety of methods to reduce selenium runoff (discharge), the farmers also chose to create a program that would allow them to trade discharge permits. If farmer Jones could reduce selenium discharge at less cost than farmer Greenjeans, Greenjeans could purchase a credit for reduced selenium discharge from Jones instead of reducing selenium on his or her own. So, discharges from individual farms could vary, as long as total discharges of selenium did not exceed the cap. The program (known locally as the Grassland Bypass Project) also included tiered water pricing to encourage farmers to use less water (a worthy end in itself), which would in turn result in less selenium discharge. Farmers and irrigation districts started to focus intensively on reducing pollution. By the fourth year of the program, the farmers had reduced total selenium loadings 23 percent below the allowable total, with some indication that total costs have been reduced at some irrigation districts. According to the Environmental Protection Agency, "Selenium loads in 1999 and 2000 were the lowest ever discharged from the drainage in the past 15 years."[6] The program also increased water use efficiency and probably reduced nutrient and pesticide pollution. Administration and enforcement of the program has been relatively easy, because only one permit was issued, and only one location has to be monitored.[7]

The Future of the Coast

Despite the unraveling of the landscape-seascape that defines the integrated coastal zone, people still flock to it. Perhaps our standards are declining, and so we are still attracted. People who don't realize what the Central Valley, the Sacramento River, or San Francisco Bay looked like before they were drastically modified by humans can't understand what has been lost. The same is true for most other coastal zones. The coastal zone retains its allure because of our collective forgetting of better times.

The accelerating settlement of people near the coast will put still more pressure on natural ecosystems. Fragmentation of wildlife habitat and the severing of vital ecological processes will continue in the absence of truly smart development (as opposed to just growth). These additional people will need more water, more food, more energy, and more infrastructure.

At the same time as more people are moving in, the coastal zone will likely shift in many areas, due to a faster-rising sea responding to global warming. Intertidal wetlands that thrive on the natural tidal cycle of submersion and emersion will probably be permanently flooded in some cases, such as in the Chesapeake. Louisiana has been losing between 24 and 40 square miles (62 to 104 square kilometers) of coastal land each year for the last four decades.[8] Sea level will likely rise by about 19 inches (48 centimeters) by 2100,[9] accelerating the loss of wetlands that can't keep up or that are blocked from migrating upland by roads and other infrastructure. The distribution of the sandy beaches that draw millions of tourists and residents each summer will change, despite our frantic efforts to "renourish" them with dredged sand. El Niños may persist longer and arrive more frequently, bringing with them large storm waves and warm, less-productive, ocean waters that kill off kelp beds and young fish.

Comprehensive land use planning, perhaps at the state level, will help us revitalize cities and reduce sprawl with all of its negative effects on quality of life. Planning will have to take on a new dimension, too — that of planning for climate change. The planet is locked into some amount of global warming, no matter how much we manage to reduce emissions of carbon dioxide and other greenhouse gases. Carbon dioxide emitted from cars, trucks, power plants, and factories persists in the atmosphere for decades. Moreover, the ocean has been storing the extra heat trapped by the blanket of gases we've put into the atmosphere since the dawn of the Industrial Revolution, and will slowly release it over time. Planning for climate change might take the shape of creating corridors to allow for wetlands to migrate upland without highways or other infrastructure blocking their way, and of encouraging people to move away from the coastline and floodways.

Connections

The coastal zones of the United States are threatened by increasing pollution, the massive diversion of water in some cases, and the fragmentation and loss of valuable habitats like floodplains and wetlands. However, decades of education, advocacy, and litigation have paid off. Society now puts a much higher value on free-flowing rivers, expansive wetlands, and rich estuaries, as indicated by enormously expensive ecological restoration programs in the Florida Everglades, the San Francisco Bay delta, and elsewhere. The connections between mountains, rivers, estuaries, and nearshore waters are more widely understood and appreciated. People will protect what they love, and can love what they understand, as the old wisdom goes. Perhaps soon we will understand that we too are part of the matrix of the coastal zone and the sea, individual waves on the ocean of being.

3

NEARSHORE WATERS: Nursery, Playground — and Dumping Ground

Beyond the estuaries, where the water is saltier, the nearshore waters begin. Also known as coastal waters, the nearshore is perhaps the most familiar part of the ocean. It is the nearshore that we gaze upon when walking on the beach. It is in the nearshore that we surf, swim, and most often fish. It all starts with the intertidal zone, that stretch of beach or mud or rocky plateau that is awash at high tide but exposed at low tide.

The Nature of West Coast Nearshore Waters

Physics seems to rule the turbulent intertidal at first glance. It certainly ruled my life as a researcher on the Oregon coast. I had to learn to bolt my field experiments down, if I was ever going to collect any meaningful data. I often felt like a beleaguered barnacle, trying to sample the sea from the beach at Yaquina Head, struggling to stay dry and intact through many a 24-hour tidal cycle.

Seaweeds sway with the surging waves, and barnacles, mussels, and limpets all hunker down against the physical forces that would sweep them away. But closer examination reveals fierce biological competition that determines to a large extent who lives where and in what numbers. Starfish and whelks roam the subtidal zone, causing mussels and other prey to grow higher up on the rocks. Different clones of anemones fight an invisible battle for turf. The brown seaweeds manufacture noxious chemicals to ward off herbivores. The red seaweeds and kelps soak up pulses of nutrients and hoard them, growing slowly but surviving the droughts between upwellings of nutrient-rich water from the depths. Green seaweeds grow rapidly and dominate during good times, only to die back in poorer times. Many different kinds of strategies have evolved for surviving and thriving in the intertidal zone.

Off the California coast, deep waters — rich in nutrients from the decomposing bodies of fish and plankton — rise into the sun-lit surface waters to fuel the fastest growing forest in the world: the kelp forest. Growing up to a foot (30 centimeters) each day, these giant seaweeds form a thick canopy where sea otters rest and play.

Once, rich populations of fish and shellfish sheltered underneath this forest canopy, in calm waters where turbulence was dampened by the thick stipes of the kelp. Sunbeams poured through the luxuriant vegetation, spotlighting sea otters and harbor seals darting among the kelps in search of abalone, urchins, fish, and clams. Enormous sea bass roamed these waters, along with boldly colored sheephead, elegant kelp bass, and scores of other species. Many of these species stayed put in the kelp forest, or on their home rock piles or reefs, at least while they were adults. The young may have wandered, but once it was time to settle down and have babies, rockfish, urchins, abalones, and many other inhabitants of both nearshore and offshore waters didn't stray far from home. Rocky reefs abounded with lively communities of rockfish, resplendent with spines.

The West Coast of North America is still the world center of rockfish biodiversity, and supports over 50 species of rockfish, along with many other species of bottom-dwelling fish such as sole, flatfish, halibut, and black cod (sablefish) — collectively called groundfish — but many of these species have declined in recent years. The young of rockfish species grow up in shallow water, then move to the rocky banks offshore where they settle down, some for a very long time indeed. Some rockfish species are thought to live up to 140 years, growing more fecund (capable of making more eggs each year) as they age. These characteristics may be adaptations to the unpredictable environment in which they live. The upwellings of rich water are sporadic, varying from year to year. Every few years, the eastern tropical Pacific Ocean warms up and affects weather around the world with the arrival of an El Niño event. Moreover, there is some evidence to suggest that the whole southern part of the Pacific Ocean flip-flops from cold and rich to warm and poor on a thirty-year (or so) cycle. The rockfish seem to be able to cope and even thrive in the face of this variability by living a long, long time, making lots of babies so that sufficient offspring will survive one year or another to sustain the species. So why have rockfish species declined?

Unsustainable Yield

Like the Cosumnes River Valley (described in Chapter 2), the Anacapa Natural Area off California's gorgeous Channel Islands offers a glimpse into the past glory of California's nearshore waters. The kelp forest has persisted in this tiny marine reserve (where no fishing has been allowed since 1978), while dying back in many other areas. Large sheephead fish cruise around, looking for sea urchins to eat. Dense populations of spiny lobsters hide warily within the caves and fissures of the rocky bottom. Kelp bass are abundant higher up in the water column.

Outside the reserve, things look remarkably different. Vast areas that once harbored rich kelp beds are now barren, save for large populations of purple sea urchins. Many of these urchins are sick and starving, having overgrazed the forest. The sheephead and lobsters have been depleted, releasing the sea urchin population from the checks and balances provided by its predators and allowing the purple urchin population to explode, at least while the kelp held out. Once the kelp disappeared, much of the other life in the area disappeared, too. Lobster populations are only about 1/6 as dense as they are in the Anacapa marine reserve, and large red sea urchins are far scarcer as well. Unlike the purple sea urchins, huge numbers of large red sea urchins were collected for the Japanese sushi market. Sheephead, favorite targets of sportfishermen, are very hard to find outside the marine reserve (their populations are more than ten times more dense there than in similar habitats exposed to fishing). While the white sea bass are recovering with the help of a hatchery, and large black sea bass can still be seen on occasion, today's populations of these fish are shadows of what they once were.

Usually, many factors interact to cause an environmental problem. According to the ancient Greeks, the rare ability to hold two conflicting ideas in our head at the same time is a major sign of intelligence. But we seem to have a hard time doing so, preferring to create dichotomies and to polarize issues. So there is a fierce debate going on about what caused the decline of the kelp forests and fish populations. Was it overfishing or was it natural variation in ocean productivity or was it pollution? The answer is all of the above.

Ocean productivity has been fairly poor since the early 1970s off the California coast. Counts of zooplankton (small animals drifting or swimming weakly in the water) in these waters declined by 80 percent between 1951 and 1993, perhaps due to global warming — water temperature rose 2.7° F (1.5° C) in some places during the same period.[1] Zooplankton are critical links in ocean food webs — the staple food of a wide range of species from sardines to whales. On top of that, El Niños that warm the surface and reduce the essential upwellings of deep water seem to be coming around more frequently and persisting longer than they used to. Some kinds of pollution dumped into the ocean are still there, decades later, while new pollution from burgeoning coastal populations adds to the burden.

It would not be surprising if ocean life declined under these circumstances, even if there was no fishing at all. Yet, lower ocean productivity and pollution would be expected to affect most if not all species everywhere in the region. Why then are populations of favorite sport and commercial species still abundant in the few tiny fully-protected marine reserves that exist (constituting only about five percent of California's waters) but depleted on the fishing grounds? Moreover, many of the species that are now depleted and seldom seen were fairly abundant just prior to the onset of the "live fish" fishery in the 1990s. Demand for dinner-plate-sized rockfish delivered live to restaurants and markets swelled, and fishermen rushed to meet it. As is the case for most new fisheries, catches rose rapidly with little management. It seems clear that fishing has been the most powerful influence on the decline of many exploited species. Moreover, fishing has probably contributed to the decline of many other species that are killed accidentally by fishermen. It seems likely that fishing has triggered some chain reactions, known as ecological cascades, affecting the kelp forest and other species as well.

Recent improvements in fishery management bode well for the future, but only if the key factor that underlies most of our fishery problems is addressed — that of overcapitalization: too many boats are chasing too few fish. Fishery managers have put into place all kinds of well-intended conservation measures, but most of the economic incentives point straight at overexploitation. The deeply-rooted sense that the ocean is the last frontier here on earth still dominates the minds of many fishermen and policy makers, even though the tragedy of the commons has obviously set in. When anyone can enter a fishery at any time, an arms race tends to ensue, with ingenious fishermen using their knowledge of the sea and sophisticated, powerful fishing technology to compete with each other. Even the most conservation-minded fishermen knows that if he or she leaves fish in the water to spawn next year's catch, or the next generation's fishery, some other fishermen will simply scoop them up and sell them tomorrow. This is the tragedy of the commons. In an open access fishery, fish only have value when they are dead and filleted.

In the 1970s, the federal government started to encourage American fishermen to buy and build boats. The idea was to "Americanize" the Exclusive Economic Zone — an area extending out from the shore 200 miles (322 kilometers) which had been dominated by enormous fishing vessels from Russia, Japan, and other countries. American fishermen responded to the call, and built up huge fleets that could easily overpower most fish populations. Most fishery managers and scientists assumed that the enormous populations of fish and shellfish found in nearshore and continental shelf waters at the time meant that these populations were very productive, and therefore allowed huge catches. Unfortunately, this assumption proved to be very wrong.

The story of the white abalone is particularly poignant. This succulent mollusk was once very abundant in Southern California waters, living in waters deeper than about 80 feet (24 meters). The dominant theory at the time was that these big populations of abalone that produced millions upon millions of eggs must be highly productive, and so could support large yields sustainably. The fishery began and continued in earnest until the abalones were depleted in the 1970s, and the fishery collapsed. Next, red abalones were depleted, along with greens, and pinks and blacks, finally resulting in a ban on all commercial abalone catch in California waters in 1997. Disease and the loss of kelp beds surely played a role in the decline of the California abalones, but we know now that individuals of many abalone species (including the white abalone) need to be within about a yard (meter) of each other to breed successfully. Perhaps we could have harvested patches of abalone, leaving other patches for reproduction. But instead, managers allowed access to all of the abalone and fishermen thinned the population out, reducing densities from 1,000 to 5,000 white abalones per acre (2,000 to 12,000 per hectare) in the early 1970s to fewer than one per acre (2.5 per hectare) in the 1990s. White abalone can hardly be found anymore, even during extensive search and rescue missions by scientists in submersibles.

The few remaining individuals are either in captive breeding programs, or growing old alone in the dark, cold water, without any prospects for reproduction and nearing the end of their life spans. The National Marine Fisheries Service declared the white abalone an endangered species in 2001, the first marine invertebrate to achieve this dubious distinction.

Nearshore rockfish, sheephead, and other delicious and slow-moving species are suffering a similar fate. Until recently, very little was known about the habits and life history of these fishes, but large catches were allowed anyway. The live fish fishery (which brings fish live to tanks in restaurants) was allowed to grow rapidly, with hardly any management intervention. Now, when we are faced with highly depleted fish populations, California is finally taking action to limit access to nearshore fisheries. The state is also beginning to institute other management reforms listed in the state's first fishery management plan, and will even create some marine reserves where fishing will be banned in order to hold onto a small part of what's left of the nearshore ecosystem.

Pressure from environmentalists, sportfishing groups, and commercial fishermen alike to protect this system and the fisheries it supports paid off in the form of California's Marine Life Management Act. This act is one of the first pieces of fishery management legislation that strives to protect whole ecosystems, rather than focusing on single species of fish. It turns rhetoric into action by insisting on marine reserves, where no fishing is to be allowed. These marine reserves will act as "fish in the bank" — insurance against the inevitable management errors and scientific mistakes that have contributed to the collapse of many fisheries throughout the world. The act also requires that a certain amount of knowledge about a fish population be obtained before allowing large-scale fisheries to exploit it — a seemingly common-sense measure that nevertheless is very rare. Most fisheries develop haphazardly, and are not managed in any significant way until they are quite large or even approaching a crisis. Perhaps this ground-breaking state law will be a model for other states, or even for reforming fisheries management for whole countries.

Reforming Fisheries Management

There have been some major fishery management reforms in recent years as a result of persistent advocacy. The spectacular failure of conventional management in Newfoundland, New England, and the U.S. West Coast has motivated action. California's Marine Life Management Act of 1999 is the first fisheries law in the nation that embodies ecological principles. It will result in some marine reserves and conservative catch limits. Implementation of the landmark reforms of the federal 1996 Sustainable Fisheries Act (amending the Magnuson Fishery Conservation and Management Act) has been spotty. But more conservative catch limits have been established for some species, and large portions of George's Bank in New England and of the continental shelf off the West Coast have been closed to certain kinds of fishing to protect and restore overfished populations. These actions may save the most highly depleted species, but do not get to the heart of the matter. Real reform must reduce the excessive number of fishing vessels plying the waters, and transform the fundamentals of fishery management.

Most resource managers have a hard time picking winners and losers — those who get to stay in the fishery and those who must be shut out. But that's what it will take to end the tragedy of the commons and put fisheries on a more sustainable path. Simply limiting access with license or permit systems will not be enough, since managers usually give permits to almost everyone active in a fishery, so as to avoid tough decisions. Moreover, limiting access to a fishery without guaranteeing a share of the catch to each fisherman maintains the perverse economic incentives of open access to compete for the fish. It just shifts the arms race from buying more boats to increasing the fishing power of the boats allowed to fish. Buying out excess fishing vessels is full of challenges, such as ensuring that vessels that have been tied up will not simply replace the vessels that are bought, but it may be necessary in the short term.

The problem of bycatch, or the accidental taking of organisms in pursuit of the target fish, persists. About one-quarter of all the fish caught in the world each year is bycatch, tossed overboard because they are not worth much economically or because regulations prohibit landing them. Moreover, tens of thousands of dolphins, sharks, sea turtles, seabirds, and other wildlife die in fishing nets and on hooks each year. Efforts to conserve the remaining fish by restricting catch have probably exacerbated this problem, as fishermen struggle to maximize the value of the dwindling amounts of fish they are allowed to catch, often by discarding the lower-value fish. Lower allowable catch limits, while necessary for preventing overfishing or for rebuilding depleted populations, can also accelerate the race for fish, at times to absurd levels — seasons shrink to a few weeks, or even a couple of days. This can result in even more bycatch, as fishermen rush to catch as many fish as possible. Bycatch, if it is not reduced, threatens to result in more closures and even in endangered species.

Nearshore ecosystems and fisheries will likely be threatened by fishery closures on the continental shelf, resulting from the collapse of the once rich West Coast groundfishery. Many more vessels exist than are required to profitably catch all of the available fish, perhaps up to several times as many. Because fishery managers have not taken steps to reduce the number of vessels, the closures on the shelf will likely squeeze fishermen back into nearshore waters (which they left years ago after nearshore fish populations were depleted). Nearshore fisheries are already overcapitalized, because fishing capacity was not effectively limited or reduced, so we appear to be heading for a train (fishing boat) wreck.

To head off this wreck, the key again is to solve the overarching problem of excess fishing capacity. What's needed are institutional changes that get at the heart of the matter — the economic incentives that encourage the catching of the most fish as fast as possible. Fishermen don't respond only to economic incentives, of course. Many other factors influence their behavior — a love for being at sea, of working alone or with a few mates, of being independent are all powerful influences. But why not try to align the economic incentives with conservation behavior, rather than with the race for fish? New governance approaches that redefine the economic incentives driving the fishery will be needed. One such approach is to use Individual Fish Quota (IFQ) programs to harness market forces and adjust fishing power to the capacity of the fish populations. Such programs divide the allowable catch into percentage shares, so that each shareholder profits by investing in conservation measures that ensure a sustainable catch. Designing equitable and effective IFQ programs is full of challenges (which will be addressed more fully in Chapter 5), but they hold great promise.

Another approach is to delegate authority for fisheries management to communities, so that social and ethical incentives can operate to ensure sustainability. The fishing community of Port Orford, on the southern Oregon coast, is experimenting with this approach. The fishermen of this small town are heeding an alarm bell that sounds like the gunning of fishing boat engines. They fear that hundreds of fishermen will migrate to their waters from the overcapitalized California live fish fishery. More fishermen might come into Oregon nearshore waters in response to the extensive continental shelf areas that were closed in 2002 in response to the collapse of the West Coast groundfishery. A couple of years before the big groundfish collapse, many fishermen saw the writing on the wall. Allowable catches had been declining for several years, and in 2000 the Secretary of Commerce declared the West Coast fishery a disaster. Port Orford fishermen had long contended that the Pacific Fishery Management Council, which oversaw the demise of the groundfish fishery, was out of touch with what was happening on the Port Orford reef. These fishermen knew that the spotty trawl surveys conducted by the National Marine Fisheries Service were unreliable and just did not reflect reality on their reef. These surveys informed the annual stock assessments that in turn served as the basis for catch projections and allowable catch limits. Port Orford fishermen had a feel for the abundance of the various species they caught with hook and line, in their small fishing vessels.

Laura Anderson grew up on the Oregon coast, the daughter of a salmon fisherman, and worked on her father's boat during the summer. She followed her love of the sea to the Philippines, where she worked in the Peace Corps and helped to set up a marine reserve. Later, Laura earned a master's degree in marine resource management from Oregon State University and hung her shingle out as a fisheries consultant. I hired her to talk to fishermen in Oregon about marine reserves, figuring that they would feel more at ease talking with her than with me, a non-fishing scientist and professional environmentalist. As Laura traveled up and down the Oregon coast having endless cups of coffee with fishermen, she began to think that perhaps one way to create an ocean governance structure that encouraged conservation and sustainable fishing would be to empower fishing communities to learn about and manage their own marine resources. Maybe one of the problems with the Pacific Fishery Management Council was that it was simply too large to be effective, with too many diverse viewpoints and political agendas to be reconciled. Decentralizing marine research and management might not only generate knowledge that was more relevant to particular locations, but also create a greater degree of psychological investment in the well-being of the living resources of the sea.

The idea of community-based management took hold in Port Orford, a small community almost entirely dependent on fishing. Progressive scientists from the Oregon Department of Fish and Wildlife, who had been surveying fish with submersibles to get a more realistic view of fish abundance and distribution than one could get from dragging nets over huge areas once every three years, got on board. The initial visioning sessions took to heart the slogan, "think globally, act locally." The list of issues people wanted to address ranged from counting fish on Port Orford reef to global climate change and the World Trade Organization. Eventually, though, with the guidance of Laura and Leesa Cobb, a fisherman, conservationist, and community leader, the list was winnowed down and a plan started to emerge.

The community would start by learning as much as possible about the ecology of Port Orford reef, with fishermen working alongside scientists, sharing insights and techniques. Then threats

to the ecosystem and to the fishery would be identified, leading
to the formulation of policy options. These options might
include such things as limiting access to the fishery so as to avoid
a gold rush by California fishermen squeezed out of the
California nearshore fishery, and perhaps even creating marine
reserves. Meanwhile, the community would seek authority from
the state and the Pacific Fishery Management Council to manage
the Port Orford reef on behalf of the public trust. The story of
community-based management in Port Orford has just started,
and it remains to be seen if the community can pull it off — and
then make it work for both the fishery and for the ecosystem that
supports it. But the time is ripe for experimenting with new ways
to manage our activities that affect the ocean. The collapse of the
West Coast groundfish and the disappearance of various
nearshore species that were once common show all too clearly
that the ways of the past have failed us.

That failure was in part caused by scientific uncertainty, partly by unanticipated changes in ocean productivity, and partly by
management errors caused by unjustified optimism. The tendency for some fishery managers to believe that fish abundance is at
the upper end of the ranges that scientists present them with may
be related to conflicts of interest on the part of some council
members. For example, members of the Pacific Fishery
Management Council are asked to simultaneously look out for
the public trust and the best interests of the nation as a whole,
and also to take care of the constituents they represent, mainly
those in the fishing industry itself. There are representatives of
state and federal agencies on the councils, as well as a few scientists and a lone environmentalist, but most council members represent various sectors of the fishing and seafood processing industry, and too many of the votes reflect a bias toward alleviating
short-term economic distress, often at the expense of long-term
sustainability.

Conflicts of interest can be reduced by strengthening requirements for council members (current and prospective) to disclose
their financial interests and by appointing more non-industry

representatives. Changes in ocean productivity will always be with us, but can be accounted for with more sophisticated monitoring, models, and catch limits that slide up and down with the capacity of the ocean to provide fish. Scientific uncertainty can be reduced through collaborative research with fishermen, more thorough monitoring of fish populations, and a greater understanding of ocean ecosystems. Marine reserves can help alleviate all three of these factors — scientific uncertainty, management error, and variable ocean productivity — by hedging against the uncertainties they cause.

Creating Marine Reserves

One reasonable way to deal with uncertainty is to take out an insurance policy. At first glance, the notion of setting aside areas where no fishing is allowed to make sure that at least some fish are left if the management system fails would seem uncontroversial. Reserving a bit of cash in a savings account, buying car insurance, and investing in the money market are common ways in which people deal with life's uncertainties. But a double standard exists in the world of environmental policy. Fishery managers had no problem allowing large scale fishing to start and continue right on through the collapse of the West Coast groundfishery, on the basis of very limited scientific understanding of the life history and productivity of the fish populations they were exploiting. But the same fishery managers demand a very high degree of scientific certainty for the common-sense idea of setting some fish aside in case of mistakes. Mounds of evidence piled up showing that marine reserves really did allow fish to grow larger and become more abundant and far more reproductively active in places where they were not being killed. But fishermen and fishery managers continue to express skepticism, this time demanding evidence that marine reserves will enhance fishery yields.

Though fishery enhancement is not a major objective of marine reserves, the available (albeit limited) evidence and theoretical considerations strongly suggest that fishery enhancement could be a nice side-effect of reserves. Most of the studies that have looked at this phenomenon demonstrate that fish do indeed swim out of reserves and onto the fishing grounds, resulting in lots of world record sport catches (in the case of the Merritt Island marine reserve in Florida) and bigger commercial catches. Many marine reserves are lined with lobster traps and fishing vessels, suggesting that some fishermen know this already. Unlike humans, many fish species make more babies as they grow older — often exponentially more. For example, a 23-inch (58-cm) vermillion rockfish is only about 1 ½ times larger than a 14-inch (36-cm) vermillion, but can produce about 17 times more young.[2] The effects of enormous numbers of larval and juvenile fish generated by the larger fish typical of reserves drifting out of the reserve on surrounding fish populations and fisheries should be even greater than the effects of adult fish swimming out of the reserve. In any case, one major reason why we can't say for sure whether marine reserves will enhance fisheries or not is because there are too few marine reserves of sufficient size to detect an effect. Steve Gaines, a scientist who devotes a lot of his time and energy to educate environmentalists, fishermen, and policy makers about marine reserves, illustrates this with a thought experiment.

Let us assume that the fish in marine reserves produce five times more larvae than fish typical of the fishing grounds. This is a conservative assumption — the empirical evidence suggests that fish in reserves are 10 to 50 times more productive than fish on the fishing grounds because they are so much bigger on average. Right now, far less than one percent of U.S. ocean waters are protected within marine reserves where no fishing is allowed. We could only expect an increase of a few percent or even a fraction of a percent in recruitment (the entry of young fish into the ranks of fishable adults) resulting from the existing reserves. This is way below our ability to detect a signal amidst the noise generated by natural variation and our spotty sampling techniques. We would probably need to set aside about 20 percent of a population (corresponding roughly to 20 percent of its habitat) to be able to detect a significant effect on recruitment. It's already clear that marine reserves protect biodiversity and allow fish populations to recover nicely within their borders. We must create more and bigger marine reserves to prove they enhance fisheries (or not). But we can't create more and bigger marine reserves until we know they'll enhance fisheries, according to the skeptics. Meanwhile, fishery managers will continue to use catch limits based on uncertain stock assessments, untested size limits, and recreational bag limits that don't even attempt to control the total fishing mortality caused by millions of sportfishermen.

Marine reserves are not primarily intended to enhance fisheries. We need reserves mostly to protect remaining biodiversity and to allow depleted fish and invertebrates (and even kelp forests) to recover within their boundaries. Reserves are the public's insurance policy against management errors, and the public's representatives ought to take this policy out and pay the premiums. Fishery managers will have to figure out how to integrate marine reserves with their own management strategies and regulations. Fishermen can play a constructive role in siting reserves so as to maximize their ecological benefits and minimize their short-term economic impacts on the fishing industry. But the question of whether marine reserves should be established is one for the people's representatives to decide, for they affect the people's marine resources and the public trust. California is leading the way, having passed a law called the Marine Life Protection Act that calls for the improvement of the state's array of marine managed areas. This array includes over a hundred managed areas, with a wide spectrum of confusing regulations. Only 17 of these areas are off limits to fishing, comprising about five percent of state ocean waters.

The state's first attempt to implement the Marine Life Protection Act violated every known principle about how best to create a network of marine reserves. The state's department of fish and game convened a team of scientists to formulate a master plan for reserves, as called for in the act, but didn't invite anyone to participate in or even observe the team's work. This exacerbated the distrust and even hatred of the department on the part of fishermen, who for decades have had to suffer the consequences of inadequate science and poor management decisions. These consequences have included the contraction of the once valuable commercial and sport abalone fishery to a sport-take-only fishery restricted to northern California; the collapse of the sea urchin fishery, once the richest in the state; the decimation of nearshore populations; the overcapitalization of the nearshore live fishery; and the list goes on. Frustrations and resentments that had built up for years were vented in some of the most rancorous "public spearings" ever when the master plan team rolled out its "draft, preliminary, conceptual" maps of proposed marine reserves that might be considered for eventual implementation. Even with long lists of qualifiers, people ripped into the maps and launched into angry diatribes, shouting matches, and name-calling. After the hotheads went home, more productive conversations ensued, and some good ideas for siting marine reserves were collected, as well as some insights into how to design a better process for implementing the act.

To its credit, the department listened to its critics and revamped its process, coming up with one that looked very much like the process that environmentalists and many fishermen had been pushing from the start. The new process (started in 2002) has been inclusive from the get-go, using small working groups of hand-picked representatives. These representatives are thinking through the objectives of the act and figuring out how to meet them in flexible ways. Ideally, they will meet the objectives not by compromising them but by choosing sites that will minimize short-term economic impacts on fishermen. For example, by looking at historical fishing patterns, it might be possible to find places that were once productive but are now fished out, and that still have high habitat quality. These might make very good sites for marine reserves, because we would expect the most rapid and dramatic biological responses to occur where fish populations have been depleted. We will still want to protect productive, high-quality areas, to be sure, but finding areas that are not fished (for whatever reasons) could lower the short-term costs of the whole reserve network without compromising performance. Not many fishermen would be using such areas, since they have been fished out already, so marine reserves there would not have a large economic impact. One hopes that the extensive knowledge of natural history that fishermen and divers have accumulated in their years on and under the water will be tapped and used to complement existing scientific information.

There is a new spirit of cooperation in the air, at least between some commercial fishermen and environmentalists. The Pacific Coast Federation of Fishermen's Associations got together with Environmental Defense to interview fishermen about their fisheries — where the fish are, where they spawn, where they grow up, and whatever else they can tell us about the sea they know so well. These data have been entered into a Geographical Information System that already contains nautical charts, data on catches for the last 30 years or so, and information on habitat types. Anyone can use this system, called Oceanmap, to sketch out prospective marine reserve sites and see what's there. We hope that Oceanmap will help build trust in the process of siting marine reserves and enhance prospects for successful negotiations. It can provide a common set of objective facts to talk about and significantly enhance the amount of quality information available for siting.

The Channel Islands Marine Reserve Network

Even before California's Marine Life Protection Act was passed, a group of elderly sportfishermen inspired what was to become one of the largest networks of marine reserves in U.S. waters.

These master fishermen were unrivaled in their ability to catch big fish in the rich waters of the Channel Islands off the Santa Barbara coast. Natural forces come together there to create a vital ocean environment teeming with life. Seasonal winds push warm surface water out to sea, enabling cold, nutrient-rich water to rise from the deep ocean. In these waters, millions of phytoplankton bloom. Tiny zooplankton feed on the plant life, creating the base of a productive food web. Biological diversity on this part of

California's coast is further enhanced as cooler ocean waters from the north mix with warm currents from the south. In this ocean "mixing zone," a diverse array of species finds just the right conditions to flourish. Massive ocean currents called "gyres" circulate the highly mobile eggs and larvae of many species throughout this ecosystem. Hundred-foot-high giant kelps shelter lively marine communities.

First granted official federal recognition as a national monument by Franklin D. Roosevelt in 1938, the Channel Islands were declared a national park in 1980. Also in 1980, in response to federal proposals to expand offshore oil and gas drilling, local residents and elected officials secured designation of all waters within six miles of the islands (1,658 square miles or 4,294 square kilometers) as the Channel Islands National Marine Sanctuary. This status affords permanent protection from new offshore oil rigs, and also bans ocean mining operations. Traditionally, fishing privileges have been granted to support a local fishing industry, under the jurisdiction of the California Fish and Game Commission and the California Department of Fish and Game.

Fishing regulations in the Channel Islands established 30 years ago were based on the assumption that populations of fish and shellfish can sustain fairly high levels of fishing mortality because they produce thousands of eggs. Despite the application of the best available science at the time, and despite the good intentions of managers and fishermen, fished populations of abalone, angel sharks, large red sea urchins, and rockfish have declined dramatically over the past 20 years.

Recent scientific studies have revealed that abalone, rockfish, and other species are especially vulnerable to fishing due to certain life history characteristics, such as the abalone's need to be close to mates, and the rockfish's tendency to grow slowly and to live a long time. Changes in natural ocean productivity (resulting from climate change, El Niños, and other environmental fluctuations), pollution, and disease have had impacts on the region's marine life in general. However, it is clear that fishing has been the major cause of the decline in several exploited species. Recent population models suggest that fishing mortality has exceeded the "surplus production" of several rockfish species (now depleted) for many years. Several studies of marine reserves have found that rockfish reproduction in the reserves is 20 or more times greater than in nearby fishing grounds.[3] This suggests that the reproductive potential of fished populations has been greatly depleted.

Some of the most compelling evidence that fishing has caused the observed population declines and attendant shifts in ecosystem balance comes from the tiny Anacapa Natural Area no-fishing reserve, the only such reserve in the Channel Islands. Densities of large red sea urchins were about 12,000 per hectare (one hectare is about 2.5 acres, or about the size of two soccer fields) when the fishery began targeting them in the early 1970s. While overall urchin densities do not differ substantially today between the reserve and the fishing grounds, there are now about 15,000 to 20,000 large red sea urchins per hectare in the no-take reserve at East Anacapa Island (called the Natural Area). In contrast, most kelp forests in the Channel Islands National Park support fewer than 2,000 large red urchins per hectare where fishing is allowed. Key urchin predators such as spiny lobsters and sheephead fish have declined dramatically in fished areas, while over the same time period they have been about ten times more abundant inside the reserve. Unexploited species remain abundant in both fished areas and in the reserve. Clearly, fishing caused the observed declines in exploited species. Otherwise, one would expect to see no major differences between areas within the no-take reserve and areas of equivalent habitat that are open to fishing. In addition, both unexploited and exploited species would tend to decline in fished areas and in the reserve if factors such as climate change or El Niños were primarily responsible for the declines.

Fishing can impact entire ecosystems and foodwebs, not just the target species or bycatch species, by removing predators and competitors, thus allowing other species to become more abundant. For example, purple urchins (which are not fished) have become much more abundant on the fishing grounds, compared with the Anacapa marine reserve. The removal by fishing of large numbers of spiny lobsters and sheephead fish (both are key urchin predators)[4] appears to have allowed the purple urchin populations to explode. Spiny lobsters are about six times more abundant in the reserve than on the fishing grounds.[5] As a result, giant kelp has been heavily grazed by the urchins, nearly disappearing entirely from survey sites in fished areas. In stark contrast, kelp has actually increased inside the reserve since 1983 by more than ten percent.[6] It's not by coincidence that the Anacapa reserve hosts one of the best kelp forests in all of the Channel Islands.[7] The very dense purple sea urchin populations that built up on the fishing grounds in the absence of predators like lobsters and sheephead tend to have high frequencies of disease, while purple sea urchin populations in the Anacapa Natural Area are much healthier.[8]

The late Jim Donlan was an experienced sportfisherman who had become concerned about the plight of the game fish he used to hunt so successfully near the Channel Islands. In his 80s, Jim created the Channel Island Marine Resources Restoration Committee, made up mostly of his old sportfishing buddies. He wrote to several environmentalists asking for advice and help in his efforts to get the state to set aside a portion of the waters around the Channel Islands as a marine reserve. We advised Jim to diversify his group to include realtors, dive tourism operators, kayaking outfits, and other people who might economically benefit from the reserve. And we asked him not to submit a map, as that would immediately polarize matters. He took our advice to diversify his membership, but a map was submitted to the California Fish and Game Commission, and (predictably) it set off a firestorm of protest.

The commission met in Santa Barbara in 1998, where Jim and his friends made one of their first pitches for the reserve. There was a lot of shouting about how there was no scientific evidence to support the creation of marine reserves and how reserves were going to wreck the fishing industry and tank the whole California economy. So I was surprised to learn that neither the commission nor the opponents of the reserve had ever been exposed to the science that did exist. My interns and I had just pulled together all the scientific papers we could find on the subject and I showed slide after slide, all with the same message: marine reserves had more fish, they were bigger, and they were making far more eggs than fish typical of the fishing grounds. Other scientists gave the commission a similar message — that the scientific basis for marine reserves as a way to protect biodiversity and allow populations to recover within their borders was very strong. After these presentations, the audience was quiet and a more deliberative tone set in. The commission decided to work with the Channel Islands National Marine Sanctuary, in which the marine reserve would be located, to create a process that would allow all the relevant stakeholders to talk through the issues and come up with a recommendation. The aim was to complete this process in one year.

Two and a half years and what seemed like millions of meetings later, the Marine Reserve Working Group convened by the sanctuary (made up of commercial fishermen, sportfishermen, environmentalists, and many other stakeholders) was close to consensus. The working group process was aided and abetted by one of the most sophisticated decision-support tools ever deployed in the service of ocean conservation. Scientists had assembled all of the available information on habitats, fishing, the distribution of wildlife, and biodiversity trends and mapped it all on a Geographical Information System. This GIS tool was used to sketch out marine reserve network scenarios, and to compare them against the criteria developed by an independent group of scientists hand-picked by the working group. The criteria were intended to make practical the lofty goals and objectives decided upon by the working group.

The working group was also aided by a socioeconomic panel charged with gathering anecdotal information from fishermen and reviewing economic impact data. Agency economists used these data to run quick analyses of the short-term economic impacts of each marine reserve network scenario submitted to the panel. Unfortunately, these analyses were deeply flawed in ways that were readily admitted to by the analysts themselves — they did not adequately account for non-market benefits of marine reserves. Such values include the benefit to future generations, the benefit of keeping one's options open in a patch of water by protecting it, and the aesthetic benefit of simply knowing that at least some pieces of the wondrous Channel Islands ocean ecosystem are protected in perpetuity — in short, most of the major benefits of marine reserves were ignored.

The socioeconomic analyses were also flawed in other, more prosaic, ways. Future fishing yields were projected from a three-year baseline, and were assumed to rise over time, when in fact all indications in the real world were pointing to further declines. Environmentalists pointed out that few rockfish populations had been assessed, for example, and that future assessments would likely reveal that a number of them were overfished, leading to closures and other kinds of constraints on fishing to protect them. Thus, they held, fishing revenues would probably decline over time with or without marine reserves. Thus, a declining baseline of expected fishing revenues was really the most relevant baseline to use for comparing the costs and benefits of marine reserves. Our expectation that fishing revenues would decline was borne out in 2002, when the Pacific Fishery Management Council closed large areas of the continental shelf to bottomfishing in response to new stock assessments that revealed that a number of species were overfished.

The official analyses also underestimated the economic benefits of marine reserves, in my opinion. They did not account for the potential of marine reserves to accelerate the rebuilding of depleted fish populations. Nor did they count as a benefit the expectation that reserves would prevent the extirpation of species whose status was unknown, in turn preventing the severe constraints on fishing that could accompany the listing of such species as endangered or threatened under the Endangered Species Act. Although we did eventually succeed in getting analysts and others to talk in terms of non-market benefits, the economic analyses that were used by decision makers markedly emphasized the short-term economic costs of marine reserves (i.e., potentially lost fishing opportunities, jobs, and revenues) and de-emphasized or ignored most of the benefits.

The way an economic analysis is framed can make all the difference. If costs and benefits can be reasonably estimated, and if economic costs and benefits are agreed to be the main criteria for decision making, then cost-benefit analysis is appropriate. But in the case of marine reserves and many other conservation measures, the main benefits are intangible or hard to quantify while the costs are fairly clear. If society (through law, regulation, or consensus) has agreed that the measure should be taken, economic analysis is useful mainly for comparing the potential impacts of various policy options, such as different reserve sites.

Though many working group meetings had been heated, the group had agreed on a strong set of goals and objectives, and had agreed that marine reserves are useful tools to conserve marine biodiversity. The group had come to consensus on several marine reserve sites around the islands that were more distant from the mainland. But they had also agreed to meet criteria established by their hand-picked scientific advisory group, which included a criterion for size (at least 30 percent of each major type of habitat in the sanctuary should be set aside in reserves) and representativeness (all three biogeographical areas — the cold waters of the north, the warm waters to the south, and the transition zone in between — had to be represented as well as all of the major habitat types like kelp forest and rocky reef). This meant that the group had to choose some areas for marine reserves near Anacapa, where most of the charter sportfishing vessels go. Sportfishing representatives wouldn't budge — even after everyone else agreed to let the 30 percent criterion slip somewhat, and even after the group had spent months playing with different scenarios to try to accommodate everyone's needs. The sanctuary had to pull the plug on a process that had run a year and half over the allotted time and way over the allotted budget.

In retrospect, the rule of consensus was a mistake, given the controversial nature of marine reserves and the diverse representation of the working group. Environmentalists called on the state and federal government to lead in the absence of consensus, and to their credit, the government responded with a well-balanced compromise that would set aside 25 percent of the sanctuary's waters in marine reserves, meet the science panel's criteria for habitat diversity, and minimize costs to all stakeholders. Still, fishing representatives supported their own alternatives, and the debate went on.

The contentious struggle to establish marine reserves around the Channel Islands started off amicably enough. Environmentalists, fishermen, and representatives of other groups with a stake in the resources of the Islands agreed that there was a problem, and that marine reserves would be a useful tool for addressing it. The various biological communities had been monitored over time, providing a basis for seeing the decline of some species. Surveys had also revealed the diversity of habitats and their locations. The best available science was applied to the development of size and siting criteria and to the analysis of proposed sites. Despite all this, however, the decision to establish the Channel Islands marine reserve network became a political one in the end. In fact, throughout the long process, proponents and opponents sought to build political will by demonstrating massive support for their positions.

Environmental Defense, for its part, produced and ran a public service announcement that persuaded people to sign up to be electronic activists. By the end of the campaign, more than 10,000 people had written letters to the governor and the commission in support of marine reserves. But environmentalists lacked the huge budgets necessary to run TV ads, and so relied on other, more creative means to educate and activate citizens. Our strategy was based on the book *The Tipping Point* by Malcolm Gladwell, [9] which lays out a theory about how ideas can catch on rapidly. Mavens who love a new idea transmit them to salesmen — naturally charismatic people who can sell anything, including new concepts. Connectors (those people who are always trying to turn you on to a new restaurant or play or movie, or who are trying to get you to have lunch with one of their friends because you have a lot in common) spread the idea by word of mouth through their extensive networks. When these three archetypes come together in a group (or in an individual), so the theory goes, ideas can spread rapidly under their own power, like a virus.

We identified a charismatic local organizer who combined features of all of the tipping point archetypes — Jesse Swanhuyser is a maven, salesman, and connector rolled into one. Jesse worked both independently for Environmental Defense and as a team with the Ocean Conservancy's Greg Helms to reach out to other local environmentalists who had been working on a variety of issues such as watershed restoration and coastal protection. At the time, there were very few marine reserve activists in the area. We invited about 15 environmental activists to a meeting to learn about marine reserves; about 30 people showed up to see my slide presentation on the science of reserves, and hear a pep talk by my colleague Richard Charter. The buzz in the room was palpable. We stayed on after our presentation, talking to excited activists about strategy. Later, we joined with other environmental groups to hold another activist training session, and about 100 people showed up. This session included an inspiring talk by Gary Davis, a scientist with the Channel Islands National Park who was one of the first to call attention to dwindling marine life populations in the sanctuary. The next day, many of the participants were treated to an exciting boat trip to the sanctuary.

Later that week, I knew that we were nearing the tipping point when I watched several of the people who had attended our training session get up during a public meeting and speak eloquently about marine reserves and why we should establish more of them. One trainee cornered me afterward and explained excitedly how she had regaled customers about marine reserves while they were trapped under the hairdryers at her beauty salon. When people are talking about ocean conservation at their hairdresser's, or in the supermarket, or during their book groups, or at their Rotary

Club meetings, we achieve our purpose — to make ocean conservation a part of community life, one of the threads that draw people together, giving each other strength and resolve.

Jesse and Greg worked tirelessly to recruit more activists, giving hundreds of presentations to community groups, dive clubs, garden clubs, and any other organization that would have them. In three years, our group of marine reserve activists exploded from that original group of 15 to over 500 people who went to public meetings and spoke out for marine reserves. We called them the Local Ocean Network. Commission meetings were extremely well attended, with up to 200 people on each side of the debate wearing red (opponents) or blue (marine reserve supporters) T-shirts. This continued right up to a special meeting that the commission convened on October 23, 2002 to decide the fate of marine reserves in the Channel Islands. The commission voted to approve the compromise proposal, a great victory for good science and ecological health, in the town where it all began — Santa Barbara.

The activist community that formed to create marine reserves around the Channel Islands will form the core of a still larger group of activists throughout California which we will build to work towards the completion of a network of marine reserves throughout state waters. Eventually, the idea epidemic will spread widely and inform the new ethic needed to heal the ocean.

Farming Fish — Solution or Problem?

Marine reserves will help protect the ocean's diverse species and bring many other benefits. One of the most important, I think, is an ocean ethic based on an understanding of and respect for ocean habitats and wildlife that will guide our actions. Place-based conservation efforts (such as campaigns to create marine reserves) replace generalities about the ocean with concrete examples that people can care about personally. A new ocean ethic (which will be explored in Chapter 8) will transform our relationship with the sea, beginning, perhaps, with one of the most basic aspects of that relationship — eating.

The demand for healthy and delicious seafood continues to increase at the same time as fishery yields are dropping off as a result of overfishing. Production of seafood through aquaculture — the farming of fish and shellfish — has increased rapidly to fill the gap and is expected to continue to increase. Aquaculture already provides about a quarter of all the seafood consumed in the world. The U.S. government is subsidizing the development of this industry through research, small business loans, and other means, and is calling for a five-fold increase in production by 2025.[10] But is aquaculture taking pressure off wild fish populations, and resulting in less environmental impact than fishing? Can we buy farmed salmon or shrimp, so prevalent in grocery stores, in good conscience?

Some kinds of aquaculture are relatively benign. The ancient art of seaweed cultivation, mastered by the Japanese and Chinese, can remove excess nutrients from the water that might otherwise cause problems. The farming of filter-feeding shellfish like oysters, mussels, and clams may also help improve water quality by removing excess phytoplankton (often the result of overenrichment by fertilizers and sewage). While living in Japan during the late 1970s, I saw a seascape full of seaweed and shellfish farms forming checkerboards within beautiful bays and estuaries. But many forms of aquaculture cause serious environmental problems, including the two most popular kinds of farming: shrimp and salmon.

Much of the farmed shrimp sold in the global marketplace appear to come from ponds that are carved out of mangrove forests and other coastal wetlands in tropical or subtropical countries. The leading producers are Thailand, China, Indonesia, and India — these four countries accounted for more than half of all farmed shrimp in 2000.[11] The mangroves that are cut down to make room for shrimp farming are incredibly valuable, not only ecologically but also for the maintenance of local fisheries. A wonderful diversity of organisms thrives among the roots of the mangrove trees. I remember snorkeling through crystal-clear waters in the mangrove forests ringing the Florida

Keys, marveling at colorful sponges and clouds of small, silvery fish. Young shrimp and myriad other creatures grow up in the safety of the tangled roots of the mangrove trees. Mangroves also keep water quality high in adjacent seagrass meadows and coral reefs. Seagrasses and corals cannot tolerate large amounts of sediments running off the land because they cloud the water, robbing plants and coral of the light they need to survive and grow. Mangroves trap sediments in their roots — and cutting them down allows all of the dirt eroding from the land to enter the water, wreaking havoc.

Happily, the felling of mangroves to create shrimp ponds seems to have slowed in recent years, in part due to NGO pressure. Even better, local groups are teaming up with international NGOs to restore damaged mangrove forests. In Indonesia, local groups (Yayasan Kelola and the Mangrove Action Project) are using a microgrant from the Coral Reef Alliance to restore 30 acres (12 hectares) of abandoned shrimp farms carved out of the mangroves. They are also using this money to build a Coastal Resource Community Center where locals can be trained in ocean and mangrove conservation. The center will be built out of sustainably-grown bamboo and is designed to have minimal environmental impact.

You might think that farming fish and shellfish helps protect wild populations, because fewer wild fish need to be caught. But that's not the case, at least for shrimp and salmon farming. It takes two to three pounds (0.9 to 1.4 kilograms) of small fish (converted into fishmeal) to make a pound (0.45 kilograms) of shrimp or salmon. The small fish that are typically caught for making fishmeal often serve as the main food sources for wild fish and birds. As in most competitions between humans and wildlife, the humans are winning. There is evidence that large-scale catches of small shoaling fishes off Norway caused mass starvation of puffin chicks and the collapse of local populations of puffins and other fish-eating birds.[12]

Most fish and shrimp farms pollute the sea in many different ways. Waste products are simply discharged into the ocean in many cases, or drift through aquaculture nets in bays and estuaries. Because the economics of aquaculture puts a premium on growing large numbers of animals in small spaces, wastes can sometimes accumulate to noxious levels. Such conditions also breed disease, the bane of aquaculture. Shrimp ponds are abandoned and whole crops are discarded when disease takes hold. Fish escape from aquaculture nets, despite the assurances of the industry that they won't. Thousands of Atlantic salmon have escaped from nets in British Columbia into the Pacific Ocean. Escapees can potentially compete with wild native fish for food and perhaps even spread disease and interfere with the genetics of these populations. Transgenic salmon have been created — but no one knows what will happen if these novel creatures escape into the ocean.

It will take time to reform fisheries management and to establish marine reserves. In the meantime, aquaculture will probably continue to grow. Increased attention is being focused on the environmental impacts of aquaculture as it is currently practiced. There is, no doubt, an alternative path for aquaculture, but the industry has to be encouraged to walk it. In many cases, the know-how is already there; all that is needed are economic and legal incentives and proper accounting of costs and benefits to encourage the spread of more sustainable practices.

Aquaculture need not be damaging to the environment. Even the impacts of shrimp and salmon farming can be reduced significantly by a combination of environmental regulations like performance standards and changes in the marketplace. National standards are needed to specify acceptable levels of pollution from aquaculture facilities and to carefully regulate the use of non-native and transgenic organisms. Standards for fishmeal content might also spur the development of innovative aquaculture feeds that have less environmental impact, while maintaining levels of healthy omega-3 fatty acids in seafood. International trade agreements need to be modified to allow countries with high standards for aquaculture to bar imports from countries that don't, without being penalized or prosecuted by the World Trade

Organization for impeding free trade. Consumers can also have a beneficial effect if they are allowed to choose sustainably-produced seafood through the provision of trustworthy labels. Certification of aquaculture products by a credible organization, labeling regulations, and a high-visibility education campaign could create a market incentive for fish farmers to meet the certification criteria.

I've seen the potential for aquaculture. In Japan, I learned how to grow tiger prawns, the delectable large shrimp that you find in Japanese restaurants, while studying aquaculture there in the late 1970s. The prawns were grown in large tanks that recirculate and treat the water, reducing pollution. Nutritional requirements were known, and I was doing research to develop a plant-based artificial food for tiger prawns that would meet those requirements and lower costs, as well as reduce dependence on fishmeal.

Research to replace fishmeal with other sources and lower the overall environmental impact of shrimp aquaculture is still underway, but on a much grander scale. For example, the U.S. Department of Commerce recently awarded an $8 million grant to a consortium to develop the next generation shrimp production system, with new kinds of feed and a closed-circuit design that should increase yields while lowering pollution.[13] Low-tech methods exist, too, borrowing from the experience of Chinese fish farmers. These ancient ecologists grew several species together, each exploiting a different niche in a pond.

It's ironic that so much aquaculture today is unsustainable, when aquaculture was invented to create a sustainable supply of food. More than a thousand years ago, ancient Hawai'ians were using fish ponds to raise fish for burgeoning human populations. They chose species that fed on plants (rather than species like shrimp and salmon, which feed higher on the food chain), greatly increasing the efficiency of food production. Each organism in a food chain dissipates about 90 percent of the energy contained in its food; by shortening food chains we can consume far less sealife. While the Hawai'ian fish ponds were filled in or fell into disrepair as traditional ocean management gave way to more rapacious, modern methods, a revival is underway. I was inspired by kids on the Hawai'ian island of Molokai, who worked hard after school and on weekends to restore a magnificent fish pond there.

Researchers are working to reduce pollution from fish and shrimp farms, and to re-formulate feeds to reduce the "ecological shadow" (that is, the larger impacts) that aquaculture casts over the ocean. Small-scale cultivation of giant clams in the Soloman Islands appears to be taking some of the pressure off wild giant clam species, most of which have been depleted for their meat and attractive shells, with little impact on nearby coral reefs.[14] Large-scale, commercially-viable examples of sustainable aquaculture are difficult to come by, however. Traditional shrimp farming is hanging on in the Mai Po Nature Reserve (Hong Kong). The shrimp ponds were constructed with minimal effects on mangrove forests, and young shrimp are flushed naturally into the ponds from surrounding wetlands with the tide. Because the shrimp farms (as well as the nature reserve) are threatened by water pollution, it is hoped that the 40,000 or so people who visit the ponds each year will communicate this concern to policy makers and help to reduce the pollution.[15]

Pollution

Communities will not only have to deal with overcapitalized fisheries, dwindling fish populations, and threats posed by fish farms, but also with the growing effluvium from burgeoning coastal populations of humans. Already, wastewater collection and treatment systems strain to keep up with the billions of gallons of sewage and storm water flowing from cities and suburbs, and too often, they overflow and dump untreated waste into the sea. Beach closings and even the spread of water-borne diseases are the result. And who knows what the impacts on marine ecosystems are? The situation is even worse in developing countries, where the lack of good wastewater collection and treatment facilities is a leading cause of death.[16] About one to three billion people do not have access to good sanitation.[17] More than seven million children die each year worldwide from diarrhea and dysentery linked to poor water quality and lack of sewage treatment.[18]

Leaders attending the 2002 World Summit on Sustainable Development (also known as Rio + 10) in Johannesburg, South Africa, pledged to double access to clean water and sanitary facilities by 2015.[19] Most likely, they have big treatment plants in mind. For some reason, politicians seem fixated on large, centralized, and very expensive sewage treatment plants that kill pathogens and remove solids just fine, but don't really remove excess nutrients that can harm the ocean, especially tropical waters that are naturally low in nutrients. These nutrients come from detergents, agricultural runoff, and sewage.

Nutrients can be assimilated by the sea to some extent, but too much nutrient enrichment can be disastrous, especially in quiet bays and estuaries that are not flushed by tides very rapidly. The little fjords of Cape Cod, Massachusetts, are cases in point. The houses surrounding these small estuaries use septic tanks, by and large, to dispose of wastewater. Ideally, wastewater slowly decomposes in the tanks and trickles out into rich soils where the nutrients glom onto minerals and are assimilated by plant roots. But Cape Cod, alas, is a sand spit with very porous soils. So the wastewater just leaks out into the water table, which is not too far from the surface, and flows into the estuaries in streams or in little springs. The water in the estuaries tends to stay put for long periods of time, renewed by the tides a little at a time. Green algae — the long filaments and leaf-like species you see near sewage outfalls and in boat marinas — love these conditions of quiet water and lots of nutrients. They grow rapidly, outstripping the ability of herbivores to consume them, and then die, building up large rafts of decaying slime. The bacteria have a field day, turning the algae back into nutrients and using up the oxygen in the water. In extreme cases, the water can become toxic, and fish, crabs, and everything else that can't get out of there quickly die by the millions. In the extreme, nutrient pollution can cause huge areas of the sea to die — the "dead zone" in the Gulf of Mexico reached 8,000 square miles (almost

21,000 square kilometers — an area about the size of New Jersey) in 1999.[20]

Humans Dominate the Planet

For eons, the oceans, the land, the water, the atmosphere, and life have existed in a kind of dynamic balance — not stable, but co-evolving and self-correcting. Essential elements like carbon, nitrogen, oxygen, and hydrogen that make up most of our bodies move from soil to plant, from plant to animal, and between organisms, the atmosphere, and the oceans. But during the Industrial Revolution (starting in the early 1700s in England), humans started to burn large amounts of long-buried oil, coal, and gas deposits, releasing ever-increasing amounts of carbon and other elements to the atmosphere. Humans now dominate the planet's carbon cycle, spewing billions of tons of carbon into the atmosphere each year, enough to bump up carbon dioxide concentrations more than 25 percent over the last century. It's astonishing, when you think about it — humans have significantly altered the chemical composition of the entire atmosphere. Carbon dioxide concentrations have risen and fallen, sometimes dramatically over the earth's long history, and species have adapted — with the occasional extinction. But carbon dioxide levels have increased between ten and one hundred times faster during the last two centuries than they have in the past 420,000 years.[21] Moreover, the fraction of carbon dioxide that remains in the atmosphere has increased, presumably because the natural processes that remove it from the atmosphere (absorption by the sea and forests) have been reduced (through deforestation) as sources have been increased (rising fossil fuel consumption). We have been removing the planet's capacity to assimilate carbon dioxide at the same time as we have been greatly accelerating the movement of carbon out of the earth and into the atmosphere.

Less widely recognized, perhaps, is the fact that we (and our wastes) also dominate the planet's nitrogen cycle. Nitrogen gas makes up most of the atmosphere, inert to most chemical reactions and therefore unavailable to life. All life forms need nitrogen to make amino acids and proteins. Specialized bacteria living in the soil and in the roots of certain plants convert or "fix" atmospheric nitrogen gas into forms like ammonia and nitrate that plants can turn into proteins. Animals eat the plants, and transfer the fixed nitrogen through food webs. The nitrogen moves into the soil from the bodies of plants and animals and is turned back into nitrogen gas by bacteria living in the soil, rivers, wetlands, and estuaries.

Through the manufacturing of fertilizers, humans have greatly accelerated the rate at which nitrogen is fixed into forms that are available to plants. The fertilizers are spread onto the land in large amounts to maximize crop yields. The excess nitrogen in the fertilizer that cannot be absorbed by the plants or the soil then flows off the neat irrigated rows of crops into streams, and then into rivers, bays, and the ocean. Nitrogen also drops onto the land and water in rain that forms in air polluted with nitrogen oxides, released from cars and smokestacks. Still more nitrogen arrives via animal feedlots and sewer systems. Whereas most animals spread their waste products on the land where bacteria can slowly process them, humans tend to concentrate their waste (and the wastes of tens of thousands of hogs and other animals) into sewage and often discharge it into rivers and bays.

Sewage treatment does not typically remove the nitrogen or other plant fertilizers (nutrients) such as phosphorus from waste water. Wetlands and mudflats were once able to turn most of the fixed nitrogen running off the land back into inert nitrogen gas, but the flow of nutrients from farms and human sewage increased as the acreage of wetlands decreased, lost to marinas and coastal developments. As a result, we have quadrupled the amount of nitrogen entering the ocean via the Mississippi River, and increased nitrogen loading (the rate at which nitrogen enters a body of water) by about six times in the Northeastern U.S., and by about tenfold in the North Sea.[22] Excessive amounts of phosphorus draining off farmland can also damage ocean ecosystems — particularly estuaries, seagrass meadows, and coral reefs in tropical waters. Globally, phosphorus runoff to the sea has increased by about three times.[23] These spectacular increases in nitrogen and phosphorus levels running off the land suggests strongly that inputs are exceeding the ability of ecosystems to transform them into relatively harmless gas (for nitrogen) or rocks (for phosphorus). We have thrown this robust planetary process out of whack, just as we have disrupted the planet's carbon cycle.

Fortunately, forward-thinking engineers have been quietly developing innovative approaches to wastewater treatment that use less energy, less capital, and lower operating expenses to achieve more — killing pathogens, removing solids, and also reducing nutrient concentrations. Some even create habitats, recycle water, and reclaim nutrients and carbon for use as clean soil amendments.

When visiting Tijuana, Mexico, if you look down the arid and highly eroded valley of the Tijuana River, you might see a patch of green that stands out against the dry brown cliffs. This is Ecoparque, an innovative wastewater treatment plant designed by Environmental Defense and the Colegio de la Frontera Norte. They were responding to the need to treat wastewater in Tijuana, and to reports that sewage was flowing from Tijuana up the coast to pollute the Tijuana Estuarine Reserve in San Diego County. The California Coastal Conservancy and the Ford Foundation agreed to fund a bold experiment to address this cross-border pollution problem with a fresh approach. Instead of focusing on the narrow problem of treating wastewater, the project's proponents chose instead to look at the big picture. They focused on figuring out how to stop the one-way processes that were not only polluting coastal waters, but also squandering precious water, nutrients, and soil carbon in this arid country. Instead, they envisioned closed loops like those typical of natural ecosystems. Unlike other cities, Tijuana had not built a sewer system that mixed domestic wastewater with toxic industrial-waste streams. So it was theoretically possible to mimic natural cycles by reclaiming water, nutrients, and soil carbon from the domestic wastewater and use it to enrich highway medians, parks, and perhaps even crops.

Environmental Defense's intrepid engineer Dan Luecke and his partners at the Colegio de la Frontera Norte in Tijuana, Mexico, endured the trials and tribulations of getting Americans and Mexicans to work together, securing the necessary permits, and developing designs and engineering plans. A vision emerged of a small, modular plant that — if successful — could be replicated up and down the Tijuana River. While they were at it, they would try to use gravity to power the plant, and design it to work with as few moving parts as possible. And why not use the clean effluent to create ponds and wetlands on the site, supporting lush vegetation that would attract birds? And why not compost the solid wastes into clean soil amendments, to nurture the poor, eroded soils of Tijuana back to health? They called their idea Ecoparque, and set to work.

Several years and many delays later, Ecoparque is up and running, capable of treating up to about 90,000 gallons (409,000 liters) of wastewater every day to exacting performance standards. The solids are processed into odor-free compost; all of it is sold to local farmers. The fruit trees, flowers, and green grass of Ecoparque contrast dramatically with the dry, eroded hillside that it once was, and is still surrounded by. Plans include creating a pond to strip the remaining phosphorus from the wastewater and a drying bed to treat the small amount of watery solids that currently remains after processing.[24] For all this, Ecoparque cost far less to build than a typical, conventional wastewater treatment plant that does not remove nutrients or recycle carbon and water, and it is relatively inexpensive to operate.

The Ecoparque approach could be adapted to almost any application. It seems especially appropriate for dry climates where water reclamation would be at a premium. But its many virtues (low energy use, ease of maintenance, good performance, soil carbon and nutrient reclamation, nutrient removal, etc.) make it suitable for almost anywhere with relatively clean domestic wastewater. Unfortunately, the original vision of replicating numerous Ecoparques up and down the Tijuana River has not been achieved. Some observers feel that the main obstacle has been the lack of sewer ratepayers in Mexico.[25]

Good wastewater treatment is just one component of sustainable development. We must also provide alternatives to unsustainable economic activities, alternatives that will generate wealth and increase the quality of life for everyone while protecting natural assets and ecosystems. There are now several environmental groups and a couple of coalitions working to generate sustainable development ideas for Baja California, and some are even demonstrating them on the ground and in the water. Environmentalists are working with fishermen and businesses to develop low-impact oyster farming operations, sustainable fisheries, and ecotourism ventures. While many kinds of aquaculture are pretty bad for the environment, people have for years been farming, with some success, mollusks such as oysters that are low on the food chain and that can actually help clean up the water.

An internationally agreed-upon set of rigorous certification standards to define what constitutes a true ecotourism operation could create powerful market incentives for sustainable development. Right now, many different certification systems exist for things such as water and energy use and decreased use of toxic cleaning agents. Some hotels in Europe (for example, Scandic Hotels, Scandinavia's largest hotel chain) have fully embraced these issues, and have gone many steps beyond, using only sustainably harvested wood, non-toxic paints, carpets made of recycled polymers, and so on.[26] The Coral Reef Alliance has developed a set of standards that define what constitutes environmentally-friendly diving, snorkeling, and whale-watching.[27] Progress is being made, but environmental groups (as arbiters of what is sufficiently protective and sustainable and what is not) must come together and jointly endorse a common set of certification standards. They and the industry should then promote the companies that meet the standards so as to create a premium in the marketplace. We can't afford to wait passively for the consumer demand to develop; we must actively create it. This has been one of the hallmarks of globalization and of McWorld[28] — Benjamin

Barber's term for the new culture and economy of image, manufactured needs, infotainment, and spin. Why not manufacture a desire for beautiful, unspoiled places and resorts that don't pollute but which instead sustain the environment and local communities?

Oil and Seawater Don't Mix

Genial, thoughtful, and quick with a joke, Richard Charter doesn't seem like a crusader, but he is. In 1969, Californians were outraged and heartsick that their efforts to prevent an oil spill were frustrated. An oil well off the coast of Santa Barbara blew out, spilling about 200,000 gallons (over 900,000 liters) of crude oil over some 800 square miles (2,000 square kilometers) and 35 miles (56 kilometers) of coast. The slick killed untold thousands of seabirds, otters, dolphins, and other ocean wildlife. Charter organized local communities all along the coast of California to fight against offshore oil drilling, shuttling ceaselessly between the West Coast and Capitol Hill — and they won. But the ban on drilling remains in place at the whim of Congress, coming up for debate each year. More than 30 years later, the debate has gained a new and compelling twist — the quest for energy independence.

Two main schools of thought (or at least, argument) exist on how to achieve energy independence, freeing us from entanglements in countries with huge oil reserves but unstable political and economic regimes. One school holds that we need to increase domestic supplies by drilling for oil and gas in wilderness areas and in our territorial ocean. Not much is made of the fact that even if oil deposits were found, it would take many years to produce usable gas and oil from them. In any case, it would only be a matter of time until swelling demand swamped domestic production. At some point, the costs of producing and transporting fossil fuels will become too high to justify domestic sources, especially if one adds the ecological costs of oil spills, the environmental shadow cast by pipelines and other infrastructure, air pollution, and global warming associated with the use of fossil fuels to the equation. The notion that increasing the supply of fossil fuels to meet ever increasing demands would result in increased air pollution and accelerate global warming does not seem to be part of the calculus of the supply-side school.

The alternative vision is that of reduced demand for fossil fuels, achieved either by top-down regulations such as fuel efficiency standards, or by bottom-up economic incentives to buy time while renewable energy sources come into their own, or by a combination of both. Reduced fossil fuel consumption does not automatically mean that we will all have to drive small cars. Standards for reduced emissions of pollution and carbon dioxide, one of the main culprits behind global warming, could harness American ingenuity to create fuel-efficient Sport Utility Vehicles (SUVs) and other vehicles. In response to the right incentives, whole new ways to move people and goods around more efficiently might be invented.

Caps on total carbon dioxide emissions and opportunities for industrial and transportation sectors to trade emissions-reductions credits could also push technology in the right direction, while at the same time reducing costs. Private interests can act, even when governments stall. Electric utilities are already buying and selling such credits for sulfur dioxide reduction (the cause of acid rain). This innovative emissions-trading program, advocated by Environmental Defense among others, has contributed to a 30-percent drop in sulfur dioxide emissions (4.8 million tons or 4.35 million tonnes), and a 20-percent reduction in nitrogen oxide emissions (one million tons or 0.91 tonnes) between 1995 and 2000.[29] Environmental Defense put together a Partnership for Climate Action that includes eight of the world's largest corporations — Entergy Corporation (one of the largest utilities in the U.S.), Alcan, British Petroleum, DuPont, Ontario Power Generation, Pechiney, Shell International, and Suncor Energy. All told, these corporations had been emitting more greenhouse gases than the entire country of Spain[30] — the twelfth largest source of greenhouse gases in the industrialized world.[31] They are now committed to ambitious emissions-reduction targets, and are achieving them. DuPont has exceeded its goal to cut emissions by 40 percent — cutting them by 63 percent and still remaining profitable. DuPont even made money by selling about 138,000 tons (125,000 tonnes) of its surplus verified carbon dioxide equivalents (gained by cutting nitrogen oxide emissions below its reduction target by voluntarily installing a catalytic control process) to Entergy, which is expanding its facilities. The Partnership for Climate Action as a whole has cut its greenhouse gas emissions 17 percent below 1990 levels, three times the amount required by the Kyoto Protocol.[32] Voluntary programs such as the Partnership for Climate Change are no substitute for mandatory, enforced, environmental standards — but they suggest that greenhouse gas emissions can be cut substantially without destroying profitability.

Switching from coal and oil to gas would reduce environmental impacts while providing the dependable supplementary power we will need while transitioning to renewable energy. Rationalizing the energy market to incorporate the full costs of fossil fuels and the full suite of benefits associated with renewables would help, of course. Perhaps we could even subsidize renewable energy to the same extent that we subsidize nuclear and fossil fuel sources.

Renewable power could be decentralized, making power supplies less vulnerable to terrorist attacks and to more pedestrian threats such as storms. In July of 1996, a tree fell on a powerline, setting off a ripple effect that cut power in 15 states throughout the western United States, plus parts of Canada and Mexico, affecting millions of people. A month later, another problem (possibly a brush fire) on the grid cut power to seven states on the hottest day of the year.[33] California has been leading the way toward greater reliance on renewable power since passage of the 1978 Public Utility Regulatory Policy Act with a wide variety of tax credits, loans, grants, and rebates to encourage investment in renewable sources. By 1996, about 12 percent of California's electricity consumption came from renewable sources, primarily geothermal, small hydropower, and wind.[34] The subsidy program was extended in 1998 with a $135 million per year program, funded by ratepayers (the charge averages about two dollars per month for residential customers). Despite setbacks due to the electricity marketing crisis of 2000 and 2001, California still aims to increase the portion of electricity demand served by renewable energy to 20 percent by 2017 with continued investments and subsidies.[35]

Emerging issues related to oil drilling in coastal waters will depend largely on which school of thought wins out. At this writing, the supply-side school clearly has the upper hand, and so the current outlook is for more pressure to drill in wilderness areas and off the coast. Where politics favor less oil pollution, it is possible to stem this new tide of domestic exploration and exploitation. U.S. taxpayers will be paying oil companies to buy their exploration leases in tracts off Florida, so as to spare the white sand beaches and tourist economy of that state the risk of oil-soaked shorelines and dying seabirds. Tax money will not, however, flow to buy similar leases off California despite the state's long history of opposition to offshore drilling. The difference? Family ties — President George W. Bush's brother was governor of Florida, not California. The nation must commit to a sensible energy policy that does not change with each new president.

Renewable energy has many advantages over energy derived from fossil fuels, and the proportion of the world's energy produced from solar, wind, and other renewable sources could increase rapidly in response to subsidies and incentives. There are also large opportunities to reduce greenhouse gas emissions through greater energy efficiency. But the time scales needed to reduce greenhouse gas emissions and transition to renewable energy could mean ecological devastation and vast human suffering from climate change. The fact that coral reefs are already bleaching, and some are dying, in response to global warming provides a glimpse of the immensity of this threat. Opposition to offshore drilling for oil off one coastline will likely shift activity to another coastline with a population that's less resistant. America should invest in a workable mix of improvements in energy efficiency and incentives for renewable energy, lest the status quo prevail. Reforestation makes sense, because it can create jobs and increase quality of life, while also removing carbon dioxide from the atmosphere. However, it seems likely that no one option — energy efficiency, renewables, or reforestation — will be able to remove enough greenhouse gases from the atmosphere on its own. Other technologies such as "carbon scrubbing" (removing carbon dioxide from smokestacks) and "carbon sequestration" (storing carbon in geological formations) may be necessary to stabilize the concentration of greenhouse gases in the atmosphere and slow climate change down so as to reduce the damage to ecosystems and human societies. Of course, vigilance and ecolacy (the wisdom to ask "and what then?" of any new technology) will be required to weigh the consequences.

These days, Richard Charter is frantically working the two phones and two computers in his home overlooking the Pacific, just as he was twenty years ago when he was in the thick of the oil wars off the California coast. But now he is working to create marine reserves and engineer buybacks of oil leases — two solutions that have emerged in recent years.

Energy from the Ocean

The search for clean domestic energy may increase interest in various ways of extracting energy from the ocean, not just drilling for offshore oil.[36] A prudent energy policy would promote a mixture of sources to stabilize supply. The ocean probably stores enough energy in heat, currents, waves, and tides to satisfy global energy needs many times over. Waves, tides, and currents tend to be more dependable than solar or wind — for example, wave power can generate useful energy up to 90 percent of the time at a site, whereas solar or wind power might be limited to just 20–30 percent of the time. Some attempts have been made to harness this energy, but technical difficulties and costs have relegated ocean energy to a minor role so far. Costs are coming down, however, and technical problems are being overcome.

Of all the current schemes for extracting power from the ocean, wave energy seems to be furthest along. The mechanical energy in waves can be harnessed to move a piston up and down or rotate a turbine, generating electricity. A small (0.5 megawatt) commercial wave-power plant was constructed by the Wavegen Company on the coast of Islay, Scotland. Called the Limpet 500, it has been feeding power into the grid since late November, 2000. A larger (two megawatts) nearshore plant and a combined wave and wind plant (3.5 megawatts) have also been designed by Wavegen. Another company, Ocean Power Delivery Ltd., is installing a small offshore wave plant near Islay that is expected to provide power for about 200 homes by 2002. The company plans to install up to 900 such plants for a total capacity of 700 megawatts. Wave-energy plants will work best where the waves are strong and steady, such as in the United Kingdom and perhaps in the Pacific Northwest of the U.S. Ocean Power Delivery won a contract to study the feasibility of building a wave energy plant off Vancouver Island, British Columbia, Canada. Wave energy costs have dropped rapidly in recent years, with the newest designs aiming to produce power for five to ten cents per kilowatt-hour, comparable to costs for energy from burning fossil fuels.

To reduce capital costs, today's wave power plants tend to be fairly small; they are therefore likely to have relatively small impacts on the environment. Of course, the cumulative impact of many small plants concentrated in one area may become significant. By converting the energy stored in waves to electricity, wave plants reduce the ability of waves to perform their ecological functions, such as mixing surface waters with deeper layers and moving sediments around. If only a small percentage of a harbor or open coastline is affected this way, the ecological consequences should be minimal. However, as the technology develops, larger plants or dense arrays of small plants covering large areas will dampen waves to a far greater extent. Ocean productivity, the flow and distribution of sediments that shape biological communities, and the nature of nearshore ecosystems could be adversely affected. In addition, the mere presence of artificial structures in the ocean may affect the distribution of animals. Structures like artificial reefs, oil platforms, or wave energy plants often attract organisms, and in some environments where stable places to live are at a premium, artificial structures could potentially increase the net production of ocean life. However, in other places, they could merely serve to concentrate fishes near highly visible structures, increasing their vulnerability to fishing.

The ocean's tides are even steadier than the waves, and could potentially generate up to 1,000 terawatts (one trillion watts) per year, though economic and political constraints would most likely reduce that potential considerably. Turbines spun by the current generated by the tide generate electricity in tidal power plants. The La Rance tidal power plant was built off the Brittany coast of France in the 1960s to take advantage of the eight-foot (2.45-meter) tidal range there; it generates about 240 megawatts of electricity. Other commercial plants exist at Kislaya in Russia, Jiangxia in China, and Annapolis in Canada.

The tidal power plant at La Rance is called a tidal barrage — it resembles a dam but allows water to flow through turbines both ways. All of the leading tidal power plant designs function this way. Theoretically, organisms, sediments, and all the other materials that naturally flow between ecosystems on either side of the plant would be unimpeded. However, large tidal barrages can block migrating fish such as salmon, as well as hindering human navigation. In addition, the construction phase can be very harmful to estuaries and bays, where these plants are likely to be located. For example, the La Rance estuary was completely closed off from the sea for several years during construction of the tidal barrage, profoundly affecting biological communities there. In addition, tidal power plants could alter circulation patterns, perhaps increasing the residence time of the water — the length of time a mass of water remains in the estuary or bay. Residence time has important effects on animals and plants. For example, long residence times can result in blooms of phytoplankton, some of which are harmful, like red tides. The impacts of pollution can also change, depending on residence time. In general, the longer the residence time, the greater the impact of pollution, because the pollution is not diluted or flushed out of the estuary as rapidly.

It is thought that Jules Verne first came up with the concept of exploiting the difference in temperature between the surface waters of the ocean and deeper layers to produce energy. He described such a scheme in his book *Twenty Thousand Leagues Under the Sea*, published in 1870. Have you ever gone for a swim in a warm lake or bay and suddenly encountered much cooler water when you dove below the surface? Because warm water is less dense than cold water, it floats on the cold water, forming a layer at the surface. This is especially true near the coast, where surface waters tend to be not only warmer than deeper waters, but also less saline. The density of the water increases with increasing salinity. Rivers and underground springs feed freshwater from the land into the surface waters, making them less dense. During warm weather, the difference in temperature and salinity between the surface and below can become very pronounced. When this happens, these differences prevent surface waters from mixing with deep water, unless an upwelling is created by other means — for example, by strong winds or currents.

About a decade after *Twenty Thousand Leagues Under the Sea* was published, the French physicist Arsene d'Arsonval theorized that warm surface water could be used to turn a working liquid into a vapor. The vapor could then be used to turn a turbine, generating electricity. Georges Claude, a French inventor, applied these principles to build the first working Ocean Thermal Energy Conversion (OTEC) plant off Cuba in 1930.

OTEC plants must be located relatively nearshore, in places where deep, cold waters are adjacent to warm surface waters. This limits OTEC to certain locations in the tropics, where the temperature difference between surface and deep water exceeds 40° F (22° C). Even so, conditions amenable to OTEC exist in some 23 million square miles (60 million square kilometers) of ocean. The warm surface water is used to heat a working fluid with a low boiling point, such as ammonia, to produce a vapor which drives a turbine. In open-cycle plants, the warm seawater itself is flash-vaporized in a vacuum to generate the steam which in turn drives the turbine. Cold water is pumped up from the depths to re-condense the working fluid.

The real beauty of the OTEC concept is that it can provide many ancillary benefits in addition to power generation. Burning fossil fuels, by contrast, produces only energy and pollution. In an OTEC plant, the cold water pumped up to condense the working fluid or warm seawater can be used to air-condition nearby offices or homes. Because air conditioning uses a large amount of energy, using cold seawater can be quite efficient. For example, the U.S. Navy is considering the construction of an eight megawatt OTEC plant to replace a 15 megawatt gas-powered plant at its base on the British island of Diego Garcia in the Indian Ocean. The smaller capacity OTEC plant is expected to suffice, because cold seawater from the OTEC plant can provide air conditioning, which would otherwise consume about five megawatts of power. Two buildings at the National Energy Laboratory of Hawai'i (NELHA), where pilot OTEC plants have produced net power, are cooled by OTEC seawater.

The cold seawater pumped up from the depths by OTEC is also rich in nutrients and free of parasites, making it ideal for use in the cultivation of marine algae and animals. Private companies have already profited by growing lobsters, fish, and high-protein algae at NELHA. In addition, warm seawater that is flash-vaporized in open-cycle OTEC plants can be re-condensed, leaving behind the salt and providing a source of fresh water.

Ocean Thermal Energy Conversion has the major advantage of generating power without emissions, save for a little carbon dioxide released from the cold water when it is pumped to the surface. The small amounts of chlorine used to keep intake pipes free of fouling organisms are not expected to create major problems. Release of the cold, nutrient-rich water into surface waters could significantly harm coral reefs and seagrass meadows that require warm, relatively stable temperatures and low nutrient concentrations to thrive. But OTEC operators will have a strong economic incentive to make use of the cold seawater for air conditioning and aquaculture, both of which would be expected to allow the seawater to warm up before release. Crops of seaweeds can be grown in the effluent prior to release to strip it of nutrients.

In comparison with fossil fuel combustion, OTEC seems quite benign. Still, care must be taken to prevent and mitigate any adverse impacts from OTEC plants. OTEC is designed to keep working fluids such as ammonia contained; releases are expected only in catastrophic situations. Environmental impacts could be minimized by keeping the plants relatively small, siting them far away from sensitive ecosystems, spacing them far apart so as to reduce cumulative impacts on particular sites, and carefully regulating the use of anti-fouling substances.

While OTEC is not yet capable of producing energy at a cost competitive with fossil fuels, there is a good case to be made for subsidization, especially for use in small island states which need sustainable energy sources at low cost. Many of these countries are eminently suitable for OTEC. Reliable power is rare, as is fresh water, on arid tropical islands such as Bonaire in the Caribbean. Air conditioning is always welcome in the tropics and local economies could benefit from food sustainably produced in OTEC aquaculture systems. OTEC has provided all these benefits, at least on a pilot scale.

OTEC could become an important source of energy for countries fortunate enough to be located in areas where the temperatures of surface waters and bottom waters are sharply distinct. But the vast stores of energy in the ocean's tides, waves, and winds could make a substantial contribution to meeting the entire world's energy demands. While large-scale ocean energy plants could have significant environmental impacts, it will be important to compare these with the impacts of continued reliance on fossil fuels. These include not only climate change, but also more immediate threats such as chronic oil pollution from drilling rigs and transport facilities, air pollution, and the occasional catastrophic oil spill or blowout. No large-scale energy facilities of any kind should be sited in sensitive natural areas, including marine reserves — that would run counter to the goal of allowing nature to manifest herself as fully as possible, free from human intervention. But the ocean could become an important source of energy for small island states, and perhaps for larger countries that have favorable conditions for harvesting energy from the sea.

A Sustainable Sea

The world is at a crossroads. For many years, conservation advocates made only slow progress, but the tipping point has arrived for some important areas like the Channel Islands. The challenge will be to transform local caring to a global ethic, so that global threats such as climate change can be ameliorated. But time is running out for coral reefs — the ocean's sensitive child.

4

CORAL REEFS: The Ocean's Sensitive Child

The Nature of Coral Reefs

Like the waters surrounding coral reefs, nature's logic seems clearer there than in most other ocean ecosystems. The transparent, warm, and (usually) calm water allows one to easily observe the busy life of the reef. You can even engage in the business of the reef on occasion. During one marvelous year, I felt like part of Carysfort Reef, about six miles off Key Largo, Florida, just another member of the biological community. I lived on an abandoned lighthouse for weeks at a time with nothing to do but conduct research, snorkel, and dive. Consequently, I spent hundreds of hours in and under the water. Eventually, I learned to identify barracudas as individuals, as well as to respect their territories. Cleaning stations buzzing with shrimp and small wrasses welcomed me, picking at my face and arms as I hovered motionless — after they were done with the groupers in front of me, of course. I hung out with big, silvery tarpon, and always welcomed a chance to have a stare-down contest with my friends the cuttle-

71

fish. Once, a trio of elegant eagle rays allowed me to join them in their graceful dance. When I was not underwater, I could watch other transactions taking place from my hammock strung high above the water. Reef sharks moved in through the spurs and grooves of the reef to hunt. And late at night, I could see fishing boats hunting, too.

Coral reefs do a lot of things that are clearly visible, and some that are not. The partnership between corals and the tiny algae (zooxanthellae) that live in their tissues is remarkable not only in its complexity, but also in its productivity. The corals capture the occasional copepod (small, shrimp-like animals) and metabolize it into nutrients, which are transferred to the zooxanthellae in exchange for the products of photosynthesis. Corals also provide shelter for their vulnerable partners. The photosynthesis by the zooxanthellae, in turn, makes it easier for the corals to turn carbonate molecules in the seawater into the limestone that shelters both the coral and the zooxanthellae. As a result of this partnership, corals have been able to build the marvelous limestone structures that attract and nurture the coral reef community.

Reefs supply most of the fresh protein for many islanders around the world and have become sources of high-priced fish for distant markets as well. The aquarium industry derives most of their specimens from reefs. In addition to all these valuable goods, reefs provide important services. Reefs protect shorelines from storm damage, and produce and sustain beautiful white sand beaches. Some of the reef's inhabitants produce unusual chemical compounds that perhaps arose in response to the constant competition for space and safety characteristic of the crowded coral reef community. Many of these compounds hold promise for alleviating human pain and suffering. Already, several compounds have been isolated from coral reef animals and plants that show strong anti-viral and anti-inflammatory properties.

Beyond all of the utilitarian values of coral reefs, they provide immeasurable pleasure for the senses and important lessons in living. One is transformed upon entering the coral reef community. The colors, the swirling patterns of silvery fish, and the beauty of the coral formations and brightly-colored animals are overwhelming. Fish reveal strange and fascinating behaviors to the patient diver or snorkeler. There's nothing quite like suddenly encountering a 100-foot (30-meter), nearly vertical drop-off in crystal-clear water after cruising through the shallow reef flats. It's what I imagine sky-diving must feel like, except slower and safer. Occasionally, huge whale sharks, dolphins, and big pelagic fish like tuna will drop by for a visit at the reef's edge.

The coral reef produces much and wastes little. The partnership between coral animals and the tiny algae that live within their tissues lies at the core of the reef. Many other organisms engage in similar mutually-beneficial relationships. Energy and materials are shared, exchanged, and tightly recycled by the community. We would do well to apply these lessons to our own communities.

Delicate-looking coral reefs are actually quite resilient, but only if conditions are right. They can recover from fierce storms and even volcanic eruptions if the dust and sediment eventually settle and are washed away. Water quality must return to clean, clear conditions for reef healing to take place. Corals, the tiny animals that build enormous limestone structures that house the coral reef community, also thrive in a fairly narrow band of temperatures. And of course, as is the case with any complex community, the coral reef needs all its members to be present and active. Each has a role to play in the never-ending drama of the reef, even if we observers can't quite figure out what that role might be.

Current Threats

Sadly, human enterprise is simultaneously destroying coral reefs directly and reducing their capacity to recover. This is the sort of double-whammy that can result in ecological collapse — and that is just what is happening to coral reefs around the world. Overfishing is rampant in many coral reef countries, driven in part by increasing demand and rising prices for coral reef fish which have become status symbols in the fancy restaurants of Hong Kong and other major cities. People beat the reef with sticks, pummeling the structures that nurture life into rubble, to drive fish out of their hiding places. Cyanide is used to the same end, narcotizing the fish for easy capture, but also killing delicate corals and sponges in the process. Reefs are even blown up with dynamite to capture fish, perhaps the ultimate in unsustainable fishing.

Meanwhile, the natural healing processes of the reef are impeded by declining water quality. Water quality is crucial for reef health, just as clean air is crucial for our own well-being. The waters surrounding coral reefs are getting dirtier, mostly as a result of inadequately treated wastewater and poor land use that allows sediments (basically, dirt) and fresh water (sometimes laden with pesticides) to run off the land and pollute the salty waters surrounding reefs. The rash of coral diseases reported in recent years remains mysterious, but may be due in part to sewage pollution.[1] The mangrove swamps that once protected reefs from sediments and freshwater flows are being removed to make charcoal and to farm shrimp for export. Sediments are also ruining seagrass meadows where many coral reef fishes go to feed every day, returning to their shelters in the reef at night like suburban commuters. The nutrients gained from eating seagrasses are also transported to the reef, added in small pulses that do not over-enrich the sensitive marine algae and corals. Seagrasses thrive in clear water, but (being plants) they cannot survive for long in waters muddied by runoff.

Perhaps most alarmingly, human activities are harming the central relationship of the reef, the one that makes it all possible — the partnership of zooxanthellae and corals. These allies part ways sometimes, resulting in the loss of color known as coral bleaching. This loss of color is much more than an aesthetic problem. The color arises from the photosynthetic pigment of the zooxanthellae, essential for photosynthesis and thus for manufacturing the food corals need to grow, reproduce, and create limestone skeletons. After bleaching, corals literally starve, shrinking in size and often dying. Corals bleach in response to any number of factors, including too much fresh water after a storm (especially when coastal highlands and mangrove swamps have been deforested, allowing water and sediments to flow freely into coral reef waters).

Extreme temperatures, which to a reef mean just a couple of degrees warmer than usual, can also cause bleaching. Starting in the late 1970s, some alert scientists were noticing that reports of coral bleaching were on the rise, and that many bleaching episodes were taking place during the warm seasons. Some field researchers were reporting that waters were especially calm and temperatures especially high during some bleaching episodes.

During the 1980s, the hottest decade on record at that point, corals bleached again and again. Many hypotheses were tendered to explain this puzzling phenomenon. Could it be a symptom of increasing threats such as poor land use, pollution, and overfishing? Perhaps, but coral reefs were bleaching in remote locations, far from human activities, as well as in places where the threats were intense. No common pathogen (disease-causing bacteria or virus) seemed to be implicated.

The factor that appeared to be common to many bleaching episodes, but not all, was elevated temperature. Laboratory experiments indicated that small increases in temperature, just one or two degrees, could induce bleaching. A few scientists showed that many bleaching episodes were correlated with the arrival of "hot spots" of warm water. Tom Goreau, Jr., a scrappy and (as it turns out) prescient coral reef ecologist, and I were among the first to warn that coral bleaching was likely to increase if global warming was allowed to proceed. Environmental Defense, Greenpeace, and other environmental groups soon joined the chorus of cautionary voices.

During the early 1990s, bleaching was not as common as it had been during the 1980s. Goreau predicted that after the dust from the 1991 explosion of Mount Pinatubo (which had cooled the earth off a little) settled, bleaching would return and become even more intense. Global warming would then continue to increase sea temperatures and induce mass coral bleaching.

Our theory that global warming would result in more extensive coral bleaching was met with disdain by many in the coral reef scientific community. It was agreed that bleaching was a problem, but many scientists held that it was not a global problem, and thus could be explained by local factors. Some accused us of being "false Cassandras" — irresponsible alarmists with a disregard for the facts. I was unprepared for such a harsh reception, having worked fruitfully with many scientists in the past. The small band of scientists and environmentalists who believed that coral bleaching would get worse as global warming proceeded supported each other, as we continued our efforts to alert the world to this threat. We managed to get some language into various international agreements (e.g., Agenda 21, signed at the Rio Earth Summit) proclaiming the importance of coral reefs and how vulnerable they were to climate change. But the lack of scientific consensus around coral bleaching, and more significantly, the lack of political will to reduce fossil fuel use, held back meaningful reforms. We recommended that the Framework Convention on Climate Change should mandate a schedule for reducing greenhouse gas emissions that would slow the rate of global warming sufficiently to give coral reefs some chance of adapting — but this recommendation was rejected.

The wrath of the scientific community is the price one sometimes has to pay for speculations on future threats, which often cannot be supported by strong empirical evidence until it's too late to do anything about them. It is one of the duties of a scientist working as a professional environmental advocate to go out on a limb and sound the alarm. There is tremendous value in having academic scientists keep out of the fray, staying focused on conducting research without a political agenda. Those of us in the environmental movement, however, have chosen to walk along a perilous ledge by trying to be objective and communicate with the public and policy makers, and at the same time making what we hope are reasonable projections of trends — projections that cannot always be solidly supported by empirical results. We need to make these projections to motivate action by policy makers before the costs of taking action become too high, or irreversible impacts are incurred. Our calculus is that the risk to the environment outweighs the risk to our careers as scientists. Scientific waffling on environmental issues, with a focus on what we do not know, is too often used to justify inaction, going with the flow of strong economic and political forces in favor of the status quo.

Environmentalists must make the case that precaution is prudent in the face of uncertainty — that inaction is sometimes a dangerous default. And by advocating action, we step away from the stout and solid trunk of academic science, and climb out onto limbs blown about by the fickle winds of politics. Most of us do not expect academic scientists to risk their status by climbing out there with us. We welcome those who want to join us; they are critically important allies. At the same time, we recognize and value the contributions of scientists who stay out of political fights, increasing knowledge and understanding through research. However, it would be helpful if scientists who disagree with our analyses of threats or suggested solutions did not seek to destroy our credibility. Increased dialogue between scientists and environmentalists could lead to increased understanding of the two cultures, increased respect, and increased effectiveness.

Despite our poor reputation among some academic scientists (and of course, among corporate flacks and anti-environmental activists who routinely accuse of us of doing junk science), the Cassandras of the environmental movement have a pretty good track record. Of course, if we were as effective as we would like to be, all of our predictions of doom and gloom would be rendered false by quick and intelligent action. Some of our predictions have not come true, whether due to faulty analysis or remedial measures. Although global population is still increasing, the "population bomb" predicted by Paul Ehrlich did not explode, perhaps because governments took the threat seriously. Fertility rates in many developing countries have dropped quite dramatically — in 33 countries, fertility rates have been cut in half or more since 1970.[2] According to the World Resources Institute,[3] these changes, especially in rapidly developing countries, may be due principally to improved education, increased childhood survival rates, and family planning. It is important to note that such changes are also often associated with economic development and changes in social conditions, particularly with increasing numbers of women entering work forces. Disease, war, and starvation have claimed millions, further dampening population growth.

In nearly every lecture I have ever given, someone states that we environmentalists nervously avoid the issue of overpopulation, which they characterize as the root of all environmental evils. I often respond that environmental impact depends on at least two major variables, population size and impact per capita. Per capita impact is hard to define, but can be approximated by consumption by an average citizen of energy, food, and building materials, or by pollution per capita. By any number of measures, an average citizen of an industrialized country has far, far more environmental impact than an average citizen of a developing country. Therefore, overall environmental impact, especially with regard to the commons of atmosphere, oceans, fresh water, and biodiversity, can be reduced either by reducing the world's population or by reducing the consumption and pollution rates of those of us who live in the industrialized world. Fewer babies, or fewer (or more fuel-efficient) SUVs? Of course, the answer is both.

As it stands, the Cassandras were right about DDT, lead (and more recently, methyl tertiary butyl ether or MTBE) in gasoline, the collapse of fisheries, global warming, the ozone hole, and many other issues — including coral bleaching. In 1998, the world suffered the worst bout of coral bleaching on record, in line with Tom Goreau's prediction. While large areas of coral reef escaped, up to 95 percent of the corals on shallow reefs in the Maldives, Sri Lanka, Thailand, Singapore, and parts of Tanzania bleached and died.[4]

Changing the Prognosis

The prognosis for coral reefs is not encouraging. But of course, the future depends on what we make of it, for the threats to coral reefs are for the most part the result of human activities and choices. If climate change is not slowed down, mass coral bleaching will probably continue and will likely worsen. Rising seas resulting from the expansion of seawater and melting ice might "drown" some coral reefs, as unlikely as that sounds.

Rapidly rising seas would increase the distance between the corals and the life-giving sunlit surface waters too rapidly for the reefs to keep pace with by growing vertically (especially if they are bleached, polluted, or otherwise hampered).

Despite the degradation of coral reefs worldwide, some beautiful ones remain. The shifting baseline phenomenon[5] keeps tourists coming to visit reefs that experienced divers, naturalists, and scientists would classify as trashed. When one lacks the historical perspective gained by studying coral reef cores that transport you back hundreds of years, or by looking at the descriptions of reefs and their fisheries by early naturalists and others, one misses the slow changes that occur on the reef. How the urchins and grazing fishes disappeared or are greatly reduced in number, and how algae cover the reef in the absence of the animals that keep the algae under control by eating them. How living corals turn to bare coral skeletons over time. How the huge aggregations of big groupers have dwindled. Where have all the fishes gone? According to eco-historian Jeremy Jackson and others,[6] fishing has dramatically altered marine ecosystems on a vast scale. Humans have removed or greatly reduced enormous herds of sea cows, sea turtles, oysters, and other animals that served valuable ecological functions, such as keeping seagrass meadows trim and diverse, and filtering the waters of the Chesapeake Bay (as explained in Chapter 1).

But to the first-time visitor to a coral reef, even the most damaged reef looks beautiful and alluring (especially after a long plane trip from some snow-encrusted city). There are still lots of colorful fish to see, and the eerie coral formations are still there to marvel at (although they are now dead). The baseline has shifted, so now overfished, polluted, and depauperate reefs are advertised as spectacular and alive with beauty. And so the tourists still flock to reefs, fueling the drive to make more and bigger cruise ships and resorts and causing more and more pollution and degradation. Large-scale coral reef tourism may continue to grow despite the demise of the reefs, resulting in a vicious cycle — unless historical awareness and an appreciation for truly healthy reefs can be increased.

In addition to educating the public about the nature and history of coral reefs, and about the impact of unsustainable tourism on reefs, we might also be able to create economic incentives for more sustainable tourism operations. Environmentalists, as arbiters of what is environmentally-friendly, could get together to support a common set of environmental performance standards for resorts, or to create their own by working with the industry so as to ensure that the criteria are practical (while being technology-forcing to some extent) and acceptable. A resort with a coral park for a front yard could trumpet the increased richness of animal life, the large populations of big fish, and the glowing health of their very own coral reef.

There is abundant evidence that coral parks (marine reserves) in coral reefs perform well, especially if the reef has been overfished in the past. The operating principles of the resort of the future would be based on the coral reef principles of maximizing productivity and minimizing waste through highly efficient use and recycling of clean renewable energy, water, waste streams, and non-toxic materials. Lush gardens could be watered with clean, treated gray water collected from the laundry room and sinks. Sewage could be composted into clean soil amendments. Hot air-conditioning exhaust could be captured and put to use. Visitors could take the next step in their diving expertise by learning environmentally-friendly diving skills and becoming amateur scientists, helping to collect data on reef health. They could participate in activities to enhance the coral park, such as reef clean-up dives. And of course, they could help finance the whole operation with a diving or visitor's fee. Studies suggest that divers would happily pay extra to see more and larger fish in a marine reserve. We already fork over ten dollars to dive in the Bonaire Marine Park which, until recently, was enough to cover the operating expenses of the park. I don't think those of us who appreciate the beauty of Bonaire's reefs, some of the very best in the Caribbean, would balk at paying a little more to protect what we travel so far to see.

Drugs from the Reef

Improved drug-screening technologies and the ongoing quest for new medicines may intensify the search for useful products from the sea. This search will probably continue to include coral reefs. Fierce competition for space and the battle for survival in complex reef communities has resulted in numerous adaptations, some of which turn out to be remarkably useful for humans. About two dozen drugs have already been derived from sea life, including chemicals that reduce inflammatory swelling, kill viruses, relax muscles, reduce pain, and work against parasites and cancer. Horseshoe-crab blood is being used to detect endotoxins released during bacterial infections. Phosphorescent chemicals from marine plankton are useful for tracking biochemical reactions. Natural insecticides have been derived from sea worms, antifouling agents from bryozoans (small, tentacled animals that form bushy colonies), and bone replacements from coral. Cone shell snails, treasured for their lovely patterns, turn out to possess one of the most potent toxins in the natural world. Being rather slow as predators go, they may need to knock out their prey very quickly. Their toxin shows promise as a super-effective pain-killer — up to ten thousand times more potent than morphine[7] — because it binds very selectively to certain receptors in the human nervous system, blocking the transmission of pain signals to the brain. The extremely precise selectivity of the toxin holds the potential of making the pain-killer derived from it non-addicting and ever-potent, capable of relieving chronic pain suffered by those who have become non-responsive to increasing doses of morphine. The Caribbean sponge *Discodermia dissolute* yields discodermalide, a possible treatment for breast cancer and some kinds of leukemia. Marine sponges have already given us the antiviral and anti-leukemia drugs Ara-A and Ara-C. New discoveries, if they pan out, could greatly boost the economic value of biological diversity. Current U.S. revenue from marine biotechnology is about $75–100 million per year.

Less developed countries such as Papua New Guinea, poor in cash but rich in biological diversity, are likely to be the focus of a new generation of bio-prospectors. Because many of the unusual compounds that ocean organisms produce cannot be synthesized in the laboratory, and because the compounds are often present in very small quantities, huge amounts of sea life are often required to extract tiny amounts of purified extracts. This can lead to overexploitation if not carefully regulated. The cultivation of organisms to meet the demands of the pharmaceutical industry could reduce the threat of overharvesting. In New Zealand, hundreds of tons of green-lipped mussels are farmed to provide the raw material for extracting the anti-arthritic compound Seatone. A new kind of imperialism could develop, too — pharmaceutical firms based in industrialized countries could exploit the biological riches of less developed countries, without benefiting the host countries very much.

New drugs from sea life can be an economic boon, especially in less developed countries where new kinds of useful compounds are most likely to be found. While the medical benefits of these new discoveries could benefit anyone who can afford them once they are brought to market, the countries that host the biodiversity at the root of new medicines will only benefit if enforceable agreements are achieved.

In the early 1990s, interest in capturing some of the economic benefits of biodiversity increased. In the past, biological diversity was viewed as a global commons that could be exploited by anyone, anywhere for improving crops or creating medicines. However, though the discovery of medicines such as vincristine and vinblastine (from the rosy periwinkle of Madagascar) benefited both cancer patients who were able to afford them and Eli Lilly and Company which developed them, Madagascar did not get a cut of the profits.[8] During the negotiations for the Convention on Biological Diversity, the notion that countries have sovereignty over genetic resources (biodiversity) began to gain ascendancy, at least in the minds of environmentalists and the leaders of developing countries. Some embarked on efforts to accommodate the interests of private enterprise with those of conservation and sustainable development.

In 1991, the National Institute of Biodiversity of Costa Rica (INBio) signed an agreement with Merck Pharmaceuticals to achieve such an accommodation. Merck agreed to pay INBio $1 million for the privilege of screening samples. INBio would also receive royalties on products that are eventually developed from these samples. It was thought at the time that royalties on just 20 drugs would exceed total revenues from coffee and bananas, Costa Rica's top export crops. With Merck's help, Costa Rica developed its own capacity to screen samples, as well. According to INBio, "bioprospecting agreements stipulate that ten percent of research budgets and 50 percent of any future royalties be awarded to the Ministry of the Environment and Energy (MINAE) for reinvestment in conservation."[9] Since 1991, such financial contributions have exceeded $2.5 million. Conservation programs linked to bioprospecting have protected significant amounts of land in the tropics — for example, four million acres (1.6 million hectares) were set aside in a reserve in Surinam.[10]

Efforts to leverage tropical biodiversity into cash, jobs, and conservation have not been without controversy. Indigenous leaders were not consulted early in the INBio-Merck negotiations, nor were they consulted in planning a bioprospecting project in Chiapas, Mexico. The Chiapas project was halted due to the concerns of local activists and indigenous people that the drug companies would privatize species that had been freely available, profiting from them in the form of new, expensive drugs.[11] Indigenous activists often object to debt-for-nature swaps and bioprospecting agreements on the grounds that biodiversity is not the property of the government, to be negotiated away in exchange for money, even if the money is to be used for conservation. In addition, some groups object to the whole idea of plugging into the global marketplace.

Tropical species have yielded many important medicines in the past. Some 80 percent of the world's population relies on traditional medicines made from crude extracts. Drugs extracted from plants and animals account for about 25 percent of all the prescriptions filled in the U.S., valued at $15.5 billion in 1990.[12] But the excitement of the early 1990s about new drugs from the rain-forest has been dampened by the failure of drug companies to produce profitable drugs from tropical organisms in recent years. The tendency of drug companies to jealously guard their secrets may be responsible to some extent for the lack of news. But Merck terminated its agreement with INBio in 1999 — they had not found any natural products with potential commercial value, but say they are still analyzing samples.[13] Other companies have found several tropical organisms that kill pain, fight antibiotic-resistant bacteria, and seem to be effective against certain kinds of cancer and AIDS. But the tedious process of isolating purified compounds from animals and plants, and then testing them clinically, has slowed the conversion of shaman's cures to modern drugs. In addition, drug companies are pouring more resources into creating new drugs through genetic engineering and chemical synthesis.[14]

Controversy over intellectual property rights, ownership of biodiversity, and just compensation to developing countries for the right to collect or screen samples for possible drug development have stalled many bioprospecting projects around the world. Many countries, such as the Philippines, now have guidelines and regulations intended to ensure that the benefits of biodiversity accrue locally, that indigenous people consent to efforts to find and extract natural products, and that natural ecosystems are not harmed by rapacious collecting.[15] Researchers and drug companies often complain about the difficulty of getting permits to collect samples from these countries. Government officials retort that frustrated applicants did not go through the whole process, or filed permit applications that were too vague.[16] Unfortunately, the guidelines intended to regulate bioprospecting and to ensure that the fruits of such research accrue at least in part to conservation and the host country seem to be dampening interest. Perhaps the answer lies in the development of drug companies and joint ventures within the developing nations themselves, such as Extracta in Brazil. The key will be national laws that link conservation to bioprospecting, without so much bureaucracy that it thwarts even well-intentioned businesses.

Coping with a Warmer World

Fortunately, the same actions that we take to reduce the direct threats to coral reefs may also help reefs cope with less direct threats like climate change. Kelp forests seem to be able to persist in marine reserves, even when kelps all around them are dying when the water is warm and unproductive (as a result of El Niños). In a similar way, coral reefs might be less subject to mass coral bleaching, or perhaps better able to recover, if other stresses were eliminated or reduced. Bleaching may be a sort of generalized stress reaction, like a headache. The reduction of overall stress in marine reserves and throughout coral reef waters by stopping destructive fishing, controlling pollution, and improving land use that affects the reefs may provide more scope for adapting to the inevitable warming that the world will experience.

The Nature Conservancy and Worldwide Fund for Nature are leading efforts to identify environmental factors that may enable corals to resist bleaching in certain areas and to help them recover from bleaching elsewhere. For example, corals that live in upwellings that bring cold water to the surface, in strong currents that dissipate any harmful byproducts of bleaching, or in turbid waters that block the harmful rays of the sun appear to be less susceptible to bleaching.[17] Setting aside such areas in marine protected areas could prove invaluable — it would be tragic to lose places that resist bleaching to more pedestrian threats such as dynamite fishing or sewage pollution. Likewise, setting up marine protected areas to reduce impacts generally on reefs to allow them to recover as quickly as possible from unavoidable bleaching would likely help.[18]

Coral reefs might be able to cope better with global warming if they are protected from other threats. But coral reefs and other sensitive ecosystems might not be able to survive the amount of warming that will occur if we do nothing to reduce greenhouse gas concentrations in the atmosphere. Coral reefs will likely be the first ecological victims of unchecked global warming. The leaders and inhabitants of coral reef countries have been among

the best spokespeople for decisive action, for their lives and livelihoods depend on success.

To save coral reefs and the people who depend on them from
the effects of global warming, we must find ways to reduce emissions of greenhouse gases such as carbon dioxide, methane, and
nitrous oxide and to increase their absorption. At the same time,
we will need to adapt to the inevitable effects of the climate
changes that will result from these gases — some of which will
stay in the atmosphere for decades. Officials in Tuvalu have
already asked New Zealand to accept its citizens when they aban-
don their country due to rising sea level. The rising sea has flooded the land, eroded shorelines and tainted groundwater supplies
of fresh water there.[19]

California will probably lead the way to a more sensible U.S.
energy policy, one of the keys to addressing global warming. The
state passed a law in 2002 (Assembly Bill 1493) that will set
standards for greenhouse gas emissions from cars and trucks, if
lawsuits filed by the auto industry are defeated. California
derives about eight percent of its total energy needs from renewable sources, such as wind, solar, and hydropower.[20] While large-
scale hydropower (huge dams and turbines) is not really sustainable due to its impacts on wildlife and natural systems, small-
scale hydropower can serve remote operations well. A diverse
and decentralized mixture of renewable energy farms, including
solar panels and small wind turbines on top of individual buildings and homes, could potentially supply significant portions of
our national energy needs. The California Public Interest
Research Group (CALPIRG) even anticipates that increasing the
amount of renewable power could create more jobs. They estimate that generating enough renewable power to meet 20 percent of California's needs could create over 100,000 person-
years of employment over 30 years. This is about four times the
employment that reliance on natural gas would produce, according to CALPIRG's calculations.[21] We can achieve energy independence more quickly if energy needs are reduced (without
necessarily reducing our quality of life) through sensible energy

conservation measures that can pay for themselves in cost savings over time.

Success Stories

The Bonaire Marine Park on the little Caribbean island of Bonaire is hard to get to, but well worth the effort. One of the Netherland Antilles, along with better-known Curacao and Aruba, Bonaire has charming villages that remind one of Holland, with colorful buildings and clean, neat streets. The coastline is spectacular, varying from the rough windward side to the relatively calm lee side, where one can gaze at the small island of Klein Bonaire. But Bonaire is distinguished most of all by the gorgeous reef that fringes the island, "just a giant stride away" (as the resort brochures put it) from your hotel room. The resorts of Bonaire offer by far the happiest combination of easy diving and beautiful coral reefs I've ever known. In most of the places I've been, one must suffer at least a little to glimpse stunning coral reefs, whether it's a week on a rocking, cramped dive boat, or balancing on a rickety canoe, or traveling far out to uninhabited atolls in the South Pacific. But on Bonaire, you need only stumble out of bed at any hour, walk to the pier in front of your hotel, grab your gear in the lockers on the way, put it on, and keep walking until you fall off, almost directly into healthy coral reefs bristling with life. For more of a challenge, you can also do a shore dive where swimming fifty yards will bring you into amazing sponge formations and again, the living reef.

Best of all, Bonaire's marvelous reef has been under the protection of the Bonaire Marine Park for 23 years, since 1979. Fishing is generally light (except for conchs, which have all but disappeared) and is mostly conducted by ordinary folk looking to catch dinner. Divers registering at some of the resorts are required to take an orientation class, where environmentally-friendly diving techniques such as good buoyancy control and restrictions on touching or taking things from the reef are emphasized. In all the resorts one must purchase a permit to dive in the park, the proceeds going to support park operations and enforcement. The annual Bonaire Dive Festival celebrates the synergy between the Bonaire Tourism Corporation, local environmentalists, the dive masters, resort owners, underwater photographers (and equipment salesmen), Rodale's Scubadiving Magazine, the Coral Reef Alliance (a U.S.-based environmental group specializing in working with divers and the dive industry), and assorted visiting lecturers. The Dive Festival is a chance to get together with like-minded tourists, scientists, and environmentalists to talk about the endless fascinations of the reef and also to dive together to experience the reef, learn more about it, and clean it up.

Even in Bonaire, which has what is generally acknowledged to be one of the healthiest reefs in the Caribbean, the shifting baseline obtains. Long-term monitoring studies have revealed that catches are small not solely due to a conservation ethic — most of the large groupers are gone, most likely fished out years ago. Spikey staghorn coral and its more massive cousin, the elkhorn coral, once grew as a nearly impenetrable thicket around most of the island. Both species have been reduced by disease to a few small clumps, as has been the case throughout the Caribbean.

Many people on Bonaire seem to recognize the importance of protecting the reef, the country's main economic engine. The country's leaders and business people celebrate the marine park, but also acknowledge emerging threats such as the increasing amounts of wastewater being discharged into nearshore waters. Resort owners such as the pioneering Captain Don advocate advanced treatment for Bonaire's sewage. At a Marine Environmental Summit held during one dive festival, I spoke of the importance of protecting water quality, and described Environmental Defense's Ecoparque project in Mexico (see Chapter 3) as an example of how Bonaire might be able to reclaim water in its arid climate (most of the Bonaire's water is claimed from seawater, at great expense). I speculated that an Ecoparque approach in Bonaire might also help to improve poor soils with carbon and nutrients recycled from sewage relatively unpolluted by industrial toxic wastes. The local environmentalists and representatives of the tourism board supported my arguments. Much to my surprise, I was invited later that week to meet with several government officials to talk about protecting water quality. And while it took a couple of years to overcome some bureaucratic obstacles, Bonaire is now moving forward to collect its sewage and treat it in a way that will not harm the reef. Whether they go all the way and close the other ecological loops of fresh water, carbon, and nutrients remains to be seen, but the new plans (and money) for sewage collection and treatment are a very promising start.

While Bonaire was reaping the economic and aesthetic benefits of their marine park, progress toward truly effective marine reserves in the Florida Keys was stalling in the late 1980s and early 1990s. During a particularly contentious meeting, I was speaking of values and rituals to protect the environment and sustainable harvests, and asked the crowd what kind of ritual we could employ to bond and come together, that would be culturally appropriate for the Keys? "Heavy drinking" was the reply, only half-jokingly. The debate over marine reserves in the Florida Keys National Marine Sanctuary had turned ugly. In fact, the consensus that had been forged to establish the sanctuary itself was unraveling. I was greeted at many meetings by angry shouts from opponents waving signs that said "Say No to NOAA" (the National Oceanic and Atmospheric Administration, lead agency for the establishment and management of marine sanctuaries). Protesters held pictures of jack-booted government officials trampling over the Keys. Billy Causey, the sanctuary manager, and others were hung in effigy, and many of us were threatened or had our tires slashed. How could we re-direct all of this anger into a constructive channel?

I saw that people were rallying around a common "enemy" — NOAA. It occurred to me that if we could swap NOAA for a real enemy that threatened the livelihoods and lifestyles of everyone in the Keys, not just the fishermen and treasure salvors who were leading the opposition to the sanctuary, we could unite. I enlisted the help of a progressive fishermen named Karl Lessard, the leader of a faction of more moderate fishermen interested in working out a compromise over marine reserves in the sanctuary.

These fishermen had worked alongside environmentalists, scientists, and many other stakeholders with diverse interests to develop an elegant proposal for a system of marine reserves. This network of reserves would have protected sections of each major biogeographical section of the Keys — the well developed reefs off Key Largo, the patch reefs of the mid-Keys, the reefs of the lower Keys, the mangrove/seagrass/reef system of the Marquesas, and the fairly pristine reefs of the Dry Tortugas. These marine reserves, which (on paper) spanned the shore to the reef crest so as to protect the essential linkages between mangroves, seagrasses, and the various zones of the coral reef, would have protected about 20 percent of sanctuary waters.[22] However, the careful compromise worked out by the sanctuary advisory committee was threatened by the increasing opposition to marine reserves and to the sanctuary itself.

In part to save the marine reserve proposal, and in part to keep the sanctuary afloat, Karl and I sought to bring a wider group of stakeholders together to restore Florida Bay. Nearly everyone in the Keys valued the bay and believed it to be threatened by pollution running off farms in the Everglades and by the massive diversion of fresh water away from the bay made possible by the vast flood control system built and operated by the U.S. Army Corps of Engineers and the South Florida Water Management District. Some fishermen had kept careful records of water temperatures, salinity, and algal blooms in the bay, and had warned scientists and officials that things were not right in the late 1980s. They reported die-offs of seagrasses and large patches of unusual colored water in the bay.

Later, scientists agreed that something strange was going on, but could not agree on what it was. One school held that the rerouting of massive amounts of fresh water to protect people from floods and to irrigate crops in the Everglades had starved the bay of fresh water, causing salinity levels to build up to dangerous levels. Some parts of the bay were registering upwards of twice the strength of normal sea water. This, the theory went, caused the once diverse beds of seagrass typical of the bay to morph into a monoculture of turtle grass, the one species that could flourish at high salinities.

The long, hot decade of the 1980s was thought to have exacerbated the adverse ecological conditions in the bay, and it had been a long time since a hurricane had flushed out accumulated organic debris. The decomposition of this debris may have contributed to an outbreak of a slime mold pathogen that killed seagrasses. The dead seagrasses then decomposed, adding more nutrients to the water, and the loose, muddy sediments that were exposed after the seagrasses died released still more nutrients. Excessive amounts of nutrients may have fueled the unusual algal blooms (resulting in colored water) first spotted by fishermen, and later seen in satellite images showing hot, salty, colored water flowing through the Bay, out through the sluice in the middle-Keys, and right out into Hawk Channel and the coral reefs. Nearly all the sponges in Florida Bay, which once provided important habitat for any number of creatures (as well as a water filtering service, I suppose) succumbed to these algal blooms.

Another scientist and his followers were violently opposed to this theory. They held that excessive nutrients from farming in the Everglades and perhaps from the Keys themselves were to blame for the devastating algal blooms and the seagrass die-offs. This sort of thing happens often in scientific debates, particularly when the debates are conducted in public hearings and newspapers rather than in person. The polarization of hypotheses may result from our natural human tendency to think in terms of dichotomies, comparing and contrasting but not synthesizing. Nature does not seem to work that way, though. More often than not, several factors contribute to the onset of an environmental problem, and it is not easy to sort out what they are or how important each is. The Greeks thought that the ability to hold two contradictory thoughts in one's head was a sign of high intelligence. The logic of synthesis and multiple causation may more accurately reflect the workings of ecosystems than Cartesian duality or competing hypotheses.

A synthesist explanation of the decline of Florida Bay would go something like this. Nutrients (from fertilizers) running off farms in the Everglades fueled algal blooms and over-nourished the seagrasses, resulting in unusually lush beds with lots of accumulated biomass. Water diversions, drought, and elevated average temperatures during the 1980s all contributed to the reduction of seagrass diversity, rendering the remaining monoculture of over-grown turtle grass (one species of seagrass) susceptible to disease. A slime-mold took advantage of a great opportunity and started to decimate the thick turtle grass meadows, setting off a cycle of decomposition and nutrient remineralization that fueled still larger algal blooms.

The workshop of diverse stakeholders that Karl and I convened in the Keys (with the help of the state's office of conflict resolution) did not get into the scientific debate over what was to blame for the decline of the bay. The participants simply stated, one after another, that farming and turning the hydrologic cycle of the Everglades upside down were both responsible. And they were mad as hell about it. After people who were fighting each other over marine reserves heard each other express this common sentiment, the whole tone of the meeting changed from one of skepticism and mistrust to one of empowerment. We broke the participants up into small groups to brainstorm solutions, and again, many common themes emerged.

By the end of the second workshop, the group had decided to incorporate as a new non-profit organization and to wage a campaign to put the hydrology of the Everglades right and reduce agricultural pollution. The Florida Keys Water Quality Joint Action Group had been born, and went on to become one of the most effective groups working to restore Florida Bay. The keys to its success seemed to be its singular focus on the bay, derived from both love of the bay and economic dependence on its health. Another strength was the diversity of its members, which included not only fishermen and environmentalists, but also fishing guides, realtors, mortgage brokers, and chamber of commerce types. The Joint Action Group brought a whole new dynamic to the debate over the Everglades and Florida Bay — it was no longer just about environmentalists against big sugar and farmers; it was now people whose livelihoods depended on ecosystem restoration versus the status quo.

Science often raises more questions than it answers, and the science around the decline of Florida Bay is no exception. A report in 2002 from the National Research Council warns that increasing water flows to the bay right now may add excessive levels of nitrogen and phosphorus, possibly triggering more algal blooms and seagrass die-offs.[23] Anticipating the potentially negative impacts of releasing polluted water into the Bay, we in the Joint Action Group called in early 1990s for the return of more natural flows of water into Florida Bay, along with measures to strip the water of nutrients resulting from agriculture in the Everglades.

I don't know whether the good will and good working relationships formed in the Joint Action Group contributed at all to the eventual acceptance of a large marine reserve in the Dry Tortugas. But due to strong opposition, the original beautifully crafted marine reserve proposal was drastically cut back to a fragmented array of marine reserves that protected only the emergent reefs (not adjacent seagrass beds or mangrove swamps, or the critical linkages between these ecosystems) and a small patch in the Sambos. The success of these little reserves in allowing fish and shellfish populations to recover after only a few years went a long way toward convincing even the most hard-core opponents of marine reserves that reserves actually could be beneficial. I think that the Joint Action Group helped tip the balance toward ecosystem restoration in the Everglades, and showed that people who are divided over one issue can still unite and achieve a common goal.

On the other side of the world in the Hawai'ian Islands, ocean conservation is taking a new (but old) twist. When I first began visiting Hawai'i in the early 1990s, I was struck by the sight of police hauling people off the beaches for camping there. Later I learned that the campers were mostly Native Hawai'ians engaging in traditional practices on lands (and in waters) that were taken from their ancestors during the annexation of Hawai'i by the United States. And the claims of the Native Hawai'ians went beyond the land and water, into the realm of culture, ethics, and metaphysics. They were seeking to reclaim the strong spiritual connections and associated traditions that served to nourish human communities, the human spirit, and nature.

Under traditional Hawai'ian governance, each of the Hawai'ian Islands was divided into political jurisdictions that followed the natural contours of the land and sea, instead of the arbitrary divisions that are now typical of most jurisdictions. The Hawai'ians wisely divided each island into wedges called ahupua'a that spanned watersheds, reaching from ridge top to ridge top and encompassing fertile valleys, floodplains, the shoreline, and the coral reef beyond.[24] The ahupua'a boundaries reflected an understanding that these ecosystems were inextricably linked and that human society and management should respect those linkages. Each ahupua'a had a clear leadership structure tied to the ecosystem.

The ahupua'a apparently functioned very well, meeting the needs of the people sustainably, even bountifully. Dozens of taro varieties (source of the staple food, poi) were grown in beautiful terraces with carefully controlled irrigation systems. The ancient Hawai'ians clearly recognized the value of crop diversity — an emphasis that is mirrored in other ancient cultures. For example, people living in the Andes mountains planted dozens of potato varieties to exploit different microclimates, reaping the advantages of not only greater production but also greater resilience to crop-destroying diseases.

Hawai'ian fishermen were not only subject to strict customary restrictions, such as alternating seasons to protect pelagic and nearshore fish,[25] but they also observed religious rituals to ensure good harvests. The ocean is of such importance to Hawai'ian culture that there are Hawai'ian words that describe at least seventeen different parts of the ocean and twelve different states of the seas.[26] Hawai'ian cultural practitioners still speak of ancestors, protectors, and guides — such as sharks and sea turtles — that protect them from the vagaries of the sea. The historical records suggest that, throughout the centuries, large amounts of fish were harvested year after year, providing for sumptuous feasts.[27]

Much has changed since the early 1900s when western civilization started to displace traditional practices. Monocultures of pineapple and sugar cane were planted for export, rather than to meet local needs. Traditional fishing regulations were abolished by the U.S. Congress, leading to a rapid decline in fisheries[28] right up to the overfishing of lobsters and bottomfish in recent years.

In the summer of 2000, I had the good fortune to spend time with a few inspiring individuals who, to me, personified the movement to restore Hawai'i's ahupua'a system and traditional practices. The brave persistence of people such as Chipper Wichman of Kaua'i, Ed Wendt of Maui, Auntie Judy Caparida of Moloka'i and many, many others has led to a strong resurgence of interest and activism to bring back traditional values and practices.

Chipper Wichman is a big, strong guy with a friendly and energetic demeanor. His grandmother, a pioneer of hibiscus cultivation, championed the protection of Kaua'i's Ha'ena ahupua'a which included the watershed draining into Ke'e beach at the end of road from Hanalei. Chipper worked tirelessly to clear the land of the many exotic species that had invaded and to unearth ancient irrigation works and farming terraces. Today, the beautiful Limahuli Garden stands as a testament to his grandmother's vision and his own hard work. Water flows through the garden in stone conduits, washing through terraces filled with many different kinds of taro and other useful plants.

Throughout the islands people catch fish to feed their families. More and more are pounding taro into poi, cultivating the traditional 'awa plant (more commonly known as kava kava). Auntie Judy Caparida took me on a bone-jarring ride around Moloka'i in her truck to show me people rebuilding ancient fish ponds and the splendors of the Halawa Valley where her family and followers camp for part of each year to live a more natural life. She spoke lovingly of children playing in the surf and of helping to provide for the community's needs, mixing in lessons in child-rearing. Ed Wendt, a natural leader, showed me the expanse of the ahupua'a in eastern Maui that he and his colleagues are trying to restore. I could easily imagine a beautiful network of traditional terrace farms co-existing with new industries that are compatible with conservation and traditional farming and gathering activities.

The combination of Native Hawai'ians living their traditional values with environmentalists proved to be powerful. Stephanie Fried, a senior scientist with Environmental Defense in their Hawai'i project office, had spent years working with indigenous communities engaged in defending their ancestral rights to protect and manage tropical forests of Indonesian Borneo before moving to Hawai'i. She has also worked in Washington, D.C., where she learned the ways of the capitol. Stephanie saw both opportunity and potential disaster when then-president Clinton announced his intention to designate the Northwestern Hawai'ian Islands (NWHI) a coral reef ecosystem reserve. This designation had the potential to provide long-lasting community-based protection for this vast and fragile region. However, Stephanie knew that if it was carried out without proper consultation, it could result in the further disenfranchisement of Hawai'ian communities from their resources and unchecked exploitation of the region. The Northwestern Hawai'ian Islands are still nearly pristine, a remote string of atolls and isles surrounded by coral reefs teeming with life — including most of the world's remaining population of 1,400 Hawai'ian monk seals as well as big fish that disappeared long ago from the main islands.

Stephanie knew that the key to success was to inform the Native Hawai'ian community about the fact that the federal government planned to seek public input into the process of protecting the NWHI and to ensure that local communities actively shaped the rules and regulations that came along with the new coral reef reserve. She worked tirelessly to ensure that information from Washington reached her Native Hawai'ian and Hawai'i environmentalist colleagues and that their voices were heard in the distant corridors of power in the nation's capital. She also worked with local activists to help launch a new coalition — KAHEA, the Hawai'ian Environmental Alliance. Under the able leadership of Vicky Holt Takamine, an articulate and well-respected Native Hawai'ian cultural practitioner, activist, and hula master, and long-time activist Cha Smith, KAHEA quickly convened a community meeting of elders, Native Hawai'ian activists, fishers, scientists, and environmentalists. It was one of the most remarkable meetings I have ever witnessed in a career dominated by attendance at meetings.

On the first night, elders rose to speak. The audience listened attentively to Uncle Buzzy Agard describe his early fishing expeditions to the Northwestern Hawai'ian Islands after World War II. He said that he would capture large schools of fish, fully expecting to come back later and capture more. But the schools did not return even 10 years later. His message, born of hard experience, was that large-scale fishing up there was not sustainable. Other elders such as Auntie Judy Caparida spoke movingly of the traditional Hawai'ian ethic that stems from a sense that human beings are in a profound relationship with nature, are actually part of nature, and must care for their family which includes the creatures of land and sea. Fisherman-turned-environmental activist Isaac Harp rose to present a document that he had prepared, supporting the proposed coral reef reserve and offering recommendations on how to implement it. By the end of the meeting, we were celebrating a community-based consensus — which included grandfathering in those few vessels that had been bottomfishing in the NWHI — achieved on the basis of Isaac's document, and community members were preparing to spread the word far and wide.

Grassroots activism combined with electronic activism strengthened the will of the Clinton administration to move forward with establishing the Northwest Hawai'ian Islands Coral Reef Ecosystem Reserve, building on the executive order issued by President Theodore Roosevelt in 1909 which provided the first protections for the NWHI. Progress continued, even in the face of fierce opposition by the politically well-connected Western Pacific Fishery Management Council (Wespac). Stephanie prepared analyses of federal government data and Wespac's own reports which clearly showed that the reserve would not have a significant negative economic impact on the bottomfish fishery since it grandfathered them in at the rates of catch that they reported to the state (and the Internal Revenue Service). Further analyses found that proposed closures were to be located outside of the zones where fishing activities had been reported, that NWHI fishing operations were not profitable, and that the NWHI lobster fishery had been "managed" into depletion. Stephanie set up a whirlwind tour to train Hawai'ian activists in the art of using the Member Action Network, a web-based electronic activism system that enables the public to submit comments directly to key government officials on issues of great concern. This network enables thousands of people to e-mail or fax the offices of key officials. Citizens from all fifty U.S. states sent over 35,000 letters to government officials in support of the reserve. Hawai'i residents participated in close to 25 state and federal hearings and consultation sessions on the NWHI over a two year period, overwhelmingly supporting strong protection measures.

Initially, the Bush administration wanted to review the executive orders which had established the NWHI Coral Reef Reserve, but for some reason (17,500 faxes to the secretary of commerce in support of the reserve, perhaps?) decided to let them stand. Hawai'i's leading gubernatorial candidate at the time, Linda Lingle, who is now the state's first Republican governor, came out in strong support of the reserve. But despite these victories, at this writing the future of the reserve is still in doubt as the federal government pushes ahead to convert the reserve to a "sanctuary" which could actually weaken the protections provided by reserve status. We can only hope that congress and the administration give proper weight to the vast outpouring of public support for the reserve, as well as to the sound scientific and economic arguments in favor of protection. If they do, they will provide for the permanent protection of the NWHI as a reserve not only for the endangered Hawai'ian monk seals, sea turtles, vast flocks of ocean-going albatrosses, and all of the other wonderful species that live there, but also for the elevation of our own human nature and values, re-learned from the ancient Hawai'ians and their modern descendants.

5

THE CONTINENTAL SHELF: The Ocean's Engine

The Nature of the Continental Shelf

Coastal nearshore waters cede to the continental shelf, with deeper waters covering a bottom gently sloping toward the precipice that defines the continental slope. The transition from nearshore waters to the continental shelf can be gradual and the shelf broad in some locations. In other places, the transition can be radical, plunging into deep underwater canyons close to shore.

Continental shelves occupy a small fraction of the ocean's area, but supply an inordinate share of total ocean production, generating ecological goods and services that some estimate to be worth trillions of dollars annually. Ecological goods include seafood, oil, minerals, and phycocolloids (compounds from seaweeds found in a vast array of products, from ice cream to cosmetics), among many others. Continental shelf and nearshore waters provide important ecological services as well, including the recycling of nutrients from the land, modulation of regional climates, and the assimilation of waste products. Beyond the utilitarian goods and services, the continental shelf is where you can get a sense of the vastness of the sea — that oceanic feeling. Shelf waters and sediments also host an astonishing array of creatures, some in almost unimaginable abundance.

Many different kinds of physical, chemical, and biological processes shape and maintain the organisms that live on the shelf. Northerly winds push surface waters south along the western edges of the continents, while forces generated by the earth's rotation deflect the water to the west. Because nature abhors a vacuum, deep water, rich in the products of decay (the ocean's compost), rushes up to replace the deflected surface waters, giving rise to the phenomenon we call upwelling. Upwellings fuel the prodigious production of kelp forests and microscopic phytoplankton in the surface waters. These in turn feed enormous populations of small herbivores, which are fed upon by their predators, which are prey for still other predators. On average, ocean food chains are (or were) longer than terrestrial food chains — but ocean food chains are getting shorter, apparently due to fishing (see Chapter 6).

Because the existence and strength of upwellings vary tremendously on many time scales, from days and weeks to years and even decades, the productivity of the shelf varies, too. Organisms have adapted to this variability in many different ways. Surface currents, gyres, and eddies that result from the interaction of the great mass movements of water with the bottom and the coastline further add to the complexity. Perhaps this variability of water movement and productivity shaped evolution, just as the variability (and isolation) of habitats spurred the origin of species on land. Even the water column, which looks homogeneous, is host to several thousand phytoplankton species. While this diversity of species is dwarfed by that of flowering plants on land (about 250,000 species), it is still somewhat surprising that seawater, lacking obvious barriers that would isolate populations and allow them to create new species, harbors so many. The mystery of ocean biodiversity continues.

Looking out on the sea, it is easy to get the impression that it is one big beautiful homogeneous ocean, where waters and organisms move freely about. But in fact, there is structure in the ocean at every level, from microscopic habitats to huge underwater mountains and canyons, and still larger fronts, eddies, and currents. Our understanding of the structure of ocean waters is changing rapidly, as we learn to look more deeply at it. Using microscopes and sophisticated analytical tools, scientists are seeing more and more structure where they once saw just water. Long strands of organic molecules, some perhaps exuded by phytoplankton, form islands of biological activity, fostering the growth of bacteria and facilitating all of the diverse ecological processes that these bacteria engage in. Perhaps these organic strands create a diversity of habitats that maintain species diversity at the microscopic scale.

Phytoplankton may be able to divide up resources and thus maintain their diversity in ways that don't depend on physical separation. Different species of phytoplankton absorb nutrients from the water at different rates and store nutrients for various amounts of time. They have different flotation characteristics, and some can even sense where the nutrients are and move up and down in the water to find the highest concentrations. Some species appear to be able to exploit ephemeral bursts of nutrients emitted by a passing copepod; others, to soak up nutrients even when they are present in extremely low concentrations.

Larger seaweeds, too, exhibit a wide variety of adaptations to the physical, chemical, and ecological (in terms of different kinds of animals trying to eat you) variability so characteristic of ocean ecosystems. Kelps can suck up nutrients during an upwelling episode and draw on them to support maximum growth rates for the next couple of weeks, without missing a beat. Many kinds of red and brown algae can do this trick. Green algae, however, tend to convert nutrients into rapid growth. Perhaps that is why they so often dominate areas that are chronically rich in nutrients —

their rapid growth allows them to cover more area more rapidly than brown or red seaweeds, which typically grow somewhat slower. On the other hand, when nutrients are only available periodically, reds and browns (including the kelps) do better.

On the bottom, the structure is more obvious to the human eye than it is in the water column. Patches of rocky reef, areas full of cobbles and boulders, and submarine canyons break the monotony of sandy and muddy stretches. But even the areas between the obvious habitats swarming with life are richly diverse. In fact, deep sea sediments may harbor tremendous species diversity (more on this in Chapter 7). On top of the loose sediments, organisms such as sponges and tunicates (colonial sea squirts) often create structures with their bodies, which in turn shelter young fishes. Fairly stable communities of rockfish, seaweeds, and various kinds of invertebrates form around rock piles, reefs, and biological structures. Many of these organisms are there for good, anchored to the rocks. Others could move on but choose to stay and make use of the shelter and food resources to be found there.

Fish and invertebrates experience lots of variation in their food supply, and the ocean conditions that support good growth of their babies vary tremendously too. One way to adapt to variability is to speciate — to diversify the genetic portfolio so that at least some relative or another will do well, no matter what. Another is to live a long time, perhaps sacrificing rapid growth for dogged persistence, so that one can take advantage of favorable periods for growth and reproduction that may only come along every ten or twenty years. Yet another trick might involve having many, many babies, again to improve the odds of survival in an ocean where 99 percent of your offspring get eaten before they even learn how to swim very well. Rockfish exhibit all of these characteristics — they live a long time (up to about 120 years for some species), have lots of babies (egg production increases exponentially with age and length), and exist in over 50 different varieties, making the North American West Coast the world's center of rockfish biodiversity. We consumers know most of them simply as "red snapper" or "rockfish", but those tender white fillets could have come from any of a number of fish that look completely different from one another.

Current Threats

As prodigiously productive as the continental shelf is, humans are appropriating a significant portion (perhaps 35 percent) of the shelf's primary production (phytoplankton growth), mainly in the form of fish.

The huge populations of groundfish that fishermen found on the western continental shelf of the U.S. in the 1970s were tempting targets. Fishery managers equated large populations with high productivity. In the ocean, large populations of organisms do indeed sometimes result from high rates of growth and reproduction. But in other cases, fast growth may result in only sparse populations, because processes that remove individuals (such as grazing, predation, or being swept away by currents) are just as fast. And sometimes large populations result not from high productivity, but from long lives and low natural mortality rates. This appears to be the case for rockfish.

While some fishery scientists, ecologists, and environmentalists have expressed concerns that rockfish populations might be more like redwood forests than sardine schools, the prevailing theory has been that rockfish are fairly productive and need to be thinned out to maximize their productivity. Based on studies using data from species not found off the West Coast, fishery managers and their scientific advisors lumped the many species of rockfish into several categories and extrapolated the optimum levels of abundance for these categories and the rates of fishing mortality (allowable catch plus discards) that would result, theoretically, in the maximum possible yield that could be sustained over the long term (called Maximum Sustainable Yield, or MSY for short).

Fishery scientists estimated rockfish abundance by surveying them infrequently, due to scarce research funds, and by scrutinizing the logbooks of fishermen, who are known to sometimes tell fish tales that don't quite comport with the facts. Even if fishermen reported their landings with complete accuracy, logbook records would still be poor guides to actual fish abundance and would only roughly approximate the number of fish killed by fishermen — two very basic statistics needed for good management. Catch per unit of fishing effort, such as days at sea, can stay constant or even increase while fish populations are declining, because fishermen are skilled at finding the remaining patches of fish. Because much fishing occurs far offshore, without observers on board, for many fisheries we simply don't know how many fish are discarded in order to maximize the value of the catch or simply to comply with regulations prohibiting the catch of certain species. Globally, this so-called bycatch amounts to about a quarter of the total catch. When catch limits for West Coast rockfish were reduced during the 1990s, the incentive to maximize value got stronger. As a result, discards have probably increased since the 1980s when the last set of scientific studies of bycatch and discard were conducted along the West Coast. Fishery managers used these old, outdated estimates to estimate the total number of fish killed each year because few data have been collected more recently.

Inadequate fish survey data and logbook data are fed into a sophisticated computer program that synthesizes the data and spits out the best estimates of fish abundance possible under the circumstances. The variation around these estimates is usually quite high; I remember staring at fisheries data as a graduate student trying to figure out how it was possible to estimate abundance or anything else from a set of points that looked as though it resulted from a shotgun blast. It takes a highly skilled analyst to make sense of these disparate data sets, with all their caveats. Fishery managers have to take these uncertain estimates of fish abundance and still more uncertain projections of future abundance, based on spotty data on fish survival and reproduction, and turn them into allowable catch levels. They then have to estimate how long the season ought to last, given the number of vessels in the fishery and how hard they fish, a variable that changes with the weather and market conditions and who knows what else. To design a bridge, a civil engineer would think twice before relying on the sort of calculations that are necessary to manage fisheries. Fishery scientists typically must multiply an uncertain estimate of abundance by an uncertain proxy for an unknown rate of fishing that should result in maximum sustainable yield to get the allowable catch, and then figure out individual trip limits and season length based on shaky estimates of actual fishing power. As this is what fishery managers have to work with, it is not surprising that mistakes are sometimes made. But what is surprising is how fishery managers deal with the high degree of uncertainty inherent in their work.

Ordinary folks usually respond to uncertainty by hedging against it somehow, whether by purchasing insurance or setting aside a nest egg. But fishery managers didn't respond this way at all. Instead, they allowed fishermen to catch lots of fish, confident in extrapolations from uncertain data. But then new information began to emerge about the rockfish — they were not as productive as once thought. Some species had not recruited (successfully produced a cohort of young fish that would become fishable adults) in years or even decades. The graphs showing trends in fish populations started to look like the Dow Jones Index in a bear market. Many were on the decline, and by the 1990s, some had sunk past the point where they were supposed to stabilize and produce maximum sustainable yield. Environmentalists and some scientists intensified calls for precautionary cuts in allowable catch.

In the early 1990s, I served on a committee to help the Pacific Fishery Management Council come up with ways to fix groundfish management problems. Over and over again, in this committee and in my testimony to the council, I called for marine reserves to be created and for the reduction of fishing capacity. The ocean — and the public trust — need insurance against honest errors, poor science, irreducible uncertainty in the ever-changing sea, and even corruption and mismanagement. Marine reserves are one of the best insurance policies we can buy, protecting real fish instead of fish spawned in mathematical models. I argued that Individual Fishing Quotas (IFQs) could reduce fishing capacity by allowing fishermen to plan their operations around a share of the catch, rather than by competing with each to catch as many fish as fast as possible (more on IFQs later).

The Pacific Council's response was to create another committee, this one to study marine reserves. The committee studied alternatives to marine reserves, concluding that marine reserves were the only way to solve certain problems, such as serving as reference areas to examine the impacts of fishing. It recommended that the council move forward to establish marine reserves. The council voted to do so, after an official analysis concluded that marine reserves could help the council rebuild depleted populations and protect biodiversity. But marine reserves had become so controversial that the council felt an extremely extensive outreach process would be necessary, far exceeding anything required for other management decisions. The high cost of this outreach process stymied any further progress toward marine reserves. Meanwhile, the council was having to close a nearly 5,000 square mile (13,000 square kilometers) area to protect dwindling populations of cowcod, a deepwater rockfish that was first decimated by sportfishermen in the 1960s and 70s, and later taken by commercial fishermen in the 80s and 90s. Bocaccio rockfish had also declined to perilously low levels.

In the early 1990s, environmentalists warned of a slippery slope of sequential depletions that the council and its fishermen were treading upon. We anticipated that more and more species would be declared overfished, resulting in reduced allowable catches and more closures. This was not due to native negativity; it was the logical consequence of the fact that of the 52 species of rockfish under the council's jurisdiction, only about a dozen had been scientifically assessed, and more than half of those had been found to be seriously overfished. As more species were assessed, the odds were that more would be found to have been overfished, because many of the species share similar life histories — long lives and low productivity.

While fishery managers and fishermen were busy blaming low ocean productivity, El Niños, and pollution for the decline of the rockfish, the few, tiny marine reserves that had been established along the West Coast told a different story. All of these factors no doubt played a role in the declines. But the marine reserves offered an unusual opportunity to compare the fishing grounds with a baseline that may not have shifted much, at least not due to fishing, because fishing had been banned within the reserves. At least one variable, fishing, had been controlled in the marine reserves during the vast experiment conducted by fishery managers on the continental shelf.

The very species that were in decline on the fishing grounds — rockfish and lingcod — were present in high abundance in the reserves off British Columbia, Washington, and California. (There were no marine reserves to study off Oregon.) Individual rockfish were far larger than their counterparts on the fishing grounds, and consequently, produced many more eggs — up to 30 times as many. Had fishing visited a double whammy on rockfish, reducing not only their abundance but also their average size — with an exponential decrease in their egg production per individual? If reduced ocean productivity or pollution had been primarily responsible for the declines in fish populations, we would expect to see reduced populations in reserves as well as on the fishing grounds.

Three lines of evidence supported the idea that fishing has been primarily responsible for the decline of the rockfish, aided and abetted by low ocean productivity since the 1970s, periodic El Niño cycles, and perhaps by pollution and habitat degradation. Declining rockfish populations correlated well with large catches. Studies suggested that catches had exceeded the ability of these populations to maintain themselves and the catches. And finally, exploited fish and shellfish populations were abundant in marine reserves, including several species that were in decline on the fishing grounds.

To be fair, some members of the council understood that too much fishing was going on, and voted pretty consistently for precautionary, conservative catch limits. Some even supported marine reserves and IFQs. But they were too often outvoted by the rest of the council, frequently in response to desperate pleas from fishermen to ignore the science or deal with uncertainty by leaving things alone, rather than by hedging bets and taking out insurance. Fear of change probably also played a role in the council's decisions. Marine reserves and IFQs represented whole different ways of managing fisheries, not just incremental changes.

Marine reserves shift the management paradigm from one of fishing down the populations that have built up over time, to one that emphasizes the protection of those characteristics of rockfish that seemed to adapt them uniquely to the vagaries of life on the continental shelf and slope. Marine reserves would allow at least some rockfish to live long lives and produce lots of young as they aged, as they did in nature. Fishermen could catch the interest on this investment, rather than spend the principal.

Individual Fishing Quotas would have completely changed the rules, taming the wild frontier presided over by the council where anyone with guts and a federal subsidy could have a go at the fish. Instead of competing to catch fish as quickly as possible (because any fish left in the ocean could just as well be caught by the next guy), IFQs would guarantee a certain percentage share of the allowable catch to each eligible fisherman. If properly cared for, the IFQ would yield fish and money for years into the future. Fishermen could think and plan like business people, matching their investments to the size of their IFQs, rather than competing for the biggest catch of fish. Perhaps that is part of the resistance to IFQs — the life of the rugged individual applying his or her skill, courage, and strength against the sea and against other fishermen seems more appealing than the life of a business person, conscientiously planning operations around expected future streams of revenue generated by his or her IFQ. But just as too many cowboys on the commons can result in congestion and overgrazing, too many fishermen engaged in the fisheries arms race (encouraged by open access or inadequate limited access management) can result in overfishing and the breaking of the public trust. Besides, the holders of IFQ I've met in the Alaska halibut and sablefish fisheries, where IFQs were established in 1995, are hardly pin-striped business people. They are highly skilled, brave men and women who are still engaged in the world's most dangerous profession, and who still love being on their own at sea. It's just that they are making a lot more money than before they got IFQs, and tend to worry about the long-term health of the fish populations (and of the value of their stake in them) more than about the next boat payment.

As fishery managers realized that too many fish were being caught, they imposed total catch limits on the fisheries. Had they been set low enough, these catch limits might have helped conserve the rockfish, but they were set too high. Even so, the reduction in allowable catch exacerbated the race for fish, because nothing was done to reduce the large numbers of vessels that had been built to fish down the rockfish when times were good during the 1970s and 1980s. Fishing vessels that once caught the valuable black cod (or sablefish) over a leisurely nine-month season now had to race to catch the annual harvest in about a week.

Alaska's halibut fishery was the poster-child for the race for fish. The season shrank to frenzied 48-hour openings, during which thousands of fishing vessels took off at the shot of the starting gun to try to catch a whole year's worth of fish. They went out in all kinds of weather, working night and day. Many men and boats were lost at sea. Gear that snared on the bottom was simply cut and left during the race, to continue killing fish unseen for years. Sloppy fishing led to lots of bycatch and overruns of the allowable catch.

Fishermen suffered economically from the catch restrictions because too many were trying to catch dwindling numbers of fish. They spoke compellingly of their financial distress. Seafood processors demanded that seasons be stretched out as long as possible, to keep the supply of fish flowing to their plants as smoothly as possible. Again failing to reduce fishing capacity, the council instead imposed limits on the amount of fish an individual vessel could catch during each fishing trip, so-called trip limits, to extend the season. As the total allowable catch shrank, the trip limits shrank as well, because the number of vessels stayed relatively constant. Soon fishermen were finding it uneconomic to fish for such small limits, or were discarding low-value fish so as to maximize the value of the small amounts they were allowed to keep. Some fish such as lingcod and shallow-water species can survive the process, but for the deeper-dwelling rockfish and other groundfish species, discarding equals death.

To the council's credit, it recognized that there was too much fishing capacity out there to profitably take the available fish, and they put a priority on reducing capacity during the mid-1990s. The council undertook a long and painstaking process to consider options for reducing capacity in the valuable sablefish fishery. Two years and many heated debates and analyses later, the council was ready to vote on an IFQ plan for this fishery, but congress stepped in, first with letters arguing against IFQs, and then with a national moratorium on all new IFQ plans. These actions were precipitated by opponents of IFQs, including some environmentalists and lots of smaller-scale fishermen who stood to get cut out of the initial allocation of individual fishing quota shares. The council's draft IFQ plan would have allocated shares in the allowable catch according primarily to the catch history of vessels, rewarding fishermen who had caught lots of fish in the past with large shares. Opponents made valid arguments about fairness — why should a big catch history be rewarded, when it could have resulted from large-scale fishing that damaged the habitat or killed a lot of fish unintentionally? Why not reward fishermen who had chosen to remain small-scale, catching fish very selectively with little waste and few impacts on habitat? But instead of working to modify the IFQ plan to address these concerns with constructive suggestions, opponents spent more time and energy getting congress to step in to solve problems that are best dealt with through good-faith negotiations at the regional level. At this writing, the congressional ban on all IFQs has been lifted, but bills that would mandate guidelines for IFQs are being debated in congress. Meanwhile, the race for fish continues.

Emerging Issues

We remain ignorant of the status of most of the fish populations that are being heavily exploited. At last count, only about one third of the species caught in U.S. waters had been assessed (i.e., their abundance had been scientifically estimated). About half of the assessed species were either overfished or about to be over-fished.[1] Along the West Coast, only a small percentage of the 82 species of groundfish that are being caught have been assessed, and nine of the assessed species were deemed to be overfished at this writing. Many of the unassessed species are rockfish that appear to be vulnerable to overexploitation because of their life history and ecology. It seems reasonable to expect that as we reduce our ignorance, the number of overfished species will rise, simply due to better assessment data.

The Pacific Fishery Management Council and the National Marine Fisheries Service has closed much of the continental shelf off California, Oregon, and Washington to bottom-fishing. Now that the true depth of the crisis is clear, congress has authorized a buy-out of the groundfish fleet, and lifted its ban on IFQs (facilitated by strong advocacy by Environmental Defense). However, these tools will take time to implement, so fishing capacity is likely to remain excessively high for the foreseeable future. Therefore, vessels that once fished for groundfish on the continental shelf are likely to target other areas and other fisheries. Some will likely transition to albacore and shrimp fishing, and perhaps to other pelagic (ocean-going) fisheries such as tuna and swordfish which are still open on the shelf. These species are thought to be in fairly good shape, but stock assessments are conducted only sporadically and are based entirely on catch statistics which may be unreliable proxies for real abundance. Others will likely pursue groundfish in the deeper waters of the continental slope which also remain open. Many of these deep-dwelling species appear to be long-lived, slow-growing, and hence vulnerable to overfishing. Perhaps some of the vessels will attempt to engage in nearshore fisheries, which are already overcrowded and have already depleted several species.

Reforming Fisheries Management

Almost everyone agrees that more and better science is needed to reduce uncertainty about how many fish there are in the sea, how many we are taking, and how many we should leave behind to spawn the next generation. The federal government should help to bail out fishermen who were encouraged to buy and build vessels with government subsidies and who are now being hurt by the consequences of those subsidies and failed management policies. One way to leverage this money might be to pay fishermen to charter their vessels as research platforms, and to use their practical experience to help scientists test fishing gear and sample populations. This approach would not only employ out-of-work fishermen, but also foster cooperation between fishermen and scientists, improve stock assessments, and build trust in the science that guides fishery management decisions.

No matter how much money we invest in ocean science, some uncertainty will always remain, because science will raise more questions and because the ocean environment will continue to vary in unpredictable ways. We need to create ocean governance systems that face uncertainty head-on and deal with it constructively. This means adopting a precautionary stance when the risks to the public trust are large, whether from overfishing or any other threat, even if the data are not all in.

New ocean ecosystem councils could capture the best features of the regional fishery management councils, while correcting some structural flaws that have resulted in overfishing and lack of adequate habitat protection. The mission of the ocean ecosystem councils would be to protect ocean ecosystems and the attributes of ocean populations that allow them to thrive and adapt to the ocean. The councils would be charged with sustaining fisheries on the interest generated from marine reserves and on allowable catches that leave plenty of the fish in the water to spawn the next generation, and to fulfill their ecological roles. Marine reserves should be an important part of any ecosystem protection strategy, as they provide insurance against errors, help rebuild depleted populations, and may even help to enhance fisheries outside their borders.

All institutions work better when their missions are supported by incentives to achieve the mission. We need to replace economic incentives to overexploit with economic incentives to conserve and steward wisely for the present and the future — incentives such as those created by a well-designed IFQ system. Performance standards for fishing gear could create incentives for innovation that would lead to lower bycatch and less damage to ocean habitats. We should experiment with smaller-scale management entities (such as the Port Orford Community-Based Management initiative described in Chapter 3) that engage in cooperative research, joint fact-finding by scientists, fishermen, and environmentalists alike that will provide a common set of facts and understandings to guide decision-making.

Ocean Aid

Creating marine reserves, limiting access to fisheries, and creating individual fishing quotas (IFQs) are all ways to divide the commons and clarify rights and privileges. Marine reserves define areas where extraction of resources is banned so as to enable natural processes to prevail. Limited access programs define who can continue to fish. Individual Fishing Quotas specify how much fish an individual fisherman can take. They are all solutions to the tragedy of the commons.

Another way to clarify rights and privileges in a commons is to simply purchase them. On land, conservancies and land trusts acquire areas harboring rare species or particularly diverse ecosystems. Timber harvest privileges have been transferred to protect valuable forests while accommodating landholders' rights to cut wood. Credits held by an individual company for reducing air pollution below permitted levels can be sold, so long as total emissions remain below a cap. Why not extend this thinking to the ocean?

The opportunities to acquire rights to ocean resources are fewer than on land, but they do exist. There are no barbed-wire fences defining patches of property in the ocean, but there are deeds to submerged lands, leases for kelp beds, fishing permits, and IFQs. Oil and aquaculture companies lease underwater tracts — why not environmental groups? Shellfish grounds could be leased and either completely protected from all harvest or restored, if necessary to allow for a sustainable harvest.[2] The Nature Conservancy has already acquired large tracts of submerged lands and shellfish beds in Great South Bay and Peconic Bay, New York; in the Virginia Coast Reserve, Virginia; and in Port Susan, Washington. Some of the magnificent kelp forests off the California coast can be leased, perhaps for as little as $40 per square mile ($15 per square kilometer) per year. And preliminary calculations indicate that to cut the overcapitalized California nearshore fishery in half (purchasing 100 fishing permits) would require about $1.5 million — a lot of money, but within the reach of a private trust devoted to ocean conservation. Analysts working for an ocean conservation trust could look for cost-effective opportunities to buy ocean conservation and for ways to leverage trust assets with other private and government money.

Ending the Tragedy

Quite a few newspaper stories have been written about problems with fisheries in New England, in the Gulf of Mexico, and now on the Pacific coast. The fishery success stories have been far less visible, but no less important to learn from.

In Alaska, fishery managers on the North Pacific Fishery Management Council (NPFMC) dealt with the frenetic race for halibut by working with fishermen to craft an Individual Fishing Quota (IFQ) plan. They learned and applied important lessons from earlier IFQ systems. The New Zealand experience taught them to allocate percentage shares of the allowable catch, rather than specified numbers of pounds of fish. New Zealand fishermen sued the government when orange roughy catches were reduced (in order to protect these long-lived fish) after scientists discovered that they had set the allowable catch too high. Because certain amounts of fish had already been allocated to the fishermen, the government had to compensate them for their loss. The NPFMC allocated percentage shares instead, that would vary automatically if allowable catch levels had to be adjusted. Furthermore, the NPFMC made it clear that IFQs were revokable privileges (rather than entitlements or rights) to harvest the nation's fish. Therefore, the government is not liable for compensation to IFQ holders for any loss in value of their quota shares.

One of the biggest concerns with IFQs has been the possibility that a single firm or individual could buy up most of the fishery and monopolize the market, or worse yet, change the nature of the fishery from one made up primarily of independent family-owned businesses to one dominated by distant executives at big corporations. Some consolidation of fishing operations is desirable in many cases, especially when a fishery is overcapitalized, but it can go too far. New Zealand allowed firms to accumulate up to 45 percent of the total allowable catch for certain species, and so a considerable amount of consolidation took place.

The first U.S. fishery to try IFQs was the mid-Atlantic surf clam and ocean quahog fishery. The program designers decided that federal anti-trust laws were sufficient protection against excessive consolidation, and so no limits were put on how much of the total allowable catch could be acquired by an individual or firm through the purchase of IFQs. Vertical integration of harvest, processing, packaging, and selling was already underway in this fishery, because clams need to be shucked to be sold. The IFQ program, without limits on IFQ consolidation, facilitated this trend and led to even more vertical integration. The NPFMC, desiring to maintain the characteristic nature of the halibut and sablefish fisheries, chose to place strict limits on how much IFQ could be accumulated by an individual or firm (one percent of the total allowable catch). To prevent absentee ownership, the NPFMC also required the owner of the IFQ to actually be on board the fishing vessel.

The North Pacific Fishery Management Council's IFQ program has been successful in many ways.[3] The race for fish has been eliminated, and the season expanded from 48-hour openings to nine months or so. The market glut of fish characteristic of the old fishery has changed to a steadier supply of fresh fish, commanding higher prices and resulting in a superior product for consumers. Fishermen are now free to choose when they want to fish, so as to maximize their profits and increase safety by avoiding bad weather. While allowable catch levels had always been set fairly conservatively for the halibut and sablefish fisheries, compliance with catch limits increased once IFQs were in place. During the frenzied race for fish, captains often cut their gear if it snagged, rather than wasting precious time retrieving it. Cast-off nets and longlines bristling with hundreds of hooks lay on the bottom, killing fish long after the season closed. This so-called "ghost fishing" was significantly reduced (by about 75 percent) after the fishery transitioned to IFQs.

Highgrading — the practice of dumping lower-value fish overboard in order to maximize the value of one's landings — might have increased under IFQ management because the overall catch of each individual fisher would be limited. Trip limits, however, provide an even stronger incentive to highgrade. While there have been anecdotal reports of highgrading since the IFQ program began, no cases have been prosecuted. However, managers will need to remain vigilant to prevent the practice.

Investing in Marine Reserves

Marine reserves are especially good for allowing fish and shellfish populations to regain their natural age and size distributions — that is, the natural balance of young, middle-aged, and old is restored. That is one reason that egg production in most marine reserves is much, much higher than on the fishing grounds — larger, older fish often produce 10, 20, or even 50 times as many eggs as smaller fish. And for species that undergo a sex change when they reach a certain size, restoration or protection of the natural size distribution of the population is even more critical.

A mainstay of Gulf fisheries, the gag grouper come together in special places to spawn (called spawning aggregations). Many different kinds of grouper get together to spawn in this way, forming large and easy-to-locate targets for fishermen. Not surprisingly, grouper populations have been depleted rapidly throughout the Gulf and the reefs of the Florida Keys and the Caribbean islands. More surprisingly, scientists discovered that fishing was probably responsible for skewing the sex ratio in the spawning aggregations. Female groupers turn into males when they get large, and fishing tends to target larger individuals. Males do seem to matter, in fish populations anyway. The viability of grouper eggs seems to have been reduced as a consequence of the scarcity of males — the females absorb their eggs if no males are around. Scientists studying the gag grouper aggregations in the Gulf teamed up with environmentalists and some fishermen to ask the council to consider establishing marine reserves to protect the grouper. The council did so in 1999, voting to set aside two areas of 100 square nautical miles (260 square kilometers) each to protect the grouper. While intense opposition delayed the closure of these areas, the National Marine Fisheries Service finally closed them in 2000. A lawsuit against NMFS by the Coastal Conservation Association (a recreational fishing organization) was settled in 2001, with NMFS agreeing to allow trolling for pelagic fishes that swim through the surface waters of the closed areas while research on the effects of this kind of fishing is conducted.

The creation of marine reserves in the Dry Tortugas and Northwestern Hawai'ian Islands (see Chapter 4), the Channel Islands (see Chapter 3), and the Gulf of Mexico was motivated in large part by dwindling populations of valuable fish species. Serious economic problems in Alaska's sablefish and halibut fishery precipitated an Individual Fish Quota system there. The open ocean and the deep sea have not been explored and exploited as intensively as nearshore waters, the continental shelves, and coral reefs. These more mysterious parts of the ocean offer opportunities for conservation before increased fishing and perhaps even hard mineral mining result in crises.

6

THE SHAPE OF THE SEA

The Nature of the Open Ocean

As I sat sipping my tea, gazing out at the ocean on an overcast day, the sun broke through the clouds to illuminate shining patches of sea. This scene illuminated for me the chat I had with Paul Dayton, the famed marine ecologist from the Scripps Institute of Oceanography. Paul had explained to me that the magnificent large fishes of the Pacific were not wandering about aimlessly; they, and the albatrosses, turtles, and sharks were focusing on patches of highly concentrated food. The sought-after squid and fishes were in turn congregating where the water was rich in plankton. The plankton in turn was concentrated where deep, nutrient-rich waters were upwelling and where eddies, gyres, and fronts were pushing nutrients, plankton, fish, and squid together.

Variable winds, currents, and upwellings create variable patches of highly concentrated nutrients and food in the ocean. But some of these patches are fairly persistent and predictable, drawing large hungry crowds of predatory fish and birds year after year. Most of these relatively persistent patches have been found close to shore, but tunas and sharks carrying tags tracked by satellites are showing us that there are patches far offshore as well. For example, food concentrations are about three times higher in the transition domain than in adjacent areas. The transition domain is a narrow corridor (40°– 44°N) in the Pacific Ocean defined by oceanic fronts where water temperatures and salinities change dramatically, attracting large and diverse populations of marine mammals, sharks, tunas, billfishes, and seabirds.[1] The transition domain also provides a good place for wide-ranging species to breed, and for their young to thrive.

The Southern California Eddy is another persistent feature, showing up pretty dependably from June to January, and more sporadically in February and March. Water is consistently upwelling in this giant eddy, which is some 125 miles (200 kilometers) in diameter, fueling the growth of highly concentrated phytoplankton and the zooplankton that feed on them. Sardine and anchovy appear to spawn preferentially inside the eddy. While the eddy comprises only about 12 percent of the total area used by the anchovies for spawning, it accounted for about 48 percent of the spawned larvae from 1951 to 1975.[2]

In their seminal article, "Marine Protected Areas and Ocean Basin Management,"[3] Hyrenbach and his co-authors identify several other particularly important areas of the ocean that could potentially benefit from "floating" or pelagic marine reserves. These include the Costa Rica Dome (a large, persistent area of high productivity, rich in whales and other marine life, off the coast of Costa Rica); the Bering Sea Greenbelt (shelf and slope areas off Alaska and Russia); the equatorial convergence (a strip of water in the mid-Pacific along the equator), the Oyashio-Kuroshio mixing zone (northwest of Japan), the Antarctic polar front (where cold Antarctic waters meet, and sink below, warmer water between 50° and 60° S latitude), and the California current (a cold current flowing south along the western margin of North America).

Prey and predators are also concentrated where currents crash against islands and underwater mountains, leaving swirls and eddies in their wake. Offshore islands, such as the Farallones off the coast of California, host rich concentrations of life in general but seem to be especially important during El Niños when food becomes scarce over most of the continental shelf. To sustain themselves during hard times, the large, wide-ranging predators congregate near the islands. Powerful jets of cold, nutrient-rich water upwelling from deep in the ocean spurt out from points jutting out from the coast. The structure of the sea is ever-changing, but at the same time somewhat predictable and even quite stable in some cases, if you know how to read the signs.

Current Threats

Of course, long before scientists figured it out, fishermen have known where life concentrates in the ocean. Schools of tuna are hard to spot, but pods of dolphins running with the tuna are easier to see, and flocks of seabirds easier still. Fishermen target concentrations of their prey, the tunas and billfishes, just as these fishes target concentrations of *their* prey. Fishermen have also learned to deploy very large types of fishing gear. Floating walls of monofilament mesh about 40 miles (64 kilometers) long were used until banned in 1992. Fishermen still use longlines that can reach up to 50 miles (80 kilometers), with thousands of baited hooks on them. Gathering diffuse resources in the vast open ocean is the main problem of making a living there, whether for man or beast.

Fishing on the open ocean, or high seas, outside of any one country's legal jurisdiction (often defined by a 200-mile or 322-kilometer Exclusive Economic Zone), has already depleted tuna and swordfish populations in the Atlantic. Indeed, some 25 percent of the world's major fisheries are thought to be overexploited or depleted, and 47–50 percent may be fully exploited.[4] Stories of biological and economic collapse similar to that of the West Coast groundfish fishery (see Chapter 5) are echoed in fisheries around the world. International organizations were set up to conserve and manage these species, but have largely failed — because international good intentions were trumped by national interests and competition. Effective governance of the high seas has been elusive.

Scientific understanding of large, wide-ranging fishes has been hard to come by too — these species are difficult to study. New techniques, such as attaching tags that can be tracked by satellite, are shedding light on the most basic of questions — where do they go to feed and breed? This research is revealing that ocean-going animals can sense and make good use of watery structures like convergence zones, gyres, and eddies. The very symbols of footloose wandering, the great albatrosses, home in on certain areas in the ocean, perhaps returning to them again and again throughout their entire lives. Tagged albatrosses from the Crozet Islands in the Indian Ocean flew up to 5,270 miles (8,479 kilometers) to specific areas in the ocean scattered from the tropics to Antarctica.[5] We now know that female great white sharks largely stay at home, while the males range widely, a lifestyle similar to that of whales, dolphins, and certain human families.

It seems as though tunas also travel great distances to feed and perhaps breed in certain areas. For example, scientists recently tagged some giant Atlantic bluefin tuna up to ten feet (three meters) long and weighing up to 1,500 pounds (680 kilograms). These fish traveled to the Gulf of Mexico and the eastern Mediterranean Sea to spawn. They also congregated in the waters over an underwater plateau in the North Atlantic called the Flemish Cap (where the *Andrea Gail* encountered the Perfect Storm), making them targets for global fishing fleets.[6]

Scientists estimate how abundant fishes are mainly by analyzing catch records, and so far, catches of most of the Pacific tunas and swordfish seem to be stable or increasing. But stable or even increasing catches can hide true trends in fish numbers, because fishermen are highly skilled at finding fish where they congregate. Catch rates can be high, sustained by these patches of concentrated fish, even while the overall number of fish is declining. Southern Bluefin Tuna have already been depleted to less than ten percent of their abundance in 1960,[7] with few signs of recovery. Total allowable catch levels are set by the Commission for the

Conservation of Southern Bluefin Tuna, but the commission acknowledges that present catch levels will probably not allow these tuna to rebuild their populations.[8] This is in direct contrast with the main goal of the commission and of the international convention that established it. Fishing nations that have not joined the commission are catching unknown amounts of this critically endangered species. The deep-swimming population of bigeye tuna in the Atlantic also appears to be overexploited,[9] and catches of young bigeye in the Eastern Pacific increased dramatically in the mid-1990s,[10] perhaps threatening future catches.

Will Pacific tunas and swordfish be depleted sequentially? The answer will depend on the effectiveness of international fishery management institutions such as the Interamerican Tropical Tuna Commission and the new Convention for the Conservation and Management of Highly Migratory Fish Stocks in the Western and Central Pacific Ocean, initiated by the Multilateral High Level Conference. This convention was signed in 2000, but has not yet entered into force.

Catching fish where they come together to breed can, of course, reduce their ability to sustain their populations. Fish caught in these biological oases can no longer go about their ecological business of culling the populations of other fish, transporting nutrients, providing sustenance for other species, among many other things. Catching fish where they feed results in the accidental catch of the rest of the diverse biological community that has also come to feed there. Drift nets were banned in 1992 because of the enormous numbers of dolphins, sea turtles, and seabirds that were entangled and drowned in the nets. Unfortunately, the use of longlines up to 50 miles (80 kilometers) long with thousands of baited hooks accelerated after the driftnets were banned. Longlines, as you might expect, also kill thousands of animals each year accidentally.

Well-intentioned environmental policies too often lead to unintended consequences. The banning of a particular kind of fishing gear or fishing practice may eliminate one threat but encourage innovations that may pose an even greater threat. A better approach is to specify performance standards for bycatch or habitat protection that all gear must meet. This sort of policy encourages innovation to meet the standards and can force technology to evolve in positive ways, with a lower risk of nasty surprises.

Fuel efficiency standards for cars could be an example of this policy approach. Instead of banning big gas-guzzlers, the corporate average fuel efficiency standards promulgated in 1975 provided car companies with a mandate to increase the average fuel efficiency of their whole fleets, but with the flexibility of choosing different ways to achieve this goal. Light-duty trucks were exempted, on the theory that holding them to fuel efficiency standards would result in higher costs to farmers and others who depended on trucks for their livelihood. Later, the definition was stretched to include Sport Utility Vehicles (SUVs), even though it's hard to see how exempting luxury SUVs (which one auto reviewer described as more suitable for hauling assets than produce) protects the farm economy. The automobile industry complained loudly (and still complains) that the 1975 fuel efficiency standards would be too costly to meet and would reduce safety. But efficiency improvements gave rise to minivans that get 22 miles to the gallon (eight kilometers per liter) and are much safer than the big station wagons they replaced. Forcing improvements in SUV gas mileage can result in a significant reduction in greenhouse gas emissions and savings on gas costs that can go a long way toward offsetting the increased purchase price of the vehicle.

Sport Utility Vehicles will probably not go away any time soon, so the challenge is to make them more fuel-efficient. Technologies that would increase the fuel efficiency of trucks already exist, including variable valve timing and more efficient transmissions. In fact, the National Research Council concluded that light-duty trucks like SUVs, pickups, and minivans offer the greatest potential for technical improvements that would increase fuel efficiency.[11] Smart regulations and performance standards can encourage technical innovations that reduce the costs of compliance without necessarily compromising safety, luxury, or convenience.

Performance standards can be used to encourage beneficial innovations not only in cars and trucks, but also in everything from household appliances to fishing gear. There is enough gross inefficiency in our use of resources that far less can be used without compromising quality of life. Increased efficiency alone will probably not save the planet, due to the large-scale effects of globalization and market forces blind to social justice and environmental protection (see Chapter 8). But perhaps more efficient use of natural resources can reduce ecological damage, buy time, and lead to a greater respect for nature and a new environmental ethic. Psychologists have found that in some cases, attitudes change only after behavior changes, rather than vice versa as one might expect. For example, people's initial distaste for seatbelts changed as they grew accustomed to using them.[12] In the same way, benevolent acts can result in an attitude of compassion and an ethic in which every act is an environmental act, as long as people realize that incremental changes are just small steps on a long journey toward sustainability.

More and Deeper Fishing

The great fishes that cruise the open waters of the Pacific Ocean could be overfished just as their cousins in the Atlantic were, unless governance of international fisheries is strengthened. Research indicates that populations of big fish such as tuna and swordfish have already been reduced by about 90 percent worldwide. Tens of thousands of ocean-going animals, including albatrosses, sea turtles, sharks, and marine mammals have been killed accidentally in fisheries.[13] Tens of thousands more will likely continue to die each year if longlines continue to be used to catch tuna and billfish. The state of the commons is even more tragic in the open ocean than it is on the continental shelf and in nearshore waters.

Fishing has not only reduced populations of targeted fish and other animals that share the fishing grounds — it may also be impacting ocean food webs by targeting organisms lower and lower in the chain, from top predators to phytoplankton. The most desirable populations (mainly long-lived, predatory fishes such as cod) were depleted first. Fishermen then started targeting less desirable species lower on the food chain (for example,

Norway pout) and creating new markets for them.[14] Organisms that occupy the lower tiers of food chains are often prey for many different species; thus, catching large numbers of them could potentially have ripple effects. Remarkably, fishing seems to be fundamentally changing the nature of ocean ecosystems by changing the relative abundance of various kinds of fish and invertebrates and by changing the relationships between them. Fishing has reduced the average number of links in ocean food chains, like the chain that links phytoplankton grazed by sardines that are turn eaten by tuna that are consumed by a shark.

Natural ocean ecosystems tend to contain lots of redundancy (at least to our eyes). A large predatory fish can choose from a number of species occupying a certain part of a food chain — so that the chains are not really independent, but linked in intricate webs. This redundancy is important for maintaining all of the parts of the food web, especially in times of scarcity, such as dur-ing an El Niño (when nutrient-rich upwellings slow down or stop) or longer-term cycles of low oceanic productivity induced by natural climatic variations or global warming. The simplifica-tion of ocean food webs by fishing means that fish may become more dependent on a few or even a single food source. Many prey species, because they have short lives, fluctuate tremendous-ly in response to variations in ocean circulation, sunlight, and other factors. When prey populations crash, predator populations may crash with them if alternatives are not available. So fishing may make predatory fish (our favorite prey) more vulnerable to variations in ocean conditions.

Many fishermen and fishery managers attribute the collapse of fisheries to changes in ocean conditions. While this may be true in some cases, there is strong evidence that fishing can deplete populations. This evidence ranges from the correlation of fishing effort to declines in fish, to the fact that exploited species remain abundant in marine reserves, where no fishing is allowed. In fact, fishing itself may be responsible for depleting species *and* for making fisheries more sensitive to changes in the productivity of the ocean.[15]

It is difficult to predict which species are "most important" in an ecosystem, and what will happen if a species is removed or depleted. Certain species interact strongly with other species and exert a measure of control on their biological community. For example, starfish help keep mussel beds patchy and diverse by eating the mussels. Likewise, sea urchin predators, such as sheephead and cabezon fish, keep purple sea urchin populations under control and prevent overgrazing of kelp forests. But many other species interact with each other in much more subtle ways, and in complex ecosystems, several species seem to occupy similar "niches" — having specific ecological jobs such as cleaning parasites off fish. Removal or depletion of one of these species may or may not have serious, adverse ecological consequences. A lot depends on what ecological attributes one decides to measure. Structural changes, like the disappearance of a kelp forest after the urchin predators are depleted, are obvious to the eye and offend our human sensibilities. Changes in invisible processes, such as energy flow or the recycling of material, may be just as important to the maintenance of the ecosystem but far less obvious. The only way to rigorously test the ecological impacts of fishing seems to be to establish marine reserves so that we can observe parts of ecosystems that are not fished. We also need to carefully observe how marine animals behave and interact and to conduct experimental studies within and outside the reserves. The prudent thing to do, when the effects of fishing are unknown, is to go slow and be careful, keeping all the ecological pieces and processes intact in at least some places.

In recent years, US fishermen started to exploit seamounts and the deeper waters of continental slopes as west coast continental shelf and reef fisheries were depleted. The vast ocean may seem capable of supplying unlimited food for humankind but, in fact, its capacity (while large) is indeed limited. About 90 percent of the global fish catch comes from the third of the ocean within 200 miles (322 kilometers) of shore because these waters are so productive.[16] This is where sunlight meets nutrient-rich water that upwells from deep layers, and where phytoplankton (the grass of the sea) grow so luxuriantly. There are other areas of high production in the ocean, such as coral reefs, oceanic fronts, eddies, and seamounts. But these areas are also limited in area and some are vulnerable to overexploitation. Coral reefs support a lot of life, but not the enormous populations of single species characteristic of colder waters. Many coral reef fishes, moreover, aggregate to spawn, forming easy targets for fishermen. Not surprisingly, they are usually depleted rapidly. Oceanic fronts and eddies attract a wide variety of species, and so bycatch and waste often result from fishing them. Seamounts support large aggregations of fish but at least some of these appear to be long-lived, isolated, and highly vulnerable to overfishing. As shocking as it may seem, there may be few places left to go in the ocean to get more fish without repeating the age-old history of overfishing, so it is imperative to protect what is left and restore the rest.

Happily, scientists have sounded the alarm about fishing on seamounts. The world has already witnessed the overfishing of seamount species such as the delectable orange roughy. Environmentalists are advocating the creation of marine reserves in places like the remarkable Davidson Seamount off Monterey, California. The top of this huge 7,200-foot (2,915-meter) high underwater mountain lies about 3,700 feet (1,128 meters) below the surface. Extremely old coral forests reach up to nine feet (2.7 meters) high and an amazing diversity of creatures takes shelter among the sponges and in rocky crevices and other habitats. The waters around and above the seamount are very productive as well, supporting albatrosses, whales, and all manner of other animals. Australia established the Tasmanian Seamounts Marine Reserve in 1999, with the support of the fishing industry. Hopefully, the idea of protecting seamounts will take hold globally before it is too late.

A Warmer World

Climate change introduces a whole new set of uncertainties. Because the ocean is still mysterious in many ways, it is unclear how global warming will affect it. There is evidence that some organisms are adjusting their ranges already. The anemones, mussels, seaweeds, and their neighbors growing at the shore don't appear to be going anywhere. Yet the intertidal (exposed to the air at low tide, awash in the sea during high tides) community near Hopkins Marine Laboratory in Monterey, California has changed over the last 60 years. Southern (warmer-water) species generally increased in abundance, while northern (cooler-water) species declined.[17] The abundance of zooplankton (small shrimp-like animals that float or swim rather weakly, graze on phytoplankton, and provide food for larger animals) declined by 70 percent between 1951 and 1993, while water temperature rose an average of 2.7° F (1.5° C).[18]

Many other strange things happened in the ocean during this period. Salmon fisheries from California to British Columbia collapsed. Seabirds, fur seals, sea lions, and gray whales died in unusually high numbers during record warm years. But the causes of these dramatic events are unclear. Natural swings in ocean temperature occur with the seasons, and from year to year. El Niños can cause warm water species to wander into areas they would normally avoid — for example, marlin were found swimming in the normally cold waters off the coast of Washington in 1997.[19] And it now appears that northern and southern waters of the Pacific take turns being warm or cold every 20 to 30 years.[20] These patterns of variation make it difficult to sort out the causes of changes in the ocean's biology.

Models of the ocean suggest that global productivity may decrease by about five percent if atmospheric carbon dioxide concentrations double. But the impacts of global warming are likely to vary tremendously in different regions, due to the complexities of ocean circulation, chemistry, and biology. Increased temperatures, altered wind patterns, and increased carbon dioxide concentrations will interact in surprising ways, no doubt. Upwelling, and thus productivity, could decrease in some areas as hotter air temperatures cause the ocean to form layers of warm water overlying cold water. Normally, the cold, nutrient-rich water rises to the surface on occasion, mixing with the surface waters and fueling the growth of phytoplankton and the rest of the ocean food web. But if the surface waters become warmer, these upwellings of cold water may become less frequent — the layers of the ocean could become more stable, like the layers in a gelatin parfait. On the other hand, altered wind patterns and intensity could increase upwelling in some areas. Some fishes could do better with global warming — for example, Pacific hake, cod, herring, and sardine all reproduced well during strong El Niño events, which may provide a glimpse of what a warmer world will be like. On the other hand, many rockfish species failed to recruit (in other words, not enough young survived to sustain the fishery or rockfish populations) during the same El Niño events.

Changes in the ranges of fish will affect food webs, too — for example, voracious mackerel moved from the tropics all the way to southeast Alaska during the very strong El Niños of 1982 and 1997. The mackerel may have eaten lots of young salmon, posing a threat to the salmon fishery and wild salmon populations. Salmon themselves are sensitive to increases in ocean temperature. Salmon catches off California, Oregon, and Washington plummeted from 1977 to 1998, when the ocean was relatively warm. Prior to that, salmon production had been high in the region.

Quite apart from the impacts of temperature, the increased carbon dioxide (which, along with other gases, causes global warming) may itself have adverse impacts. Too much carbon dioxide can increase the acidity of the ocean, just as carbonation increases the acidity of water or soft drinks. Many phytoplankton in the open ocean build their skeletons of calcium carbonate using processes that are hampered by acidity.[21] The increased acidity of seawater due to growing carbon dioxide concentrations in the atmosphere could dissolve the limestone skeletons of coral reefs.

Oxygen, nutrients, and carbon dioxide circulate through the ocean on a giant conveyer belt driven by cold water sinking in the North Atlantic. Deep beneath the surface, this cold, dense, salty water flows south, turns east around the Cape of South Africa, and then slowly warms and, centuries later, rises to the surface in the Indian Ocean and western Pacific Ocean. It brings oxygen and carbon dioxide to deep waters and nutrients to surface waters where phytoplankton can use them. Global warming could potentially alter this global respiratory system by slowing or even stopping it. If this were to happen, deep waters would be deprived of oxygen and food from the surface, and many deep sea animals could be affected — before we even discover them. Upwelling could be reduced, diminishing the ocean's productivity. This sounds like science fiction, but there is evidence that the global ocean conveyer belt has slowed or stopped in the past. Like most other aspects of global warming, its effects on the conveyer belt are very difficult to predict. Some scientists believe that it is likely to be affected by warming while others think not. The bottom line is that while the impacts of global warming are uncertain, the enormous magnitude of some of the potential impacts calls for actions to reduce the risks by reducing greenhouse gas concentrations in the atmosphere.

Dangerous Decibels

Because the ocean interacts with the atmosphere and climate in so many ways and over such large areas, climate change will probably affect most of the ocean one way or another, in addition to its effects on specific places or ecosystems. Human activities affecting the ocean have increased in number and scope. Small incremental changes, multiplied by millions of coastal dwellers or fishermen, add up to large impacts. Some technologies are so powerful that they have the potential to affect most of the ocean all by themselves. The sequestration of waste carbon dioxide resulting from burning fossil fuels at a scale large enough to significantly reduce carbon dioxide concentrations in the atmosphere may be one such planet-altering technology (see Chapter 7). The U.S. Navy's plan to permeate the ocean with sound waves in order to detect submarines may be another.

The navy is not the first institution to transmit powerful sounds through the ocean. During the 1980s, the eminent physical oceanographers Walter Munk and Carl Wunsch developed a brilliant approach for measuring global warming much more accurately than had previously been possible. Measurements of

air temperature are highly variable, and the mish-mash of read-
ings from ships, airports, and various other platforms bounce up
and down a lot. The long-term trend of global warming can
only be observed by looking at decades worth of air temperature
data because it is hidden by the variability of the data. Munk
realized that measuring temperature change in the ocean could
offer a major advantage: temperature is much less variable in the
ocean than in the atmosphere, and so perhaps the signal of global warming could be detected over a shorter time period.
Because the speed of sound increases in proportion to temperature, it is possible to measure changes in temperature by measuring changes in the speed of sound. Munk proposed to transmit sound waves through the Sound Fixing and Ranging
(SOFAR) channel, a layer of ocean water about 3300 feet
(1,000 meters) deep whose temperature, salinity, and pressure
combine to create excellent conditions for transmitting sound
over long distances. Within this channel, an imploding light
bulb can be heard 600 miles (965 kilometers) away. Munk
thought that global warming could be detected this way in
about ten years.

I was intrigued by this experiment, having wrestled with interpreting the highly variable atmospheric temperature data. The
concept was elegant, and the idea of an accurate and precise record
of global warming was appealing. But several concerns arose as I
and my colleagues read through technical documents describing
the experiment that Munk and his team proposed to test the theory, called Acoustic Thermometry of Ocean Climate (ATOC).
They wanted to transmit loud (up to 221 decibels) low-frequency
(averaging 57 hertz) sounds from a site near Heard Island in the
southern Indian Ocean.[22] We found out, by talking with marine
mammalogists concerned about the project, that whales were
thought to use the SOFAR channel to communicate with each
other over long distances. The ATOC project would make use of
low frequency sounds — the same kinds of sounds that whales
use. We thought that ATOC could interfere with whale commu-
nication, which presumably is important for mating, feeding, and

perhaps other social functions that we know nothing about. I thought that for the whales, it might be a little like trying to get to know someone at a noisy party. Large colonies of seals and birds breed and feed on and near Heard Island. Perhaps their prey would be scattered by the loud noises emanating from the ATOC array or they themselves would be disturbed in some way. Very little is known about the effects of sound on marine mammals, and still less about how fish and invertebrates might react.

We communicated our concerns with the project to the ATOC team. They agreed to look carefully for any signs of adverse impacts on whales. We remained concerned that, because the monitoring program would only passively monitor whales that could be sighted at the surface or detected with underwater microphones, it could miss important changes in behavior underwater. But the experiment went forward.

The ATOC team seemed slightly puzzled that an environmental group would object to a project whose aim was to clarify one of the greatest threats to the environment — climate change. But we were already fairly confident that global warming was real — even though air temperature records were variable, they had been collected for a long time and the increase in global average temperature was statistically significant. We didn't think that a more accurate record of warming that wouldn't be available for at least ten years would influence the debate over what to do about global warming. Far more powerful factors were at work to preserve the status quo than uncertainty over the temperature record. Fossil fuel use was (and is) deeply entrenched, supported by massive investments and subsidies.

In 1991, Munk and his colleagues dangled an underwater speaker array from a ship off Heard Island. From this isolated location, the sound had a clear run to several distant receiving stations around the world, creating an opportunity to make several independent measurements over very long distances. The experiment was a remarkable success — receivers as far as 11,801 miles (19,000 kilometers) away from the speaker array picked up the sound signal.

The ATOC team assured us that no harm had been done to the ocean environment. But their standard was low — no dead whales were sighted, and that was taken as evidence of no effect. There were some indications that beaked whales and minke whales changed their distribution when the sound source was on. Pilot and sperm whales actually stopped singing, or left the test area. But these observations were deemed statistically insignificant, because so few samples were obtained.[23]

The success of the Heard Island experiment led the ATOC team to propose other experiments off Hawai'i and California. These proposals were met with skepticism and concern by a number of environmental groups. Some opposed the projects altogether, while others agreed to discuss modifications, such as much more extensive studies of the impacts on marine mammals and changes in the experimental protocol designed to minimize potential impacts. In the end, Environmental Defense, the ATOC team, and several other environmental groups signed a document laying out conditions that must be met to reduce the chances that ATOC would harm marine mammals, including the location of the ATOC sound source away from known concentrations of marine mammals. In exchange, the environmental groups that signed agreed not to try to kill the experiments through litigation.

In the end, scientific and engineering considerations outweighed environmental concerns. During the fall of 1995, the ATOC team decided to locate the sound source near the Pioneer seamount, an area frequented by whales and many other kinds of animals. This site is relatively close to shore but adjacent to the deep waters of the SOFAR channel. The ATOC marine mammal researchers argued that the sound source had to be located near concentrations of marine mammals; otherwise, not enough observations could be made to rigorously test the effects of ATOC. Instead of waiting for the planes and ships that would be used to survey the area for whales and carry out the marine mammal research to get into place, ATOC engineers tested the sound source before the experiment was to begin. Several days after the experiment, three dead humpback whales were found, washed up on nearby beaches.[24] The whales were not examined because ATOC's vessel was too small to pick them up, and were promptly buried without being autopsied. We will never know for sure whether the ATOC sound source caused or contributed to their deaths.

The National Marine Fisheries Service stopped the experiment and initiated studies to determine whether the sounds had harmed marine mammals. But since very few marine mammals were sighted during the experiment, and because the three dead whales were not autopsied, investigators had little to go on and concluded that the ATOC sound source probably did not harm any marine mammals. The deaths of the three whales were thought to be an unfortunate coincidence by the NMFS investigators, although environmentalists pointed out that the death of even a single whale in this area was highly unusual.

As troubling as ATOC was, the 185-decibel ATOC sound source paled in comparison with the navy's high-powered Low Frequency Active Sonar (LFA). The navy wanted to "light up" the ocean with sounds that could travel and be detected over thousands of miles, so they could track the next generation of silent submarines. The environmental community and many marine mammalogists expressed strong concerns that the loud, low frequency sounds generated by LFA could harm whales and other ocean creatures. We were not reassured by the navy's insistence that no harm would be done to the environment.

In 2000, sixteen Cuvier's beaked whales beached themselves in the Bahamas hours after the navy had conducted mid-frequency sound source tests nearby. The ears and brain cases of many of the whales had hemorrhaged; eight whales died. Whale experts considered these injuries to be consistent with exposure to loud noise. Many whales are thought to have abandoned the waters around the Bahamas. In theory, any animal with an air-filled cavity that could resonate with the sound could be harmed by underwater noise. An extensive investigation by the National Marine Fisheries Service concluded that the navy's test had probably caused the deaths of the whales — and the navy admitted as much.

Environmentalists asked the National Marine Fisheries Service to deny permission for the navy to conduct more LFA tests. Thousands of concerned citizens sent letters and voiced their opposition to the tests in dozens of public hearings. Nevertheless, in July of 2002 NMFS exempted the navy's LFA tests from the Marine Mammal Act, effectively approving the tests — with some restrictions, such as a requirement to stay at least 14 miles (23 kilometers) away from the coast. Environmentalists, led by the Natural Resources Defense Council, have sued to stop the tests. In a great victory for the whales, the court agreed, and issued a preliminary injunction against the LFA tests. However, further legal action is pending as of this writing.

The heads of nation states are naturally concerned to protect the safety of their citizens, and the U.S. government's focus on strengthening national security increased tremendously after the events of September 11, 2001. More measures to beef up defensive capabilities and improve intelligence-gathering may be considered necessary in the future, and the imperatives of war will no doubt continue to outweigh the need to protect the environment. But perhaps other military activities, such as LFA tests and training exercises, can be modified to reduce their environmental impacts without compromising national security.

Some activities conducted in the name of national security have caused serious environmental problems. The use of Vieques Island in Puerto Rico for bombing practice set off protests by environmental groups and local community activists, resulting in a decision to stop the bombing. Many military bases have been indifferent to environmental laws and regulations, resulting in massive toxic waste problems and expensive efforts to clean them up. It seems fairly clear that national security would not have been seriously compromised by complying with environmental regulations and avoiding needless pollution on the bases. But activities such as the bombing Vieques Island, the testing the LFA, and many other military activities pose a special problem to the solutions-oriented environmentalist. Often, disagreements can be resolved by understanding the real interests and goals that lie behind the public positions of each disputant, and coming up with a way to accommodate those interests and goals (a "win-win" solution). But environmentalists are not privy to the strategic thinking and intelligence that guides military activities, and I for one do not feel as though I am in a position to judge their benefits, nor to develop compromises that could meet strategic goals while minimizing environmental impacts. All I can do as an environmentalist in this case is point out the dangers and actual damages, and act as the ocean's advocate.

Ending the Tragedy of the Open Ocean Commons

The same trends that are causing fisheries to collapse in nearshore and continental shelf waters are likely to cause open ocean fisheries to decline and collapse, unless they are reversed. Just as in the nearshore, governance on the high seas must be strengthened, fishing capacity must be reduced, and marine reserves should be established. All of these reforms will be more difficult on the high seas than within national jurisdictions, due to the lack of clear lines of authority and mechanisms for enforcement. However, progress is being made on many fronts to prevent the collapse of open ocean fisheries and to protect ecosystems defined by circulation patterns, temperature, and salinity rather than by rocky reefs or sandy bottoms.

The United Nations Agreement on Highly Migratory and Straddling Fish Stocks represents a major advance in international fisheries management, at least on paper. The agreement was worked out in 1995 and entered into force in 2001.[25] In part due to the increased attention being given to fisheries management by the media, environmentalists, and scientists, the agreement contains strong language directing signatories to apply the precautionary principle. That is, fishing nations and coastal states abiding by the agreement should take action to prevent overfishing and adverse ecological impacts, even if conclusive evidence of harm is lacking. Because so many fisheries have already been fished to their capacity or beyond, however, there is an urgent need to reduce current levels of fishing on overexploited marine populations. Fishery managers should also consider carefully whether existing estimates of maximum sustainable yield are truly sustainable, given our limited understanding of the biology and ecology of these species.

The key to addressing existing fishery problems on the high seas, I think, will be to reduce the number of fishing vessels, which has increased since the 1970s in response to national subsidies[26] and the race for fish. According to the United Nations Food and Agriculture Organization (FAO), growth in the number of fishing vessels is slowing and subsidies are being reduced — yet some 1.2 million fishing vessels continue to roam the seas, and this number represents only the vessels with decks. When small boats are included, the number is probably double that.[27] The World Wildlife Fund estimates global fishing capacity might be more than twice what is needed to achieve sustainable yields.[28]

Why are there so many fishing vessels chasing a dwindling supply of fish? One reason is that the open ocean, to an even greater degree than nearshore and continental shelf areas, is a commons. The same economic incentives that drive fishermen to build more and bigger vessels to compete for fish (see Chapter 5) drive nations to do the same on the high seas. And just as within the territorial waters of nations, governments subsidize fishing in the open ocean — to the tune of about $13 billion each year[29] — with Japan far in the lead, followed by the European Union, the United States, Canada, Russia, and Korea. These subsidies, often intended to help fishermen survive hard times, have played a major role in destroying several major fisheries, and the economies that depended on them. For example, subsidies drove the overfishing of a valuable whitefish (hake) fishery off Argentina, of the North Atlantic cod fishery, and of West African coastal fisheries (destroying the livelihood of small-scale African fishers).

Recognizing the fundamental importance of reducing the number of fishing vessels, not just on the high seas but within national EEZs as well, the U.N.'s Food and Agriculture Organization (FAO) brought nations together in 1998 to develop and sign an agreement to do just that.[30] The FAO Consultation on the Management of Fishing Capacity, Shark Fisheries, and Incidental Catch of Seabirds in Longline Fisheries includes measures to phase in reductions in fishing capacity — but the measures are voluntary. Strong constituencies for environmental protection are needed to ensure that plans of action are actually implemented. Some nations have taken preliminary steps toward reducing subsidies, as has the World Trade Organization. The path is fraught with difficulties, not the least of which is the task of determining which subsidies are good (e.g., government investment in measures to improve safety at sea) and which are bad (e.g., subsidies designed to expand fishing fleets aimed at already overexploited or overcapitalized fisheries).[31] But the world must embark upon this path, because the goal is worthy — a global fishing fleet in harmony with the ocean's productive capacity.

The U.N.'s FAO also brought nations together to sign an agreement to protect sharks and seabirds, two groups of animals that are killed in the tens of thousands in high seas fishing operations. In 1996, Environmental Defense board member and seabird aficionado Charlie Wurster first alerted me to the fact that seabirds, including vulnerable populations of albatross, were getting hooked and drowned. Longline fishing vessels make tempting habitats — they toss thousands of pieces of bait on hooks into the water with every set and dump fish offal over the side as well. While some birds make off with a meal, many seabirds trying to feed on the bait get hooked and pulled under the water, where they drown. Some albatross species, such as the short-tailed albatross of the North Pacific, were decimated for their feathers and eggs long ago. But as longlining expanded in the late twentieth century, it became an increasingly important source of mortality for more and more species of albatross, including critically endangered species such as the short-tailed albatross, as well as for other kinds of birds including petrels, fulmars, shearwaters, penguins, and skuas.

To their credit, Alaska longliners began working to reduce seabird bycatch on their own long before it became a national and international issue. They knew that killing just one or two endangered short-tailed albatross could trigger the Endangered Species Act and close their fishery. Environmental Defense and other groups encouraged the National Marine Fisheries Service to adopt regulations and require measures to reduce the kill of seabirds. Longliners operating around Antarctica, forced to reduce seabird bycatch by the Convention on Antarctic Marine Living Resources, had developed several cost-effective methods such as streamer lines (to scare birds away), avoiding the dumping of offal when fishing lines are being set, and setting at night when birds can't see the bait. As a result of the longliner's initiative and advocacy by environmental groups, fishermen began testing such methods in the North Pacific. After two years, researchers[32] found that streamer lines were extremely effective in preventing seabird deaths. Night setting was not effective in the North Pacific, because night-active birds like Northern Fulmars were present — showing the importance of developing regulations tailored to the ecosystem of interest. Regulations are now in place to protect seabirds in U.S. waters of the North Pacific and the Western Pacific (for vessels based in Hawai'i).

The fact that animals such as albatross and tuna range widely across whole ocean basins is a major challenge for ocean governance and conservation. The nation-state and its jurisdiction does not fit the scale of oceanic ecosystems and migratory species. Industries in each country complain that constraining their activities to protect such species would be futile, because they will just be killed when they cross the border. Bold leadership by a single country in this context can produce a ripple effect, as other countries acknowledge a changing ethos and international political pressure. In other cases, international bodies take action at the behest of non-governmental organizations. The International

Union for the Conservation of Nature (now known as the World Conservation Union) provides a forum in which NGOs and governments can work together toward effective international conservation.

Shortly after Charlie Wurster brought the plight of seabirds to our attention, my intern, Angela Kalmer, took their cause to heart. Angela pored over reams of data and voluminous technical documents to identify the major causes of seabird mortality. She also consulted with experts around the world to come up with workable solutions. She even traveled to Midway Atoll in the remote Northwestern Hawai'ian Islands to observe albatross colonies first-hand and help with a research project there. We distilled the information she gathered into a short background paper[33] for the October 1996 Congress of the World Conservation Union (WCU) in Montreal, Canada. The WCU is unique in that it includes representatives of both governments and nongovernmental organizations. In advance of the meeting, we worked with Defenders of Wildlife and the World Wildlife Fund to craft a motion to reduce the kill of seabirds by longline vessels and persuaded nine other WCU members to co-sponsor it. In the end, the motion passed and created momentum that resulted in a United Nations plan of action for seabirds in 1998, along with plans to protect sharks and reduce global fishing capacity. The United States, in part due to the support of the fishing industry and environmentalists, has made progress toward protecting seabirds (with new requirements for vessels to carry streamer lines, which have proved very effective in scaring birds away from hooks), sharks (with new prohibitions on "finning" — the wasteful practice of cutting off a shark's fins to sell at a high profit for shark-fin soup, then dumping the rest of the shark overboard), and sea turtles (with the closure of huge areas to longliners, by a U.S. federal district court).

Conflicts between countries that host migratory species, or species whose ranges straddle national borders, can also precipitate changes in international governance. For example, the ground-breaking United Nations Agreement on Straddling Fish

Stocks and Highly Migratory Fish Stocks[34] (the U.N. Fish Stocks Agreement, for short) was concluded in 1995, shortly after Canada sent a gunboat to arrest a Spanish trawler fishing on a stock of turbot (a halibut-like flatfish) that straddles Canadian and international waters on the Grand Banks. When the *Estai* tried to flee, the Canadian ship fired across its bow and gave chase.[35] This was the culmination of years of tension between Canada and foreign fishermen, during which huge vessels decimated straddling stocks which, along with Canadian overfishing, resulted in devastating fishery closures. Canada went on to lead negotiations toward the 1995 United Nations agreement.

In 2000, the countries ringing the Pacific Ocean and distant-water fishing nations (nineteen in all, including the United States) signed the Convention for the Conservation and Management of Highly Migratory Fish Stocks in the Western and Central Pacific Ocean, modeled on the U.N. Fish Stocks Agreement. The convention covers a vast swath of the Pacific,[36] encompassing the cold waters south of Australia, the tropical Central and Western Pacific, and part of the North Pacific. Once it enters into force (when 13 signatories ratify it), the convention promises to provide a framework for a new ocean governance regime in the Pacific. At present, many nations fish for tuna, swordfish, and other migratory species, many of which travel around the entire North and South Pacific Ocean basins. In some cases, effective conservation action has been held back by the perception that conservation measures undertaken by only one nation or in only one portion of a species' range will have little benefit if similar measures are not taken comprehensively wherever the species is found. This was a persuasive argument in the debate over what the Pacific Fishery Management Council in the U.S. should do with respect to the fisheries it manages. That argument may be countered by information that is emerging on how wide-ranging species such as tuna and billfish use special areas in the ocean. In any case, coordinated action by all nations fishing for these species can only help.

The new Convention for the Conservation and Management of Highly Migratory Fish Stocks in the Western and Central

Pacific Ocean could bring together existing scientific and fisheries management entities such as the Interamerican Tropical Tuna Commission, the Commission for the Conservation of Southern Bluefin Tuna, and the Indian Ocean Tuna Commission to coordinate management of species that range across their jurisdictions, such as bluefin, skipjack, and big-eye tuna as well as various billfish species.[37] Basin-wide allowable catch levels could be set, with portions allocated to the parties to the convention.

Bycatch (the accidental killing of species that are not targeted by a fishery) continues to be a problem in the fisheries covered by the convention. Allowable bycatch levels could be set for various species — such as sea turtles, seabirds, marine mammals, sharks, and non-target fishes — ranging from zero (for highly endangered species) to limits designed to foster the conservation of robust populations of these species. These bycatch limits, if enforced, could spur innovations in gear and fishing practices as fishermen seek to maximize their catch of target species by avoiding the constraints imposed by catching too many species accidentally, constraints that can include total fishery closures.

Conventional fishery management often creates conflicts, waste, and overfishing because of inflexibility. Fishery regulations should not compromise on ecological goals such as catch limits, but must be flexible enough to adjust to inevitable changes in the abundance and distribution of fish — that is their nature. Inflexible regulations can result in nasty fishery conflicts, as exemplified by the "salmon war" between the U.S. and Canada in the late 1990s. The Pacific Salmon Treaty specified fixed allocations of certain runs of salmon to each nation, based on where their home watersheds were located. When salmon born in Canadian watersheds mixed with salmon born in Alaska watersheds, Alaskan fishermen started to catch them while pursuing the Alaska fish. In 1997, Canadian fishermen became so upset that they blockaded a ferry terminal in Prince Rupert for four days.[38] Negotiations to resolve the crisis were often heated and difficult. Ultimately, the two countries reached an agreement in which each country's share will be percentages of the actual abundance and distribution of the salmon, so that catches can increase and decrease according to environmental changes. This should reduce conflicts, as well as improve the conservation of these shared salmon resources.

Inflexible regulations also sometimes force fishermen to throw fish overboard. This wasteful practice can amount to a substantial portion, or even multiples, of the catch in some cases. Why? Because fishermen are prohibited from retaining and landing certain species that may be depleted or targets of another fishery — so they must throw them overboard when they encounter them in their nets or hooks. If allowances to individual fishermen for bycatch species could be traded in real-time, with administrators keeping track of the trades to ensure that the total bycatch does not exceed allowable limits, one fishermen who has run into a bycatch species could buy an allowance to land it from another fishermen, reducing waste while keeping total bycatch levels under the allowable limit.

If these new international fisheries agreements are to be based on science, the science will have to be greatly improved. Currently, all assessments of high seas species are based solely on catch statistics — which can be seriously misleading. A recent study suggests that China, for example, has been massively over-reporting its catch. As a result, the conventional wisdom that global catches were increasing during the 1990s now appears to be wrong — catches may in fact have been slowing decreasing by about 0.7 million tons (0.6 million tonnes) per year.[39] In addition to simply getting the catches right and interpreting them properly, we will need more natural history studies that provide insight into the most basic features of the biology of high seas species, such as where they breed and feed, and how fast they can replace themselves. Information on population growth rates, life spans, and the age at which individuals become sexually mature can tip us off as to which species might be most vulnerable to fishing.

Marine Reserves on the High Seas

Marine reserves may at first blush appear to be an unlikely tool to apply in the ever-changing and rapidly-moving open ocean. How can the fastest swimmers in the sea, fish that migrate for thousands of miles, benefit from a stationary reserve? Just as ocean-going vessels and long-distance aircraft depend on certain areas (ports, airports) to refuel and re-provision, migratory animals depend on highly productive places like wetlands (and in the case of geese, parks and golf courses). It is becoming increasingly clear that some spots in the ocean are more important to migratory fish than others, because food is concentrated in some areas and diffuse in others. Marine reserves, where fishing activity is banned or heavily regulated, could serve to protect some of these disproportionately important areas on the high seas. If the oceanographic processes that sustain these special areas are relatively stable and predictable, the marine reserve could have traditional fixed boundaries. In the case of less stable processes, or features that are relatively stable but move around a lot (such as the warm and cold core rings of the Atlantic), the boundaries could conceivably be defined by sharp changes in salinity, temperature, or nutrient concentration.

Success Stories

Despite the difficulties inherent in managing high seas fisheries prosecuted by many nations, there have been some bright spots. For example, the number of dolphins killed in the tuna fishery has decreased dramatically in the last 20 years.

For some reason that remains mysterious, big tuna tend to swim in nearly pure schools under pods of dolphin. The dolphin pods are easily targeted by tuna fishermen, and can result in a very "clean" catch of big tuna with little bycatch — except for the dolphin. Before 1990, the most common way to catch tuna in the Eastern Tropical Pacific (called the ETP) was to chase and then surround a dolphin pod with a circular net, called a purse seine, and then draw the bottom up, trapping tuna and drowning dolphins. Over 100,000 dolphins were killed in the pursuit of tuna each year prior to 1989 in the eastern tropical Pacific Ocean alone.[40] U.S. fishers, who dominated the fishery in the 1970s, employed several methods to reduce dolphin deaths to less than

21,000 per year in response to the Marine Mammal Protection Act (MMPA) of 1972. However, other nations started to increase their participation in the ETP fishery, and because they were not subject to the MMPA, they killed more than 110,000 dolphins per year in the early 1980s.[41] Congress amended the MMPA to crack down on dolphin mortality in the tuna fishery by both U.S. and foreign fishers.

Courageous environmentalist Sam LaBudde, working undercover as a cook on a tuna boat, documented the carnage. Media coverage and the resulting outcry fueled a strategy led by the Earth Island Institute that included a consumer boycott of tuna caught by killing dolphins. The tuna canning industry was highly consolidated into just a few major firms. These companies voluntarily agreed to buy tuna only from fishermen who could prove that no dolphins were killed or seriously injured, meaning that no dolphins were encircled with purse-seine nets. The Interamerican Tropical Tuna Commission, one of the best of the international fishery management institutions, managed a voluntary dolphin conservation program for all nations fishing in the ETP.

In 1992, these nations signed the La Jolla Agreement which committed them to reducing dolphin mortality each year over seven years, with the ultimate goal of eliminating dolphin deaths entirely. Meanwhile, tuna fishermen in the eastern tropical Pacific had learned to set their purse seines on pods of dolphin, pull in a clean catch of big tuna, and release most of the dolphin alive. In another example of how incentive-based policies can work, the allowable dolphin mortality was divided into individual quotas and distributed to each tuna vessel. Skilled captain and crews who learned how to release dolphins alive were able to stay under their dolphin quota and keep fishing, while less successful vessels hit their limit and had to stop fishing. The fittest survived, and the weak left the fishery.[42]

By the time the La Jolla Agreement was signed, dolphin deaths in the ETP tuna fishery had been reduced to about 15,000 per year.[43] Nets were only partially closed to allow dolphins to escape. New kinds of nets were used to reduce the entanglement of dolphins. In some cases, divers enter the purse seine while it is being drawn closed, and dip the edge of it under water so that the dolphins can swim away. This must be pretty exciting and risky for the divers — I can only imagine what it must be like to swim through the middle of a net roiling with big fast fish, dolphins, and who knows what else.

The combination of dramatic video footage, environmental activism, consumer pressure, government trade restrictions, industry cooperation, and at-sea monitoring and enforcement resulted in one of the most spectacular environmental successes ever. Dolphin deaths in the eastern tropical Pacific tuna fishery plummeted from 132,000 in 1986 to less than 2,000 by the year 2000, far less than one percent of the estimated dolphin population.[44] However, the tremendous success of this program was not without a downside.

Fishermen need to solve their fishing problem and to apply their ingenuity in order to keep catching fish throughout all the regulatory changes. Catching tuna successfully depends on finding the places where tuna aggregate — places where they feed, breed, or find shelter. In the open ocean, tuna are attracted to floating objects of all kinds. Tuna may also be attracted to places where rich, deep water comes to the surface to nourish great blooms of phytoplankton and the complex food webs they support. Many, many other creatures are also attracted to these oases of high production and activity in the midst of thousands of square miles of relatively empty blue ocean. Sea turtles come to feed on jellyfish, seabirds feast on small fishes in the surface waters, and the big predators — such as tuna, billfish, and shark — feed on the wild variety of animals who hang out under floating objects (generically called "logs") and in upwelling zones. As a result, fishing nets cast in such places and near Fish Aggregating Devices (artificial floating objects that attract fish) catch not only tuna but a whole community of animals. About five to ten times the number of juvenile tuna have been caught by nets set on tuna schools and logs, compared with sets on dolphin pods. Tens of thousands more fish and sharks were caught by fishermen avoiding dolphins.

Kills of sea turtles in the tuna fishery increased several-fold.[45] One author equates one dolphin saved to the killing of an average of 25,824 small tuna, 1,845 other fish, 27 sharks and rays, and 1 billfish.[46] Nevertheless, tuna caught in this way was dolphin-safe, and so was allowed to enter the U.S. market.

Humans have many different kinds of relationships with wildlife. Some view wildlife as prey, with a goal of catching enough animals to sustain human life. Others view animals as gods, willing to give their lives to sustain mankind. These relationships revolve around giving thanks and sustenance back to wildlife through rituals and sacrifices. Some try to catch enough to make a living by selling them. Others see the protection of wildlife as a conservation issue; their goal is to allow some level of killing, while conserving enough animals to sustain their populations and the ecosystems they live in. And still others value the lives of individual animals and are sensitive to their suffering. The debate between environmentalists over the dolphin-safe labeling issue was full of arguments about scientific evidence and about what kinds of incentives various policy options were creating and would create; but the basic disagreement, that of conflicting values, lay hidden for the most part.

Unfortunately, the conflict between environmental groups was not resolved and the community divided. Environmental Defense, the Worldwide Fund for Nature (WWF), the Center for Marine Conservation (now the Ocean Conservancy), the National Wildlife Federation, and Greenpeace began working with Latin American countries to hammer out the details of an agreement that would, among other things, make possible a change in the dolphin-safe label. With this change, the owners of vessels who had developed ways to encircle dolphins and release them would be able to sell their tuna in the lucrative U.S. market — but only if they could certify (with on-board observers) that no dolphins were killed or seriously injured.

These environmental groups were motivated by a desire to lock in the voluntary programs that had so dramatically reduced dolphin mortality and to reduce the enormous bycatch of fish,

sharks, and sea turtles associated with setting tuna nets on floating objects and tuna schools.[47] They tried to address concerns
about trauma to dolphins by making the agreement contingent
on scientific evidence that the dolphins were not unacceptably
harmed by being captured and released from purse seines. These
serious concerns were based on the reasonable expectation that,
while these dolphin escaped death by drowning, the process of
being chased, surrounded by a net, and then released could so
traumatize them that their health, reproductive capacity, or more
subtle aspects of their complicated social lives could well be
adversely affected. Also, these environmental groups were concerned that Latin American countries that had been reducing
dolphin deaths voluntarily would no longer do so if they were not
allowed access to the large U.S. market. Other groups, like the
Earth Island Institute, Defenders of Wildlife, and many others,
were arrayed against any changes in the dolphin-safe label
because of their concerns that dolphin deaths might increase
again and that encircling dolphins might be harmful to them,
especially over the long run.

In 1995, several Latin American countries signed the Panama
Declaration, in which they agreed to limit dolphin deaths to no
more than 5,000 per year and participate in a voluntary dolphin
conservation program. In turn, the U.S. agreed to change the criteria for the dolphin-safe label, if research showed that dolphins
released from purse seines were indeed unharmed.[48]

Environmentalists and policy makers had to decide whether
the current definition of dolphin-safe tuna was encouraging the
use of fishing methods that killed huge amounts of other species
in addition to tuna, and whether it was time to change the label
to allow U.S. sales of tuna caught by surrounding and then
releasing pods of dolphin. The initial results of the research (man-
dated by congress) on the effects of purse seining on dolphins
were uncertain. The effects of stress were studied only by reviewing the literature. Although this literature review suggested that
stress induced by encirclement could plausibly have negative
effects on dolphin populations, the major conclusion in the

National Marine Fisheries Service (NMFS) Report to Congress[49] was that there was not enough evidence to conclude that chasing and encircling dolphins with purse seines was harming them. Despite the huge decrease in dolphin deaths attributable to the tuna fishery, three dolphin populations are not recovering as rapidly as expected. NMFS concluded that the tuna fishery was probably not responsible for delaying recovery, and speculated that these depleted dolphin populations may not have had enough time to respond to the dramatic reductions in dolphin deaths over the last decade or so. So NMFS decided that tuna caught by encircling dolphin pods with purse seines could be granted the dolphin-safe label, as long as captains and observers certified that no dolphins were killed or seriously injured in the process.

The conclusion of NMFS that there was insufficient evidence to show that purse seining harms dolphins, and therefore, purse seining should be considered to be dolphin-safe, illustrates a very common problem in the creation of public policy. Agency officials very often take a lack of evidence or high degree of uncertainty to mean a lack of effect (purse seining does not harm dolphins) when this interpretation facilitates economic activity, versus the alternative explanation that effects may not have been detected for some reason (purse seines might harm dolphins, we just can't tell at the moment, so let's restrict or ban it). Reasons for a lack of sufficient evidence can include poor experimental design, small sample size (a common problem when studying marine mammals), or insufficient time for the manifestation of adverse impacts. This difference in how scientific uncertainty is interpreted is also related to where the burden of proof lies. In our society, despite language in laws to the contrary, the burden of proof usually rests squarely on those who are concerned about potential impacts of economic activities on wildlife or the environment in general. If there is no proof that pursuing an economic activity harms wildlife or the environment, that activity is generally allowed to continue, though there may be good reasons to expect harm, or even if few or no studies have been conducted.

The new labeling criteria were to take effect in January of 2000, but a lawsuit filed by Earth Island Institute and several other environmental groups resulted in a judgment that delayed any change in the label until the final results of scientific research on the impacts of purse seines on dolphins became available. Unfortunately, the final results are also equivocal and difficult to interpret. In the absence of hard scientific evidence, the weighing of the potential harm to dolphins of getting netted and released versus the possibility of reducing the huge amount of bycatch associated with fishing on logs and oceanic oases is difficult, and depends largely on one's value system. Do you care more about the trauma to dolphins than about the loss of tens of thousands of other kinds of wildlife? It's difficult to know if this is even the right calculus. Would allowing fishermen to target dolphins, release them, and then label the tuna caught in this way as dolphin-safe actually result in less fishing on logs and oases, and therefore less bycatch of other animals? There is also a risk of countries eschewing the U.S. tuna market altogether and simply selling their tuna to other countries that lack restrictions to protect dolphins if the dolphin-safe label is not changed. This could result in a return of the bad old days of high dolphin death rates.

The answer to these daunting questions, I think, is to set comprehensive bycatch standards that apply not only to dolphins, but to all other creatures of the sea. This policy could create incentives for fishermen to develop different kinds of gear and practices to catch tuna. The bycatch problem has persisted only because enforceable standards and reliable monitoring have not been implemented in most fisheries. Where they have, technical innovations that reduce bycatch without compromising fish harvests have occurred. Regulations and educational programs aimed at reducing seabird bycatch in longline fisheries off Alaska and Hawai'i have resulted, for example, in the use of inexpensive streamer lines that flap in the wind, scaring birds away from the hooks that drown them. Scientists are developing different kinds of baits that appear to appeal to only certain kinds of fish, potentially reducing bycatch, because such baits could dramatically increase fishing opportunities (i.e., increase revenues).

Other policies can create positive economic incentives to reduce bycatch. When access to fisheries is restricted with permits or Individual Fishing Quotas, one of the criteria for gaining access to the fishery or for allocation of a share of the catch should be the selectivity of the fishing operation — that is, does it meet the bycatch standard? Deducting measured bycatch mortality from the catch quotas of different fishing sectors, so that allowable catch increases as bycatch is reduced, would encourage fishermen to reduce bycatch as much as possible so as to increase their allowable catch. In many cases, a single estimate of bycatch mortality is deducted from the allowable catch for whole fisheries, so that clean fishing operations have no advantage over operations that result in lots of bycatch.

Marine reserves can also help reduce bycatch by keeping fishermen out of areas where many different kinds of organisms live together. If they don't live together, chances are that they won't be caught together. Lowering bycatch rates and absolute numbers of animals that are killed accidentally by fishermen will not only help protect the integrity of marine ecosystems, it will also increase fishing opportunities. Because species vary tremendously in their growth rates and reproductive capacity, if a group of species is caught together in a net or on a longline, some of the less productive species will decline faster than the others. When fish populations start to dwindle, as is the case in many fisheries in the U.S. and around the world, bycatch of a depleted species can result in the closure of productive fisheries, so as to protect or rebuild the depleted species. This is the crux of the problem with what are called multispecies fisheries — fisheries that take many different species because they inhabit similar (or the same) habitats.

Other attempts to protect wildlife on the high seas have not been as successful as the dolphin-safe label, but illustrate innovative ways to achieve conservation where national jurisdictions don't apply and international governance is weak. In 1991 and 1993, the U.S.-based North Atlantic Salmon Fund (a non-profit organization supported by the sportfishing industry) bought and retired the annual fishing rights of fishermen from Greenland in an attempt to conserve dwindling populations of Atlantic salmon that were expected to return to watersheds in Maine and New Hampshire. The conservation results are difficult to assess because, although more salmon made it back to New England watersheds following the retirement of these fishing rights, fewer salmon were being harvested overall because of the increasing availability of inexpensive farmed salmon during this period.[50]

International agreements have sometimes succeeded in protecting resources, wildlife, and ocean ecosystems. For example, Australia and New Zealand were able to force Japan to comply with provisions agreed to by the Commission for the Conservation of Southern Bluefin Tuna, to which all three nations belong. Japan had sought to continue fishing this depleted population under the guise of "scientific fishing" until the International Tribunal of the Law of the Sea ruled against it. The Law of the Sea is the only environmental treaty with such a tribunal — similar provisions are needed to improve enforcement of other international agreements.

But despite the occasional success, strong treaty language is too often not backed up by strong enforcement actions. Compliance with the 1972 London Dumping Convention and the 1973 International Convention for the Prevention of Pollution from Ships (MARPOL) has generally been poor.[51] International treaties are quite difficult to enforce, particularly at sea. Nations are often loathe to slap trade sanctions on a country that is violating an international environmental agreement or national environmental laws. At the same time, the World Trade Organization works against the use of trade sanctions — one of the only viable means for a nation to enforce international agreements and to live up to its national commitment to environmental protection. For example, in 1998 a WTO dispute resolution panel ruled against a U.S. law forbidding the import of shrimp from countries that did not require the use of turtle-excluder devices (TEDs) which dramatically reduce sea turtle deaths in shrimp fisheries. A second WTO dispute resolution panel partially reversed this decision on appeal by the U.S., upholding the U.S. law but requiring several changes. As a result, the U.S. now allows individual shipments of shrimp caught by fishermen using TEDs. But this reduces pressure on exporting countries to pass national laws requiring TEDs, increasing the risk of sea turtle deaths by fishermen who sell shrimp to companies that don't export to the U.S.[52]

Benjamin Barber, in his book *Jihad vs. McWorld*,[53] argues that free trade and free markets can be dangerous to democratic institutions that are supposed to protect non-market goods and values such as social justice, human rights, and the environment. Even when market forces are constrained and economic activities are regulated, the constant pressure to make money from natural resources strains the system and too often prevails against precautionary action or even obviously necessary conservation measures. The most effective international conservation measures and institutions seem to benefit from strong scientific support which leads to credibility and hence buy-in by the parties (e.g., the Interamerican Tropical Tuna Commission). Widespread public acceptance of the value of protecting certain places, certain kinds of wildlife (charismatic megafauna like dolphins), and certain kinds of resources (e.g., the ban on whaling, and the International Dolphin Conservation Program) is also important for ensuring the effectiveness of such conservation programs.

Globalization cannot be stopped; it is already upon us. But if enough people express the desire, globalization can evolve to comport with, or even encourage, our most deeply held values — values that the market is blind to. New trade rules can create economic incentives that encourage conservation and good stewardship to replace existing incentives that encourage waste, overexploitation, and ecosystem damage. Positive incentives, such as increased market demand for sustainably caught fish, can supplement the use of negative incentives such as trade sanctions. Such incentives can be built into international agreements or can support them from the outside. The success of the Dolphin-Safe label in dramatically reducing dolphin demonstrates the power of the market to influence fishing practices. The next step is to set the bar higher — whole ecosystem protection that does not trade dolphins saved against the deaths of thousands of other creatures. Increased consumer awareness of the ecological impacts of fishing, coupled with credible certification systems, has the potential to create incentives for conservation not only in nearshore waters but also on the continental shelves and the high seas, where enforcement is more problematic and incentives become even more important.

Already, one can observe fastidious consumers pulling out small cards to check their menu choices against the recommendations of the Monterey Bay Aquarium, the Audubon Society, or Environmental Defense, and then purchase the product that allows them to enjoy a seafood dinner, knowing that it was caught using sustainable practices. Since most Americans apparently prefer to buy fish in processed form, either in the frozen food case or in a restaurant, it will be important to persuade large institutional purchasers of seafood to insist on sustainable products, whether harvested from the sea or pulled from a fish or shrimp farm. As the market demands more and more sustainable seafood, fishermen and fish farmers will change their methods and increase compliance with regulations to meet that demand — if the labels signifying sustainability are credible, backed up by effective monitoring and enforcement programs.

The new Convention for the Conservation and Management of Highly Migratory Fish Stocks in the Western and Central Pacific Ocean is promising. The new, heightened level of awareness about the dire status of fisheries also resulted in a pledge by world leaders attending the 2002 World Summit on Sustainable Development in Johannesburg to better protect fish stocks. These new international agreements will need support from economic incentives, reforms in free-trade institutions and agreements, and massive grassroots support to be successful in protecting ocean wildlife and sustaining high seas fisheries, many of which are already depleted. There is an opportunity to intervene early and prevent the despoilment of the deep sea, where unique species and whole ecosystems new to science flourish on top of fabulously rich mineral deposits.

7

THE DEEP SEA:
In Over Our Heads?

Until recently, the deep sea was thought to be a barren biological desert, devoid of life save for a few hardy species. We now know that the cold, pressurized waters of the deep sea are home to an almost unbelievable variety of clams, worms, amphipods, and other creatures. We do not even know what we don't know about the deep sea. As a measure of the profound depth of our ignorance, consider that just in the past few years hydrothermal vents full of gold were discovered, lying right on the ocean's bottom within the Exclusive Economic Zones (EEZ) of certain countries. Because the EEZs are exempt from the stringent international regulations of the International Seabed Authority (set up under the Law of the Sea), these new discoveries may set off a gold rush. This could in turn destroy one of the most bizarre and fascinating ecosystems on the planet — the only one that doesn't run off solar energy. Mining companies are already signing underwater leases with developing countries hungry for foreign exchange and mineral riches. New underwater technologies are bringing commercial exploitation of deep sea resources ever closer to commercial feasibility. How can we prevent a gold rush from destroying hydrothermal vent communities, which we only just discovered?

The Nature of the Deep Sea

Sir John Ross and his nephew Sir James Clark Ross knew that animals flourished in the deep sea as early as the 1840s. They lowered their "deep-sea clamm" with sounding lines up to 4.3 miles (6.9 kilometers) long into Antarctic and Arctic seas, and brought up various kinds of sea life. However, at about the same time, Edward Forbes was also sampling the ocean, and showed that animal abundance generally increased near the surface and decreased with depth. Forbes concluded that animals became scarcer with increasing depth. His followers, illustrating the dangers of extrapolation, took the logic a step further by saying that no life at all could possibly exist in the deep ocean, because of the great pressures, lack of light, and near absence of oxygen characteristic of deep waters.[1] This theory persisted despite the empirical evidence of the Rosses to the contrary. It even gained strength as the perception developed of the deep sea as a quiet, homogeneous place — everybody knew that high biological diversity was found only where habitats are diverse and subject to the occasional disturbance to shake things up a bit.

The pressure in the deep sea is indeed intense (up to 1,000 atmospheres in the deepest trenches), it is indeed dark, and cold too (usually below 37° F or 2.8° C), but the deep sea somehow supports plenty of life. Some parts of the deep sea are incredibly rich in biodiversity — among the richest in the world. A 1989 survey that covered less than 200 square feet (about the size of a living room) yielded 798 species, more than half of which were new to science. Some scientists speculated that if so many species could be found in so small an area, the deep sea should contain millions of species. Even conservative estimates range up to half a million species, and that accounts for only the large animals like mollusks, crustaceans, and worms. Who knows how many species of smaller creatures might live in the deep sea? Only about 275,000 ocean species have been described to date, but we've only sampled the tiniest fraction of the ocean. And in terms of higher-level biodiversity — the major branches of life called phyla — the ocean far exceeds the land. All but one of the 40 or so animal phyla live in the sea, and about half of them live only in the sea — perhaps because life originated there. What mysterious processes gave rise to the tremendous diversity of the deep sea?

The deep sea was once thought to be a quiet, dark place where not much biological activity was going on. Bacteria operate on such a slow track that a bologna sandwich retrieved from a lost submersible still looked fresh after 11 months in the deep.[2] But recent, more detailed observations by scientists in submersibles and Remotely Operated Vehicles (ROVs) provide a strikingly different picture. Strong currents give rise to eddies and underwater storms lasting for days or even weeks. Millions of tons of sediment sometimes slide into underwater canyons, the muddy torrents persisting for hundreds of miles. When examined closely, the soft sediments on the ocean bottom vary tremendously in particle size, texture, and density. The animals themselves make the habitat even more diverse by burrowing through it, sweeping the surface with their tentacles, pumping water, feeding, excreting, and doing all the things that animals do. They depend on the rain of organic manna from the surface waters above — dead plankton, often clumped together in marine "snow"; large groups of dead jellyfish drifting slowly to the bottom; and the occasional bonanza provided by dead fish, dolphins, seals, or even whales. Variable currents and patterns of surface production result in variable degrees of marine rain and snow. The diverse patterns of food supply add to the diversity of habitats and the occasional disturbance from storms to promote biological diversity in the deep sea.

Strange creatures abound in the deep sea, exquisitely adapted to life there. Many of the fishes have huge mouths and extensible stomachs to make the most of meals that must be quite few and far between. Some animals glow with bioluminescence, the only light available in the perpetual darkness. Owlfish may use their large eyes to collect this limited amount of light in order to find their prey. Other fish have small eyes but are sensitive to other energies in the environment — the gulper eel can sense the tell-tale vibrations of its prey.[3]

The mystery of the deep sea is so profound that only 25 years ago, an entirely new kind of ecosystem was discovered. In 1977, Robert Ballard and his team of adventurous scientists discovered a hot spot of geological activity deep in the waters off the Galapagos Islands. Here, the seabed had fractured and given rise to hot geysers of seawater, up to 350° F (177° C). Much to their surprise, a thriving community of large animals had grown up around these hot vents. Giant worms, up to three feet (one meter) long, waved in the current, their red "lips" protruding from white tubes. Crabs and shrimps scurried about amongst numerous species of filter-feeding animals. I will never forget my first glimpse of the huge vent clams — they were about ten inches wide, with bright red flesh — lying in the seawater tanks of the Marine Biological Laboratory in Woods Hole. They had been discovered just before I started my graduate studies there, and the whole lab was buzzing with excitement.

Primary production, that is, the production of "new" food from inorganic materials, was several times higher at the vents than in most surface waters. As a result, the total amount of biological material ("biomass") at the vents was much, much higher per unit area than elsewhere on the ocean bottom. The vent communities are not the most diverse in the sea, but about 300 vent species have been described, and (most remarkably) about 90 percent of these were new to science. Whole new families (groups of related species) had to be created to accommodate the unique life forms of the vents. Intense research ensued, aimed at elucidating how this strange ecological community could thrive in the deep sea, more than 8,000 feet (2,400 meters) away from the sunlight that was thought to be essential.

The secret to life near the vents lies in tiny bacteria that can transform the otherwise toxic hydrogen sulfide flowing out of the

vents into food. Cold water vents supporting biological communities similar to those of the hot vents were discovered in the
1980s, showing that high temperatures were not necessary for
high primary productivity. The vent animals have many physio-
logical adaptations for life in what might appear at first to be a
hostile environment. The tube worms have no mouths or guts;
instead, they have special organs filled with symbiotic bacteria
that convert hydrogen sulfide into organic food molecules for the
worm. The clams have a unique molecule that they use to transport the otherwise deadly hydrogen sulfide through their tissues
safely. The shocking red color of the worms and clams is the
result of high concentrations of hemoglobin (the same molecule
that makes our blood red), which is necessary for absorbing and
transporting oxygen in the low-oxygen waters near the vents.
Somehow, the vent animals propagate themselves, colonizing far-
flung vents scattered through the deep ocean.

Despite all of these marvelous adaptations for life under
duress, the vent communities may have now met their match —
humans lusting after the mineral riches piled up all around them.
The crushing pressure, cold temperatures, and perpetual darkness
of the deep ocean that gave rise to the amazing adaptations of the
animals that thrive there also afford some protection from human
activities. It's hard to imagine an environment more hostile to
humans. But remotely-operated vehicles and underwater robots
which will soon be operating autonomously for months at a time
are extending our senses (and our power to extract resources) all
the way to the bottom of the sea.

Mining the Bottom of the Sea

New discoveries of rich veins of gold on land are rare these days.
But our ignorance of the ocean is so deep that a large new species
of squid was discovered just a few years ago, and an ancient fish
(the coelacanth) thought to be long extinct showed up at an
Indonesian fish market. The discovery of hydrothermal vents and
their strange biological communities set off a frenzy of scientific
research. It was soon discovered that the hot water spilling out of

the vents was laying down deposits full of gold and other valuable metals.

This was by no means the first time that valuable minerals have been found on the seafloor. As far back as 1873, the Challenger expedition discovered lumps (nodules) of minerals, including manganese, copper, iron, nickel, cobalt, and platinum lying on the bottom in deep water.[4] In some areas, the nodules contain metals in concentrations much higher than is typical for ores on land. The eastern Pacific Ocean between Hawai'i and Mexico is particularly rich in nodules, scattered more than two-and-a-half miles (four kilometers) below the surface. The nodules are about the size of softballs, but may be very old. They appear to build up extremely slowly, on the order of four one hundred thousandths of an inch (0.001 millimeters) every thousand years.[5] The process by which they are formed is still a mystery; it could be steady and very, very slow, or it could be characterized by relatively rapid but infrequent bursts of accretion.

Interest and investment in deep sea mining increased quickly during the 1960s and was sustained during the 1970s. Projections of vast riches to be had from mining the nodules were fueled by the prospect of increasing mineral prices and concerns about the political stability of countries where most of the world's strategic minerals are located. The United Nations Law of the Sea Conferences were also initiated during the 1970s and culminated in the Law of the Sea Treaty in 1982. The signatories to this treaty recognized deep seabed minerals (outside of Exclusive Economic Zones, up to 200 miles from a nation's coastline) as the common heritage of all countries, to be regulated by a new International Seabed Authority. Private companies, nations, or multinational consortia would be required to pay fees for a mining claim, be subject to international mining regulations, and fund not only their own mining operations but a parallel operation by the United Nations for the benefit of less developed countries. One hundred and thirty nations signed the treaty, four voted against it (the United States, Israel, Turkey, and Venezuela), and 17 abstained (including Belgium, Italy, the

Netherlands, the former Soviet Union, the United Kingdom, and West Germany),[6] all of which had an interest in deep sea mining.[7]

Countries objecting to the Law of the Sea signed a separate agreement called the Provisional Understanding Regarding Deep Seabed Matters.[8] Under this agreement, four international consortia were awarded licenses to explore seabed mining. Seabed mining was regarded, by the U.S. at least, as a "freedom of the high seas", analogous to catching fish on the high seas — "title to which has historically rested upon capture" — recognizing that this freedom can be exercised only to "reasonable" limits that don't infringe on the rights of other countries.[9] The Law of the Sea came into force in 1994. The U.S. signed after the deep sea mining provisions were modified in the 1994 Agreement Relating to the Implementation of Part XI of the U.N. Law of the Sea Convention, largely to meet the objections of the U.S. and other industrialized countries. The main objections concerned decision-making, the mandatory transfer of private technology, disincentives to deep seabed mining that the U.S. maintained were inconsistent with a free market philosophy, and uncertain access to seabed minerals in the future.[10]

As a result of the 1994 agreement, the U.S. is now assured a seat on the decision-making council of the International Seabed Authority in perpetuity. A special review procedure that would have made it easier for developing countries to amend the convention was eliminated. Technology transfer is no longer mandatory, but instead is guided by a set of general principles. Disincentives to mining were addressed by getting rid of production limits on seabed mining, replacing the $1 million annual mining fee with a set of principles, reducing the $500,000 application fee for a mining permit to $250,000, and removing the special privileges accorded to the Enterprise (the mining arm of the International Seabed Authority) under the original convention and subjecting it to the same rules that apply to countries. The Law of the Sea Convention and the 1994 Agreement were submitted for ratification to the U.S. Senate in 1994, but it has not yet acted upon it.

Meanwhile, interest in deep sea mining had cooled off considerably. Metal prices did not increase as expected. Perhaps of equal importance, the Law of the Sea provisions (even after the 1994 modifications) create many disincentives inhibiting exploration and exploitation of deep sea minerals in international waters. In addition, the fact that manganese nodules are not concentrated in large single deposits but are instead scattered in deep water makes mining them costly. Some deep sea mining claims were as large as Switzerland, and would have produced trainloads of tailings. Experimental disturbance of the bottom, intended to mimic the effects of nodule mining, showed that recovery of animal communities in deep sea sediments is extremely slow.[11] The plumes of sediment kicked up by mining activities could affect ecosystems miles away.

The discovery of mineral deposits associated with hydrothermal vents removes many of the barriers that have inhibited deep sea mining, and so could encourage a new gold rush to the bottom of the sea. The same mineral-rich hot water that nourishes the giant vent worms, clams, and the rest of the hydrothermal vent community also deposits precious metals in large chimneys and domes, some up to the size of Capitol Hill. Some of these deposits (called polymetallic sulfides, because they contain many different kinds of metals) occur within the Exclusive Economic Zones of individual countries like Japan, the Soloman Islands, and Papua New Guinea, and so are exempt from international law. These deposits are much shallower than the manganese nodule beds — they occur in waters about 300 to 6,000 feet (91 to 1,830 meters) deep, potentially making their extraction much less costly. Unlike the nodules, polymetallic sulfide deposits are highly concentrated. Some contain gold at concentrations up to ten times the levels typical of a commercial mine on land.[12]

Mining companies are already staking their claims in this new gold rush. Papua New Guinea granted a license in 1997 to the Nautilus Minerals Corporation for exploring and exploiting hydrothermal vent mineral deposits in a 1,930-square-mile

(5,000-square-kilometer) area in the Manus Basin. Nautilus plans to extract 10,000 tons (9,072 tonnes) of ore from this claim over the next two years in the course of prospecting, and planned to start commercial mining operations by 2003.[13] Japan has begun to study the feasibility of mining a large sulfide deposit in the Okinawa Trough. The U.S. is developing programs to explore and mine polymetallic sulfides on the Gorda Ridge off Oregon and Northern California.[14]

The environmental impacts of ocean mining are hard to predict, but some educated guesses are possible. Environmental impacts will depend strongly on the kind of mining that takes place, and where. The International Seabed Authority believes that strip mining and open cast mining are the likeliest candidates for mining polymetallic sulfide deposits near hydrothermal vents.[15] While mining on soft sediments for manganese nodules would probably result in vast plumes of resuspended sediment that could choke biological communities for miles around, mining near vents would probably result in less resuspension because the mineral deposits are relatively new and are generally covered with thin layers of sediment.

Miners would probably avoid the active vents because of the dangers associated with operating near such hot water (hot enough to melt metal). But significant biological communities extend far from the actual vents in some cases; vent crabs, for example, have been found foraging far from the vents. Some sediment will inevitably be resuspended, even though the detritus from hydrothermal vent mining will likely be quite heavy and return to the bottom sooner than would finer sediments. Toxic metals released in the course of mining or of processing the tailings could harm marine food webs. Accidental damage to conveyance systems bringing ore to the surface could lead to catastrophic toxicity and burial of organisms. Ore slurries brought up from the depths will also be cold and rich in nutrients. Accidental or deliberate discharge of waste-water from mining operations into surface waters could seriously harm marine ecosystems, particularly in tropical seas that are naturally low in nutrients.

Disturbance of soft sediments on the continental slopes and abyssal plains by mining could result in very long-lived changes in animal communities, due to the slowness of life processes in general in these habitats.[16] Mining on vents, in contrast, could destroy a vent community, but the site could be recolonized relatively rapidly because these communities are extremely productive and appear to be adapted to sometimes catastrophic changes in their environment. The hot water vents can shut down or burst forth with little or no warning. One's perception of the seriousness of such impacts depends to a large extent on one's view of the intrinsic worth of the relatively ephemeral vent communities (they may last for several decades, a short span of time in ecological terms). Environmentalists tend to value the vent communities, regardless of how long they persist, whereas at least some mining engineers and scientists tend to believe that their ephemeral nature renders their loss less of a problem; for this reason, some have compared vent mining to farming.[17]

Other kinds of underwater mineral deposits are also attracting interest. The government of the Cook Islands is accepting proposals to mine cobalt-rich deposits within its territorial waters. In the U.S., state and federal task forces are studying the feasibility of mining cobalt crusts off the Hawai'ian Islands.[18] Deposits of muds, rich in metals and up to 80 feet (24 meters) thick, have been discovered in the Red Sea, and exploratory dredging is already underway.[19] While some countries have regulatory frameworks that apply to ocean mineral deposits, many others do not. And it's not clear that existing regulations would actually protect ocean ecosystems, about which little is known.

Mining has a rather bad environmental record on land. Mining operations in the ocean will probably be even more difficult to observe and hold accountable. Once large investments in ocean mining are made, it may be much more difficult to impose environmental regulations on mining operations.

Deep Energy

The deep sea contains a resource even more valuable than gold — immense deposits of natural gas. On the continental slopes and rises under more than 1,000 feet (305 meters) of water, the remains of countless marine organisms decay giving rise to methane or natural gas. At these temperatures and pressures, the methane molecules combine with water to create crystals called methane hydrates (or clathrates). Some estimate that about ten percent of the ocean could contain methane hydrates[20] — a small percentage but one that adds up to an enormous area, exceeding the total extent of the world's continental shelves.

Reserves of natural gas of this size are naturally attracting interest, especially as the United States looks for ways to reduce its dependence on foreign oil and gas. But the extraction of methane hydrates from the sea is fraught with difficulties, at least conceptually. No technology for mining methane hydrates currently exists. And quite apart from the technical difficulties of exploiting hydrates, accidental releases of methane could have profound effects on the entire planet. Some scientists believe that because methane hydrates are not buried in hard rock, but rather exist as unstable masses of semi-frozen crystals, they could be released suddenly in giant burps. Because methane is a potent greenhouse gas, trapping heat 20 times more effectively per molecule than carbon dioxide, large releases of methane from the sea could result in the catastrophic acceleration of global warming. Indeed, some theorize that such releases might have helped tip the climate system into warm phases in the past.

Hiding the Carbon

The flip side of taking natural gas out of the ocean is putting carbon dioxide back in. Fossil fuel addicts such as the United States can only keep the petroleum party going by increasing the supply of fossil fuels, by getting rid of the greenhouse gases that result from fossil fuel combustion, or both. As the realities of global warming sink in, there will probably be in increase in efforts to engineer the environment, rather than modify ingrained habits and upset financial interests in continuing to find, exploit, and burn fossil fuels. Some methods of absorbing carbon dioxide from the atmosphere — which could buy time by reducing the extent and rate of global warming — could be relatively benign and perhaps even beneficial. Planting trees in urban areas can not only remove carbon dioxide from the atmosphere, but also significantly reduce air conditioning needs (a relatively large source of energy consumption and therefore of greenhouse gas emissions). Reforesting areas that have been logged can also bring improved ecological services such as flood control, reduced erosion, and better water quality. Trees absorb carbon dioxide, converting it to leaves and wood. But vast areas and huge amounts of nutrients would probably be needed to remove enough carbon dioxide from the atmosphere to make a difference. All the forests on earth constitute a relatively small reservoir of carbon when compared to the ocean: the ocean stores some 17 times the amount of carbon stored on land.

The potentially huge capacity of the ocean to absorb wastes has generated interest in using the ocean as a waste dump for all kinds of things, ranging from radioactive waste to (more recently) carbon dioxide. Some of the same principles that make the ocean unsuitable for conventional and nuclear wastes apply to carbon dioxide. The ocean, and the deep sea in particular, is hard to monitor; thus, waste of any kind on the seafloor would be difficult to monitor and regulations difficult to enforce. Wastes that are injected directly into the ocean or which are released accidentally from corroding containers can be dispersed over vast distances. Two-dimensional oil spills are hard enough to clean up; no technology currently exists for cleaning up three-dimensional spills in the water column.

Injecting carbon dioxide into the deep ocean poses a unique set of problems, too. Schemes for dumping carbon dioxide into the ocean have taken two forms so far: pump liquefied carbon dioxide directly into the deep sea; or fertilize the ocean to stimulate gigantic algal blooms that would absorb atmospheric carbon dioxide through photosynthesis, and then carry it down to the deep sea for burial.

Both approaches to sequester carbon dioxide in the sea suffer from major, perhaps fatal flaws. To pump liquid waste carbon dioxide into the sea, one would first have to collect it somehow from smokestacks and then expend a considerable amount of energy to liquefy it. Next, the liquid gas would have to be transported to the coast. Facilities would ideally be located in areas close to very deep water, such as Monterey, California, where a canyon up to 10,000 feet (3,048 meters) deep sits right off the beach, so that pipes can be kept to a minimum. If the costs (both economic and environmental) of dumping the carbon dioxide into the deep sea seem justifiable, another set of even more pressing issues comes into play. What if it works? What if we manage to inject large amounts (say a billion tons per year or so, or about 20 percent of annual carbon dioxide emissions) of carbon dioxide into the ocean? In the atmosphere, carbon dioxide acts like a blanket, trapping heat. But in the ocean, it is more likely to act as an acid. Ocean water is heavily buffered against any change in its acidity or alkalinity. But large amounts of additional carbon dioxide could conceivably increase the ocean's acidity, at least near the dump site and perhaps for quite a way beyond. Marine animals and bacteria have evolved in a very stable environment. The effects of even slightly increased acidity on animals — and perhaps more importantly, on critical ecosystem processes such as decomposition — are unknown but seem risky.

Fertilizing the sea to remove carbon dioxide from the atmosphere may be even trickier than pumping liquid carbon. Scientists have shown that adding iron to surface waters in certain areas of the ocean does stimulate large phytoplankton blooms that can persist up to ten days or so. However, as anyone who has ever tried to grow phytoplankton in the laboratory knows, it is difficult to control the species that bloom in response to the addition of nutrients. The kind of phytoplankton that bloom might be important, because phytoplankton are very diverse and probably decompose and sink at different rates. To efficiently transfer carbon dioxide from the atmosphere to the deep ocean, one would like to grow phytoplankton that absorb the carbon rapidly, fend off grazers, and sink quickly. If the phytoplankton that respond to the fertilization happen to be favored food species, they could be eaten by voracious herbivores who would rapidly convert the carbon absorbed by the phytoplankton back into carbon dioxide in the surface waters where it could pop right back up into the atmosphere. Furthermore, if diatoms predominate (as they have in the iron fertilization experiments), their growth may become limited by another mineral — silicon — in certain waters. For example, ocean waters surrounding the Antarctic, where nutrient-rich deep waters come to the surface, become depleted in silicon as they flow northward. Adding iron to such waters might not increase phytoplankton growth, unless large amounts of silicate were also added. If all these conditions are met and the phytoplankton actually do sink to deeper waters before they are eaten, a different problem could occur. Deep ocean waters are already fairly low in oxygen. The influx of millions or even billions of tons of more organic carbon in the form of phytoplankton could overwhelm the system and tip it over, at least in some areas, to completely anoxic (zero oxygen) dead zones.

The concept of dumping waste carbon dioxide in the ocean also raises important policy questions, quite apart from technical questions about their feasibility or environmental impacts. Plans to fertilize the ocean or inject liquid carbon dioxide into deep waters would have to be fairly large scale to reduce the rate and extent of global warming (perhaps covering 20 percent of the ocean or so), and thus could be viewed as planetary engineering (with highly uncertain planetary consequences) to support our fossil fuel habit. A far more reliable approach would be to reduce fossil fuel combustion, plant trees, and encourage renewable sources of energy. A global cap on greenhouse gas emissions, combined with a system for trading credits earned by either reducing emissions or removing greenhouse gases from the atmosphere, could create positive incentives for technical innovations. As the reality of climate change sinks in, the innovations are starting to increase. For example, Tasmanian inventor John Harrison has created a new kind of concrete that generates only half of the carbon dioxide during its manufacture than conventional concrete and absorbs additional carbon dioxide from the atmosphere — sort of like trees do.[21] Organic wastes such as rice husks, which currently release carbon dioxide by rotting or by being burned, can be incorporated into this cement in far greater quantities than is the case for regular cement. According to Harrison, complete replacement of all cement currently being manufactured and used with his new formulation could eliminate over one billion tons of carbon dioxide per year — a substantial improvement in the climate system. Human creativity and ingenuity, spurred on by the desire to save the world or just to make a buck, can be a force to be reckoned with. But it will be critical to ensure that new technologies do not create more problems than they solve.

A New World Ocean Order

The deep sea, like the open ocean, is for the most part a global commons. Many other commons, such as freshwater resources, the atmosphere, biodiversity, and open ocean fisheries, seem to be suffering from various forms of the tragedy of the commons. This tragedy ensues because individuals (and nations) tend to ignore the cumulative impacts of their activities in pursuit of their narrow self interest. It seems reasonable to expect that the same tragedy will play out in the deep sea as soon as it becomes profitable to exploit its resources, unless some form of effective ocean governance evolves. The key issue to be resolved is that of ownership. Are ocean resources the province of the whole of mankind, or do they go to countries that can exploit or buy them? Is there a middle way?

Answers to the fundamental question of who owns the ocean have evolved over time, since Hugo Grotius penned his *Mare Liberum* (Free Seas) in 1609. Grotius' contention — that the oceans are the common heritage of all nations and thus owned and controlled by none — was enshrined as the Freedom of the

Seas doctrine, which is still invoked today. The development of powerful navies and the corresponding importance of controlling the seas for national defense and international adventures spurred intense controversies over ocean jurisdiction, especially near the coastlines of sovereign nations. Cornelius van Bynkershonk came up with a practical solution in 1702, articulated in his *De Dominio Maris* (Domain of the Sea): a nation's jurisdiction extended three miles offshore, probably because that was about how far a cannon ball shot from the land could reach in those days.[22]

These old doctrines prevailed until 1958, when the United Nations convened the first conference on the Law of the Sea. Industrialized nations were starting to exploit ocean resources such as fisheries right up to the nearshore waters of weaker countries. Increasingly, it was recognized that this inequitable situation — where might made right — would grow worse as the capability to exploit oil, gas, and mineral wealth in the oceans increased. A treaty was produced, pronouncing that countries had exclusive rights to control prospecting and mining for minerals on the continental shelves lying off their shorelines. Unfortunately, the treaty defined the continental shelves as extending to where the slope gets significantly steeper, a blurry distinction that was interpreted in different ways.[23] As with most poorly defined boundaries, disputes between countries ensued. In addition, approaches to the international governance of commons such as the ocean were evolving.[24] A split developed between industrialized countries (including the U.S.) which wanted the freedom to exploit resources in the open ocean and deep sea and less developed countries which maintained that these resources were the common heritage of all humankind, to be shared by all. The industrialized countries generally had the technological prowess to mine the ocean, while the developing countries generally lacked such capacity.

The second conference on the Law of the Sea, held in 1960, failed to resolve these disputes, and so it was left to the third conference to create a new ocean governance regime. This took a long time (the third conference lasted from 1973 to 1982) but did result in clear definitions of several kinds of jurisdiction in the sea. Under the treaty signed at the Conference, countries had absolute authority over a 12-nautical-mile (22-kilometer) territorial sea. They had only to allow "innocent passage" of ships. A so-called contiguous zone was established out to 24 nautical miles (44 kilometers) from shore, in which nations could assert their immigration, customs, fiscal, and pollution laws. Countries could also claim an Exclusive Economic Zone (EEZ) out to 200 nautical miles (370 kilometers) — or even beyond to 350 nautical miles (648 kilometers), if the continental shelf off a nation's shoreline happened to be very broad in which the nation could exert its jurisdiction over fisheries, mineral resources, and pollution.

The provisions of the Law of the Sea clarified the boundaries of ocean governance and were generally acceptable to all. But the Law of the Sea did not create a way to govern the exploitation of fisheries in the vast stretches of ocean between the EEZs of coastal nations, leading to a free-for-all and overfishing (see Chapters 5 and 6). It did, however, include a provision governing the minerals lying on the seafloor in these areas, which quickly became highly controversial (as outlined above).

Since then, ocean governance has become a patchwork of treaties and international agreements. Treaties were developed and signed to ban the dumping of wastes into the sea (the 1972 Convention on the Prevention of Marine Pollution by Dumping of Wastes and Other Matter — the London Dumping Convention for short) and to prevent pollution from ships (the 1973 International Convention for the Prevention of Pollution from Ships, or MARPOL, amended later to cover the dumping of plastic debris). The United Nations Convention on the Conservation and Management of Highly Migratory and Straddling Fish Stocks entered into force in 2002, and the Convention for the Conservation and Management of Highly Migratory Fish Stocks in the Western and Central Pacific Ocean was signed in 2000. The Food and Agriculture Organization of the United Nations held technical consultations that gave rise to new codes of conduct for fishermen and fishing nations and to new agreements to protect sharks, sea turtles, and sea birds. In addition, numerous regional fishing agreements between nations exist.

The most recent of these treaties and agreements embody a new understanding of what will be required to protect the ocean and its resources. They articulate the precautionary principle — the concept of taking action to protect ecosystems and resources even if scientific evidence of harm is uncertain — but they all suffer from fundamental flaws. They too often fail to establish strong systems of international governance with enforceable standards that would put into practice their fine rhetoric. They continue to treat individual species as disconnected commodities, rather than as wildlife inextricably linked together in complex food webs and ecological relationships. They mostly ignore the economic incentives and subsidies that encourage overexploitation and pollution, even as they rail against the effects of these incentives.

The substance of international treaties can be altered by amending them. Scientific consensus has caught up with the exhortations of environmentalists and traditional wisdom. Reflecting the old philosophical and mystical view that all things are one and that everything in the universe is hitched together, the scientific literature is now replete with calls to protect whole ecosystems. In practical terms, this translates into regulations that acknowledge and protect all of the ecological roles that species play — even if we don't quite know what they are.

The more difficult reform has to do with overhauling the market forces that cause the overexploitation of resources held in common. Environmental groups such as the Worldwide Fund for Nature are working to get countries to reduce or eliminate the subsidies they provide to their fishing fleets, which amount to about $13 billion each year.[25] Perhaps the World Trade Organization, so diligent in freeing up global markets and removing barriers to trade, can be persuaded to crack down on fishery subsidies that are strongly distorting the market — and pushing fishermen to exploit vulnerable fish populations on the high seas and around seamounts. Between $700 billion[26] and $1 trillion[27] is spent each year on subsidies that harm the environment by encouraging overfishing, the use of pesticides and fertilizer, and the like. Protests by environmentalists, social justice activists, fishermen, and other working men and women at WTO meetings represent a groundswell of support for the protection of cultural values, human rights, and natural ecosystems and wildlife that completely free markets do not and cannot uphold.

Ecosystem management is called for in the deep sea, albeit on a grander scale than in nearshore waters. This elusive concept has been defined in several ways, but I prefer my own. If it is to be effective, I think that ecosystem management must be conducted in accordance with the following principles:

- Preserve and protect whole ecosystems by establishing networks of marine reserves, reducing bycatch, and minimizing habitat damage;
- Manage and reduce uncertainty with the precautionary approach;
- Stimulate research, learn from experience, and adapt to new knowledge;
- Create an ocean conservation ethic by fostering economic incentives for stewardship, by building communities around ocean conservation, and by inspiring individual action as well as engagement in policy reform.

Working from these principles, ecosystem management of the deep sea would entail a much-improved system of ocean governance, including marine reserves on seamounts and hydrothermal vents. A new treaty restricting ocean pollution that flows across the borders of Exclusive Economic Zones would crack down on existing sources of such pollution on land and also guide the development of new technologies to reduce or prevent altogether such "migratory" pollution from new activities, including deep sea mining. Increased metal recycling and improved environmental performance of terrestrial mines could stave off a deep sea gold rush until the impacts are better understood.

This wish-list may seem implausible right now. Attention has been focused on the failure of the international community to deal with global warming, with high seas overfishing and bycatch, and other tragedies of the commons. But there have been some successes in international environmental conservation, providing us with lessons for motivating international action. And there is a trend toward stronger and more effective regimes for global governance, perhaps starting with the Montreal Protocol on Substances that Deplete the Ozone Layer (the Montreal Protocol). Unfortunately, all too often the motivation for international action is a crisis. The Montreal Protocol is generally regarded to be the first to address a potential environmental threat before the adverse impacts became incontrovertibly clear.[28] It is also thought to be the most effective of all international environmental agreements.[29]

Like the high seas and the deep ocean, the stratospheric ozone layer is a commons. The ozone layer protects us and all other life on earth from the sun's harmful ultraviolet radiation. Chlorofluorocarbons (CFCs), a class of very useful chemicals, had been thought to be harmless because they don't react or combine with other materials. It is precisely this property of CFCs that makes them so useful as propellants in spray cans, as refrigerants, and as cleaning agents for delicate electronic components. However, in 1974 scientists advanced a theory that CFCs could persist in the atmosphere for decades, eventually rising up into the stratosphere. There, powerful UV rays from the sun could break them apart, releasing chlorine that in turn could catalyze chemical reactions that destroy ozone. Individual countries had different policy responses to this theory. The U.S., responding to a growing environmental movement in the 1970s, banned the use of CFCs in spray cans (over industry objections, of course). But the less visible, non-spray-can uses of CFCs accelerated in both the U.S. and in other countries. Scientific consensus that CFCs could harm the ozone layer gelled in the mid-1980s, and citizens became alarmed by projections of millions of deaths from skin cancer caused by the breakdown of the ozone layer.

The United Nations Environment Programme (UNEP) galvanized nations to engage in negotiations aimed at creating a global solution to this global threat. During these negotiations (in 1985), scientists discovered a massive hole in the ozone layer over Antarctica, providing a compelling visual for this hard-to-visualize problem. Monitoring also revealed a two-percent reduction in the ozone layer globally since 1978. Though hard evidence of increasing skin cancer rates or other impacts of ozone depletion was lacking, a strong theory coupled with evidence of depletion provided sufficient motivation for the parties to sign the Montreal Protocol in 1987, only 13 years after the scientific theory that CFCs might deplete the ozone layer was put forward and just two years after the start of negotiations. The fact that corporations felt they needed an international agreement to ban CFCs to spur the development of commercially-viable alternatives no doubt helped, as well.

While scientific evidence was certainly a major factor in the success of the Montreal Protocol negotiations, scientific evidence is usually not enough to address problems in the global commons. Several factors are often at play — the importance of maintaining sovereignty versus the need to cooperate internationally, hegemonic power exercised by single nations to either force agreement or to veto it, creation of political blocs of a few nations that can influence many others, and the potential for economic benefits, to name just a few. But the potential for some combination of these impersonal factors to result in an effective international agreement also depends to a large extent on how citizens and their leaders perceive reality.[30]

There is always a great deal of diversity among humans and institutions regarding the way they think the world works, but nevertheless one can identify dominant paradigms — sets of widely held beliefs and values — that have evolved through history. And of course, globalization, market economies, and trade

— so successful in increasing wealth (at least for some) — are extraordinarily effective mechanisms for spreading ideas and culture. Perhaps early on in our history, humans felt themselves to be fully integrated and at one with nature. As humans began to modify local ecosystems to meet their needs, strong connections to nature were maintained through ritual and animism — we were weak, the gods were powerful. Animals and plants gave their lives so that we could survive, and we restored those lives through rituals. But these connections were weakened, at least in human perception, as the dominant paradigm shifted to the view that humans had no part in nature except to dominate and use it. People and institutions that adopted this view accumulated wealth and power; social paradigms spread in some proportion to how useful they are, of course. Free markets would inexorably maximize human welfare. Natural resources were essentially infinite because technological innovation would steadily increase efficiency and overcome natural constraints. Science, so effective in splitting the atom and deciphering the genome, would solve all of our problems. Wealth resulting from the extraction and processing of natural materials and wildlife was all that mattered in economic accounting — the loss of natural wealth in terms of depleted resources was ignored.[31]

We are now in the midst of a transformation of beliefs and values — in other words, a paradigm shift. This transformation may seem slow, especially in view of the great urgency of many environmental problems. But in fact it is lightening-fast in historical terms, occurring over decades rather than centuries as is usually the case. Social paradigms, like scientific theories, change when a critical mass of people experience enough dissonance between their assumptions and observed reality to make them first question, then change their assumptions. Rachel Carson's 1962 book *Silent Spring* and all of the popular environmental writings since then have gone a long way toward increasing such dissonance. Textbooks and lesson plans have also evolved over time to accommodate new understandings about how unsustainable the old paradigm really is.

The rise of the mass environmental movement in the late 1960s led to an increasing number of global institutions and treaties that recognize the primary importance of protecting the atmosphere, the oceans, and other global commons. An alternative paradigm arose during the 1970s and 1980s which posited that depletion of the earth's resources was indeed possible, even inevitable, if business went on as usual. We learned that technology does not automatically arise to solve our problems, and that it can create serious new problems as well. Technology must be guided by intelligent policies to help us increase the efficiency of resource use, reduce pollution, and move toward a more sustainable economy — markets are blind to these values. Scientific understanding is limited, not omniscient, especially with regard to natural ecosystems — the planet's life-support systems. The arrogance of science-based natural resource management has been tempered by spectacular failures, such as the collapse of fisheries that once seemed inexhaustible. Opposition to the new paradigm is still strong at the highest levels of government and corporate power. But increasingly, people and institutions recognize that rapacious exploitation of nature imposes an unacceptably high cost on our health, well-being, and human spirit.

The new paradigm is being institutionalized in many ways. Sustainable development — the idea that present economic activities should not compromise our own future needs for resources, or those of future generations — is one element of the new paradigm. After years of advocacy by groups like Environmental Defense, multilateral development banks are confessing that the old ways are indeed unsustainable, and have begun to speak well of sustainable development. Some government bureaucracies have also embraced sustainable development. The torrent of verbal support for this concept culminated in the United Nations Conference on Environment and Development, held in Rio de Janeiro, Brazil, in 1992. The framework conventions on climate change and biodiversity signed at Rio lacked specific, enforceable measures designed to achieve their lofty goals — but other international agreements have evolved from weak and ineffective instruments into more powerful treaties. The International Convention for the Regulation of Whaling of 1946 eventually produced a ban on whaling in 1985. A treaty riddled with loopholes gave way to the International Convention for the Prevention of Pollution from Ships (MARPOL) and later, the even more stringent London Dumping Convention, the first to allow coastal states to enforce its measures. In the same way, we can hope that the conventions on climate change and biodiversity will, over time, incorporate protocols (like the Kyoto Protocol to the Climate Change Convention) with enforceable standards and practical measures to meet their goals.

The most recent manifestation of the new paradigm was signed at the World Summit on Sustainable Development, held in Johannesburg, South Africa, in 2002. A concerted effort by NGOs, the UN, and some governments succeeded in placing ocean conservation on the agenda. These efforts were rewarded with agreements to establish representative networks of marine protected areas by 2012 and to restore depleted fish populations by 2015. These agreements have been hailed as two of the most significant outcomes of the summit. Will the goals of the summit be translated into national action plans that will really create MPA networks and restore fisheries? That will depend on the development of sufficient political will to overcome opposition to reforms — and to support a new vision for the governance of the planetary commons.

Environmental treaties and institutions have come a long way, and have met with a degree of success. Millions of dolphins have been saved. Ozone-depleting chemicals are being phased out. Some illegal fishing of depleted populations of Southern Bluefin Tuna was stopped by the International Tribunal of the Law of the Sea. The bans on whaling and driftnets have been enforced with both economic pressure and Coast Guard cutters. The United Nations Environment Programme has brokered over 170 environmental agreements, providing leadership on many of them. The Food and Agriculture Organization, after a history of promoting unsustainable development of forests and agriculture, has been reorganized to promote sustainable development. It is showing signs of environmental responsibility in the form of its new code of conduct for fishing and plans of action to reduce fishing capacity and protect sharks and seabirds.

But there is a long way to go toward effective international governance of the ocean. More environmental agreements need to include powerful dispute resolution and enforcement mechanisms, like the International Tribunal of the Law of the Sea. Environmental protection should become at least as high a priority as free trade. After all, natural resources are the main engine for economic growth and natural ecosystems constitute the very life support systems for the planet. The dozens of environmental treaties on the books are fragmented. There are good reasons to keep some treaties focused on solving regional problems such as land-based sources of pollution. But many environmental issues transcend regions and require global coordination. For example, if a regional fishery agreement is successful in enforcing catch limits and fishing effort, vessels are very likely to simply move to another fishery, potentially causing overcapacity and overfishing there.

While many scholars, environmentalists, and even some governments have called for the creation of a new World Environmental Organization, no plans to do so were made at the 2002 World Summit on Sustainable Development (the Johannesburg Summit). However, plans to strengthen the United Nations Environment Programme (UNEP) and to increase coordination of United Nations environmental programs were endorsed at Johannesburg.[32] I think the ideal lies somewhere between these two poles, in the form of strengthened regional agreements combined with a new global environmental institution or a stronger version of UNEP empowered to enforce certain measures that are global by nature.

After analyzing the evolution of ten environmental treaties, Gareth Porter and Janet Welsh Brown concluded that states with the power to veto these agreements eventually came around to support them because of new scientific evidence, a change in political leadership, or a combination of domestic pressure and concern about international criticism.[33] These external, impersonal factors have been and will continue to be important for inducing incremental progress toward a new dominant social paradigm. Progress toward global environmental protection and sustainable development will depend on creative ideas, strong advocacy, and skillful political maneuvering — exercises of the mind. But on a deeper level, the development of the new paradigm will be energized by a new ethic based on a perception of, and feel for, our fundamental connection to nature.

8

CREATING A NEW OCEAN ETHIC

The prescription for healing the ocean is clear. The ebb and flow of tides, the growth of salt marshes, the consumption of little fish by big fish, and all the other natural processes that make ecosystems work must be protected and restored to maintain ecological health. Marine reserves are needed to preserve habitats like coral reefs and kelp forests, along with less spectacular areas like underwater boulder fields and mud bottoms. These special places nurture the ocean's biological diversity, and provide settings for the complex interplay between species — and between life, physics, and chemistry — that drives evolution itself, maintaining life through the eons. Smart regulations that specify environmental goals and encourage industry to find cost-effective means to achieve them can remedy problems ranging from pollution to overfishing. Better enforcement and market incentives such as consumer demand for sustainably caught seafood are needed to back up noble international intentions. Only then will the international community realize its full potential to protect global wanderers such as tuna and the great billfishes, the still-mysterious life of the seamounts, and the teeming hydrothermal vents of the deep sea.

This prescription has been partially filled. Dams are being decommissioned, floodplains are being restored, and barriers to tidal circulation are being removed to help watersheds, rivers, salt marshes and estuaries recover. Large new marine reserves are being created to protect habitats ranging from the kelp forests and rocky reefs of California's Channel Islands to the seamounts of Tasmania. Transferable pollution and bycatch reduction permits are helping farmers to reduce farm runoff and save money. California is implementing a new fisheries management regime that has ecosystems at its heart, rather than as an afterthought. A new treaty covering a vast area promises to protect the magnificent migratory fishes of the Pacific Ocean. All of these efforts are laudable, and must be continued. We are starting to learn the lessons of nature — to extract wisdom, rather than just fish, minerals, and other things. As Janine Benyas reminds us in her book *Biomimicry,*[1] life has learned to harness the sun's power, to exploit the profoundly cold and pressurized deep sea, to transform minerals into energy, to maintain a profusion of species without waste, and to master innumerable other tricks. These lessons from life can help us live in harmony with the world, if we are wise enough to mimic nature and not destroy it.

But despite these advances, fish populations continue to be overexploited, millions of tons of marine life are still killed accidentally in fisheries, coral reefs are dying as a result of global warming, and polluted runoff still sullies coastal waters. Population growth, coupled with increasing rates of consumption in the rich countries, is still a major contributor to coastal pollution and the depletion of fisheries. About 6.2 billion people now inhabit the earth,[2] and population is increasing rapidly in many developing countries.

On top of all that, new issues are emerging. The mining industry is poised to extract gold from deep sea hydrothermal vents, threatening destruction before we even get to know these wonderfully bizarre biological communities very well. The rush to develop secure sources of energy threatens to open up the continental shelves of many nations to exploration for gas and oil, threatening seabirds, marine mammals — and the fishing industry. Schemes to re-engineer the planet by turning the ocean into a dump for the carbon dioxide waste of our profligate fossil fuel use are still alive and will likely become more attractive as global warming proceeds. Even technologies that could help us harvest clean renewable energy from the sun, wind, waves, or tides could pose some risks when pursued at large scales that will need careful evaluation.[3]

Enforcement of existing ocean conservation laws and regulations is, in general, far from adequate. Resource managers veer from crisis to crisis, in part because they still think of fish as isolated market commodities rather than as wild members of complex communities. But the ocean is not a fish farm. A different approach is needed — one that protects whole ecosystems and the ecological processes that maintain healthy and diverse populations of animals and plants in the sea. Furthermore, fundamental governance problems facing the ocean's commons have not yet been resolved. Does "free" trade (between countries with heavily subsidized industries) trump a nation's environmental laws or preclude the use of trade sanctions to enforce international agreements?

Technology is Necessary, but Not Sufficient

New technologies hold promise but, as always, are only part of the answer. Satellites can track fishing vessels carrying Vessel Monitoring Systems (VMS), transponders that signal their locations continuously to enforcement officers.[4] The U.S. National Marine Fisheries Service (NMFS) has used VMS to track and capture illegal driftnet vessels on the high seas since 1988. NMFS also uses VMS to successfully monitor compliance with huge areas of the North Pacific closed to longliners to protect endangered species and reduce overfishing. The service will embark on a similar program in U.S. waters of the Gulf of Mexico, the

Atlantic coast, and off the West Coast. Scallop vessels fishing northeast waters carry VMS units so that authorities can enforce restrictions on how many days they can fish each week. These units also help NMFS monitor compliance with the boundaries of a large closed area on Georges Bank (off Cape Cod, Massachusetts) that is allowing depleted cod and haddock populations to recover.

VMS is catching on internationally, as well. Several Pacific Island countries now require vessels fishing their waters to carry VMS.[5] Vessels participating in an experimental pollack fishery in the Central Bering Sea are required to carry VMS, and if the fishery is expanded, all the new entrants will be subject to the same requirement. And almost all the vessels fishing in the fertile waters of Antarctica must carry VMS.[6]

Satellites can do much more than track fishing vessels. They can also shine a light on problems that would otherwise escape notice because they occur far out at sea, or on remote islands. The European Space Agency's Treaty Enforcement Services Using Earth Observation (TESEO) program is specifically designed to improve the implementation of international environmental treaties covering issues such as marine debris, ocean dumping, and wetland conservation using satellite images.[7] Law schools are organizing workshops to examine the legal ramifications of using satellites to enforce environmental treaties and regulations. So far, the U.S. Supreme Court has ruled that satellite images can be admitted as evidence without violating Fourth Amendment protections against illegal search and seizure.[8]

Enforcement technology is improving but it can only serve us if there is sufficient political will to put marine reserves in place, improve regulations, craft meaningful treaties — and enforce all of these. A mass outcry on behalf of the ocean, as well as popular support for conservation measures, will be needed to generate that political will. Powerful forces are arrayed against attempts to heal the ocean. Perhaps the most potent of these are the false "jobs versus the environment" dichotomy, ignorance of how the ocean works and what the threats are, and lack of a pervasive ocean ethic that would guide our individual and collective actions toward greater harmony with the ocean's rhythms.

Jobs versus the Environment — A False Dichotomy

Opponents of environmental protection often use the hackneyed argument that the jobs created by the fishery, marina, port, housing development, or power plant (choose one) that they are promoting are more important than protecting the environment. Yes, conservation sometimes requires the downsizing of an industry, or a readjustment to reflect new understandings about the sustainability (or lack thereof) of an activity. While such adjustments may result in the loss of jobs in one economic sector, these jobs would likely be lost anyway due to the unsustainable exploitation of natural resources. And downsizing does not necessarily mean the loss of the entire industry, despite rhetoric to the contrary. The transition of economies away from near-total reliance on natural resource extraction to more sustainable enterprises — including the maintenance of farming and fishing cultures — can be a good thing. In fact, the shifting of jobs from one economic sector to another is characteristic of the way market economies adapt and survive — so-called "creative destruction."[9] If sweeping generalizations are set aside ("Those environmentalists want to put us all out of business!" or "Every industry is out to rape the environment!"), reasonable accommodations of competing interests — economic development and environmental protection — can often be made.

More fundamentally, the jobs-versus-environment argument is often based on a disagreement about what economic development really means. Development, properly understood, is not simply economic growth or more tax revenues or greater profits for a few already wealthy people or corporations. It is not just about generating more money to protect the environment or leaving enough for future generations, as important as that is. True economic development is an increased quality of life, wherein people prosper not only in financial terms, but also in aesthetic and spiritual terms, sustained by natural beauty, wildlife, and healthy ecosystems.

In recent years, one of the most dramatic threats of wrongheaded economic growth (as opposed to real development) is pointed straight at the long, rugged peninsula of Baja California and the Sea of Cortez that it cradles. The coast of Baja still evokes the sense of a pristine wilderness, with arid desert meeting clear blue ocean waters. Whales, manta rays, and spectacular billfish take advantage of deep waters adjacent to the coast and injections of cold, nutrient-rich waters from the depths that make this a haven for marine wildlife. The laid-back culture and spectacular natural assets that were, and remain, so powerfully attractive to me and millions of others are still there. You can still get inexpensive grilled lobsters and good Mexican beer at a ramshackle seaside eatery after riding your horse for miles along deserted beaches. You can still feel like you are on a real adventure as you drive along the lonely highway through the desert. The coast is dotted with beautiful little resorts, colorful tiled monuments to the dreams of small-scale entrepreneurs. The impulse to defend this way of life is strong in Baja. Little villages host fishery cooperatives that are trying their best to fend off trawlers that come in to suck all the shrimp up. And local activists are joining with national and international environmental groups to create a vision for the future in which the natural beauty of the desert and coast co-exists with true economic development.

But Mexican tourism officials have another vision — they want to update this culture with a string of large marinas dotting the Baja coast, called Escalera Nautica, or the Nautical Stairway. The idea is to attract people with yachts to luxurious resorts, golf courses, and even a highway bypass across the peninsula to shorten one's cruise to the Sea of Cortez. Advocates of an alternative vision of smaller marinas, high-end ecoresorts with marine reserves for front yards, small-scale and sustainable fisheries, oyster aquaculture operations, and other sustainable enterprises are putting up a powerful resistance to Escalera Nautica. If they win, Baja California could well become the sustainable development showcase of the world, showing the rest of us how it can be done. If they lose, Baja could become a Nautical Stairway leading to unsustainable, glitzy "development" — like Cancun, the realization of the government's development dreams to the east, in the Yucatan.

Overcoming Ignorance

The most obvious way to overcome widespread ignorance about the ocean and threats to its health is to educate people. But where to start and how to focus? There is a great need for enhanced environmental education programs, for specific curricula on oceans, and for a general increase in scientific and environmental literacy. But the ocean is already beset by serious and urgent problems. About 75 percent of the world's major fisheries are fully exploited or in decline; colorful coral reefs are turning a deathly white at a massive scale throughout the world due to global warming; and oil tankers continue to break up at sea, ruining fisheries and ecosystems alike, to name just a few. Traditional education from primary schools on up will be essential for transforming society over the long run — but the need for corrective action is urgent. Other kinds of education will be required.

Scientists, the creators of new knowledge, can play a key role in reducing ignorance. The best of the scientific communicators can elucidate the ocean's lessons vividly, in terms most people can understand. A few, such as James Hanson (who warned of global warming during the 1980s) and E.O. Wilson (one of the world's foremost advocates of protecting biological diversity), have led the way toward conservation, drawing on both their scientific knowledge and on their love of nature. They have lit the fire of activism with compelling books and moving speeches.

These outspoken scientists are rare. Scientists often hotly debate the role of science and of themselves in environmental policy making. The debate almost always centers on issues for which the underlying science is uncertain. Science can deliver near-certainties in some fields like physics, chemistry, and molecular biology, where variables can be carefully controlled in elegant experiments that clearly support or disprove hypotheses and theories. The scientific method, based on asking questions and designing experiments that can answer them with relatively little ambiguity, is the basis for "strong inference." Strong inferences result in the clear understandings that provide the foundations for powerful technologies through which most people experience science. But the environmental sciences, such as marine ecology and fisheries science, can rely on strong inference only rarely. Variables such as ocean temperature, nutrient concentration, and the abundance and distribution of organisms are difficult or impossible to control, making experiments in the sea much murkier than experiments in the laboratory. Most ocean and fishery scientists are like naturalists seeking to sample a forest by running around in it in a dense fog, armed only with butterfly nets. New technologies, such as high-resolution underwater video cameras, remotely operated vehicles, and deep-diving submersibles are extending our senses farther and deeper every year. But we have still explored only the tiniest fraction of the ocean, and experiments are still difficult to conduct there. Almost all aspects of the ocean remain uncertain. New species of large animals are still being discovered in the ocean, such as the "mystery squid" — a whole new family of squids with 20-foot-long tentacles. Hardly inconspicuous, these squids were discovered only a few years ago. So it is no surprise that many ocean conservation debates — what to do about fisheries management or whether to create marine reserves — remain highly controversial. The facts, including very basic facts such as how many fish there are in a given population, remain uncertain.

In the face of this uncertainty, scientists often argue about what to do within the context of policy controversies. Does one advocate a precautionary approach to policy, erring on the side of cutting back fish catches or creating protected areas even before conclusive proof is obtained? Or does one stay out of the policy debate altogether, content to do science and publish scientific papers? In my view, academic scientists should be allowed to conduct research without pressure to support one policy position or another. They must protect their scientific credibility and objectivity. The generation of new knowledge and understanding, the goal of science, is a noble pursuit — one that is crucial for the advancement of conservation and sustainable development. Accuracy and objectivity can only benefit the cause of ocean conservation. After all, cracking down on actors or actions that are causing no harm will not protect the ocean.

It is important to recognize, moreover, that science can only point out the likely consequences of various courses of action. The choice to protect biological diversity, while supported by some utilitarian arguments (e.g., the potential for new medicines and for ecological "services" such as flood protection or clean water rendered by ecosystems), really depends on values and ethics. Science cannot make this choice for us. Scientists who want to engage in public debates over policy choices should be free to do so. Their professional judgments of which remedies are most likely to work are invaluable, given the uncertainties that persist regarding the impacts of fishing, pollution, coastal development, and other threats to the ocean. The science of both purists and scientist-advocates can, of course, be criticized with respect to the data, analysis, and inferences drawn. Such constructive criticism is a hallmark of good science. But we should all refrain from personal attacks. Instead, we should acknowledge that both scientists and advocates must play their roles well if environmental policy is to reflect the best scientific understanding and to be effective.

Spreading the Word

High-profile media campaigns to communicate simple messages that appeal to the eye and to the heart can greatly increase awareness of environmental problems, albeit only temporarily — until the next big issue comes along. Beautiful public television and radio documentaries that thoughtfully explore issues in depth will always be important, but they capture only part of the public. Environmental education must adapt to this age of strong images and brief attention spans. Many television commercials now only vaguely allude to the products they are pitching, focusing instead on humor, entertainment, and drama. Ocean education campaigns are beginning to reflect this trend as well, promising to reach millions of people who don't wish to look at the talking heads of experts interspersed with beautiful footage of ocean wildlife for an hour or two. Instead, dramatic or funny images and sound-bites about the ocean will be needed to capture the imagination — to connect to people's core values of health, family, community, or the pocketbook.

Awareness of the crisis in the ocean is critical but awareness alone is usually not enough to motivate action. Campaigns to increase awareness about an environmental issue are usually intended to influence attitudes — on the assumption that a change in attitude will result in changed behavior. But the psychological literature indicates only a weak correlation between attitudes and behavior. Context matters a lot. For example, some observers believe that cleaning up the graffiti on New York City's subway cars and cracking down on fare-beating in the early 1990s were important factors in the spectacular fall in murder rates at that time — they dropped by two-thirds in only five years. The context of the subways had changed from chaos — in which people felt that "anything goes" — to cleanliness and order: a context for good behavior. By the same token, normal, healthy volunteers turned into vicious, sadistic "guards" in a mock prison during the famous Stanford prison experiment.[10] Also, we are social creatures and are more likely to do as others do — we litter more when others are littering; we tend to buy solar power when we know others who have done so.[11] That's why making environmental protection an integral part of community life is so important — the context of our everyday lives figures importantly in our choices and actions.

Ideally, media campaigns should be combined with grassroots campaigns that can convert the momentary awareness generated by compelling images and catchy sound-bites into activism sustained for years by good ideas and good old-fashioned community. Environmental Defense, for example, aired a television spot featuring beautiful music and gorgeous images of dolphins and whales cavorting near the Channel Islands off California. This spot guided viewers to a website where they could learn more about our campaign to create marine reserves there. Over 13,000 people sent letters to California's governor and other key decision makers in support of our campaign. This media and web-based campaign complemented a large-scale grassroots community organizing effort.

This organizing effort employed a "Tipping Point" strategy designed to leverage meager resources to speed the diffusion of the marine reserve concept through communities. We started by finding and activating key types of people. Every community has these archetypes — mavens (who love new ideas), connectors (who build relationships and networks), and salesmen (loaded with charisma, who can sell ideas).[12] Our core activists motivated hundreds of people to get involved in public hearings and meetings that stretched over three years. This strategy was a major factor in the creation of one of the largest marine reserve networks in the world, off California's Channel Islands.

People love the ocean, but for many it may be more like a teenage infatuation with the ocean's superficial beauty than a mature love based on deep understanding and respect. Knowledge about habitats and animal behavior is essential for solutions like marine reserves to make sense. Such knowledge, and the passions that can spring from it, can be spread through the Internet and traditional lectures. But perhaps the best way to spread not only knowledge but passion is to educate the tipping point archetypes in a community, perhaps hooking them with a whale-watching excursion or some other exciting wildlife adventure, as we did in the Channel Islands — and then turning them loose. Some messages are more motivating than others: they must be tailored to specific audiences. In the Florida Keys, it was the threat posed by agricultural pollution and water diversions on the mainland that galvanized the community; in the Channel Islands, it was the serial depletion of abalone, large red sea urchins, sharks, and long-lived rockfish that motivated activists. When combined with practical solutions, these messages can engage both the mind and the heart — an unstoppable combination.

The core activists-archetypes will educate more people, and so on, until an "idea epidemic" is launched. This is education that people can own — it is constructed by peers through dialogue. In this way, ocean conservation can build communities of people learning from their neighbors and friends, instead of from professional advocates and mass mailings. Ocean conservation can be the main buzz at the hairdresser's, in the supermarket, and at the Rotary Club — I've seen it happen. Activism can spread quickly across countries, and across borders — witness the extremely rapid mobilization of millions of people in 2003 to protest against war in Iraq. The very connectivity engendered by globalization can be harnessed to link activist communities around the world. So far, much of this activism has been directed against globalization. But rather than opposing globalization, which is already a fact of life, we can use the Internet to work together toward positive solutions. Instead of acting out of anger and frustration at the way things are, grassroots campaigns can be based on celebrations of and love for the ocean's beauty and bounty: sustainable activism for a sustainable future.

Creating an Ocean Conservation Ethic

Much has been written in the scientific, technical, and environmental literature about how to regulate environmental impacts and to increase wealth and well-being sustainably. Ideas by themselves, however, are not enough. The key to healing the ocean lies in developing an ethic that pervades the actions and guides the choices of individuals, of businesses, of governments, and of the international community. All tools are deployed in service of an ideology, or ethic, or value system. The challenge is to change these intangibles so that the ideas that promote sustainable living and ocean conservation come to life in the hearts and minds of people.

To paraphrase E.O. Wilson's *The Future of Life*, the juggernaut of global capitalism, fueled by technology, cannot be stopped — it will ultimately either destroy nature or be re-directed toward the task of saving it.[13] Science can only help clarify the options and the consequences of various actions or inaction; science cannot choose for us. We must develop that part of human nature that expresses itself in beautiful art, inspiring music, brilliant literature, and genuine spiritual experience. From that higher human nature, an ocean ethic — and the right choices — will flow naturally.

The Spirit of Biophilia

Many a late-night conversation in dorm rooms and living rooms across the world has centered on the world's problems, only to end with a resigned acknowledgment that nothing short of a spiritual transformation can save life on earth. The tacit understanding is that such a transformation is impossible. But I believe that humans are evolving, as all species do, and that we are capable of a higher human nature that includes a widening circle of compassion, starting with other humans and extending to all things. In fact, we may be predisposed to loving nature. We are, after all, only recently removed, in evolutionary terms, from our natural habitats of forests, savannah, and the seashore. Just as a fish prefers the sheltering interstices of a coral reef to the dangerous surrounding waters full of predators, we may be drawn to the natural habitats that nurtured our ancestors.

Like many parents, I have observed my young daughter and her friends taking a natural interest in wild animals and plants that can easily grow into love and compassion, if it is not stamped out by materialism and the constant stimulation of places and things constructed by humans. There is now scientific evidence to support this view. The vestiges of our biophilia, or innate love of nature, apparently still remain even in adults. For example, experiments show that adults recover from stress more rapidly when in beautiful natural areas, even if they are merely looking out the window at one.[14]

The momentary awareness and compassion for wildlife and nature that arises after watching an ocean documentary film or

seeing a photograph of sea otters covered with oil can be extended into continuous awareness that guides attitudes and actions.
Buddhists call this state "mindfulness." Others might call it a
state of grace or flow. Many religious and spiritual traditions
share the basic truth that nature is sacred and that the distinction
between humans and nature, between the self and non-self, is
illusory. The atomistic world of dualisms and dichotomies where
we spend most of our time is an artifact, perhaps the legacy of
our rapidly increasing power to control nature in the absence of
a concomitant increase in wisdom. We have all at some point lost
ourselves while watching the sun setting over the ocean, during
a hike amidst towering redwood trees, or while taking in the
transcendent beauty of a flower. Many spiritual and religious
leaders have taught that these moments of unity reflect the ultimate reality.

> In one sheet of paper, you can see the sun, the
> clouds, the forest, and even the logger. The paper is
> made of non-paper elements. The entire world con-
> spired to create it and exists within it. We,
> ourselves, are made of non-self elements — the sun,
> the plants, the bacteria, the water, and the atmos-
> phere. Breathing out, we realize the atmosphere is
> made of all of us. I am, therefore you are. You are,
> therefore I am. We inter-are.
>   — Thich Nhat Hahn[15]

> Human beings destroy the ecology at the same
> time as they destroy one another ... Healing our
> society goes hand in hand with healing our person-
> al, elemental connection with the phenomenal
> world
>   — Chogyam Trungpa[16]

Unfortunately, the extensive moralizing within the
ecological movement has given the public the false

impression that they are being asked to make a sac-
rifice — to show more responsibility, more concern,
and a nicer moral standard. But all of that would
flow naturally and easily if the self were widened
and deepened so that the protection of nature was
felt and perceived as protection of our very selves.

— Arne Naess[17]

A human being is part of the whole called by us
universe, a part limited in time and space. We experience ourselves, our thoughts and feelings as
something separate from the rest. A kind of optical
delusion of consciousness. This delusion is a kind of
prison for us, restricting us to our personal desires
and to affection for a few persons nearest to us.
Our task must be to free ourselves from the prison
by widening our circle of compassion to embrace all
living creatures and the whole of nature in its beauty. We shall require a substantially new manner of
thinking if mankind is to survive.

— Albert Einstein[18]

A new manner of thinking, and a new manner of being, will
be necessary. Indeed, scientists have shown that the areas of the
brain responsible for maintaining the sense of self shut off during
deep meditation and mystical experiences.[19] The walls between
humans and nature can come down at any time, anywhere, if we
stop actively trying to isolate ourselves from nature. James
Austin, the neuroscientist thought to be the father of the new
field of neurotheology (the study of how the brain reacts to or
generates mystical experience), suddenly became aware of the
ultimate nature of things and touched infinity while waiting for a
train in a grimy London underground station.[20]

After spending weeks living in a coral reef community miles
from shore, I felt a unity with the animals and plants of that reef

that I had not experienced before. This experience motivated me to leave academic science and become an environmental advocate. Years later, I again lost my sense of self, this time on the streets of lower Manhattan. I became aware of the universal nature shared by all of humanity. This state of grace continued during a month-long visit to Hawai'i with my wife. For about two weeks, I felt indescribably joyful and at one with nature while swimming through clear tropical waters and walking through mountain rain-forests. I had boundless energy and required little sleep. This extraordinary ecstatic experience faded over time. But mindful-ness and the ability to be fully alive in each moment can be culti-vated with a regular meditation practice and the occasional retreat. It is no accident that monastics dedicated to cultivating mindfulness and spirituality are so often also dedicated social and environmental activists. They want to relieve the suffering of all beings and they recognize that we "inter-are" with nature.

Activism motivated by ideology, stereotyping, and "claims of inherent moral superiority" (as E.O. Wilson puts it) must give way to the realization that we cannot really choose between "put-ting people first" and "protecting the environment."[21] The peo-ple and the environment are one. We must improve the quality of human life, while simultaneously safeguarding wildlife and the wild places that sustain us. Moreover, activism rooted in anger or frustration is unsustainable. We will still need to adduce com-pelling arguments, find innovative solutions, and demonstrate mass concern in order to generate the political will necessary to address the serious threats facing the ocean. But the cultivation of a peaceful nature and of our innate biophilia will nourish the great movement necessary to instill a widespread ocean conser-vation ethic. This ethic will in turn guide the formulation of intel-ligent policies, the wise use of technology, and the countless actions of individuals.

To heal the ocean, we must heal ourselves.

ENDNOTES

Note: all online citations below were made in 2002–2003.

Chapter 1. Turning the Tide: An Introduction

1. Jeremy Jackson, et al., "Historical Overfishing and the Recent Collapse of Coastal Ecosystems," *Science* 293(5530), pp. 629–634.

2. Jeremy Jackson, et al., "Historical Overfishing and the Recent Collapse of Coastal Ecosystems," *Science* 293(5530), pp. 629–634.

3. Deborah McArdle, *California Marine Protected Areas: Past and Present*, California Sea Grant College Program, Publication T-047, 2002. <www-csgc.ucsd.edu/publications>

4. George S. Howard, "Ecological Psychology: Creating a More Earth-Friendly Human Nature," University of Notre Dame Press, 1997.

5. Garrett Hardin, *Filters Against Folly: How to Survive Despite Economists, Ecologists, and the Merely Eloquent*, Viking, 1985.

6. Deborah Du Nann Winter, "Some Big Ideas For Some Big Problems," *American Psychologist* 55(5), pp. 516–522.

7. B.R. Barber, *Jihad vs. McWorld: How Globalism and Tribalism are Reshaping the World*, Ballantine Books, 1996, pp. 268–288.

Chapter 2. The Coastal Zone: From the Mountains to the Sea

1. Natural Resources Defense Council [online]. <www.nrdc.org/greengate/water/divertedv.asp>

2. CVP Long-term Contract Renewals Workshop, handout, Nov 17, 1999. (contact: Laurence J. Baumann, U.S. Bureau of Reclamation)

3. David and Lucile Packard Foundation [online], "Cargill Salt Ponds: Summary and Terms of the Deal." <www.packard.org/pdf/saltbayannounce.pdf>

4. U.S. National Oceanic and Atmospheric Administration, *Trends in U.S. Coastal Regions, 1970–1998*, Addendum to the proceedings, *Trends and Future Challenges for U.S. National Ocean and Coastal Policy*, NOAA, National Ocean Service, Silver Spring, Maryland, 1998.

5. T.F. Young and J. Karkoski, "Green Evolution: Are Economic Incentives the Next Step in Nonpoint Source Pollution Control?" *Water Policy* 2(3), pp. 151–173.

6. U.S. Environmental Protection Agency, "Grasslands Bypass Project: Economic Incentives Program Helps to Improve Water Quality," *Section 319 Success Stories*, Vol. III, 2002. <www.epa.gov/owow/nps/section319III/CA.htm>

7. T.F. Young and J. Karkoski, "Green Evolution: Are Economic Incentives the Next Step in Nonpoint Source Pollution Control?" *Water Policy* 2(3): 151–173.

8. National Assessment Synthesis Team of the U.S. Global Change Research Program, *Climate Change Impacts On The United States: The Potential Consequences of Climate Variability and Change*, U.S. Global Change Research Program, 2000. <www.usgcrp.gov/usgcrp/library/nationalassessment>

9. National Assessment Synthesis Team of the U.S. Global Change Research Program, *Climate Change Impacts on the United States: The Potential Consequences of Climate Variability and Change*, U.S. Global Change Research Program, 2000. <www.usgcrp.gov/usgcrp/library/nationalassessment>

Chapter 3. Nearshore Waters: Nursery, Playground — and Dumping Ground

1. D. Roemmich and J. McGowan, "Climatic Warming and the Decline of Zooplankton in the California Current," *Science* 267(5202), pp. 1324–1326 [online] Cited by U.S. Global Change Research Information Office, <www.gcrio.org>

2. Partnership for Interdisciplinary Studies of Coastal Oceans, *The Science of Marine Reserves*, PISCO [online], 2002. <www.pis-coweb.org>

3. W. A. Palsson, "Marine Refuges Offer Haven for Puget Sound

Fish," *Fish and Wildlife Science: An On-line Science Magazine* [online], Washington Department of Fish and Game, April 2001. <www.wa.gov/wdfg/science/current/marine_sanctuary.html.> Also M.J. Paddock and J.A. Estes, "Kelp Forest Fish Populations in Marine Reserves and Adjacent Exploited Areas of Central California," *Ecological Applications* 10(3), pp. 855–870.

4. M.J. Tegner and L.A. Levin, "Spiny Lobsters and Sea Urchins: Analysis of a Predator-Prey Interaction," *Journal of Experimental Marine Biology and Ecology* 73, pp. 125–150; R.K. Cowen, "The Effect of Sheephead (*Semicossyphus pulcher*) Predation on Red Sea Urchin (*Strongylocentrotus franciscanus*) Populations: An Experimental Analysis," *Oecologia* 58(2), pp. 249–255.

5. Partnership for Interdisciplinary Studies of Coastal Oceans, *The Science of Marine Reserves*, PISCO [online], 2002. <www.piscoweb.org>

6. P. K. Dayton, M. J. Tegner, et al., "Sliding Baselines, Ghosts, and Reduced Expectations in Kelp Forest Communities," *Ecological Applications* 8(2), pp. 309–322.

7. Partnership for Interdisciplinary Studies of Coastal Oceans, *The Science of Marine Reserves*, PISCO [online], 2002. <www.piscoweb.org>

8. K.D. Lafferty and D. Kushner, "Population Regulation of the Purple Sea Urchin, *Strongylocentrotus purpuratus*, at the California Channel Islands," pp. 379–381 in D.R. Brown, K.L. Mitchell and H.W. Chang, eds., Proceedings of the Fifth California Islands Symposium. Minerals Management Service Publication, 99-0038, 2000.

9. Malcolm Gladwell, *The Tipping Point: How Little Things Can Make a Big Difference*, Little, Brown, 2000.

10. Pew Oceans Commission, *Sustainable Aquaculture: Potential Topics for Recommendations by the Pew Oceans Commission*, 2002. <www.pewocdeans.org/inquiry/fishing/2002/01/31/fishing_23487.asp>

11. United Nations Food and Agriculture Organization, "Shrimp Analysis," UN FAO Globefish Unit [online], 2001. <www.globefish.org>

12. W. Vader, R.T. Barrett, K.E. Erikstad and K.B. Strann, "Differential Responses of Common and Thick-Billed Murres to a Crash in The Capelin Stock in the Southern Barents Sea," *Studies in Avian Biology* Issue 14 (1990), pp. 175–180. W. Vader, T. Anker-Nilssen, V. Bakken, R. Barrett and K.-B. Strann, "Regional

and Temporal Differences in Breeding Success and Population Development of Fisheating Seabirds in Norway After Collapses of Herring and Capelin Stocks," *Transactions of the 19th IUGB Congress*, Trondheim 1989.

13. Oceanic Institute Press Release, "Department of Commerce Awards Funds to Accelerate the Commercialization of Shrimp Aquaculture" [online], November 7, 2001. <www.oceanicinstitute.org/news&info/02ATPaward.html>

14. Worldwide Fund for Nature International, *The Role of Major Groups in Sustainable Oceans and Seas*, Background paper for the Commission on Sustainable Development, Seventh Session, April 1999. United Nations Department of Economic and Social Affairs, Division for Sustainable Development.

15. Worldwide Fund for Nature International, *The Role of Major Groups in Sustainable Oceans and Seas*, Background paper for the Commission on Sustainable Development, Seventh Session, April 1999. United Nations Department of Economic and Social Affairs, Division for Sustainable Development.

16. Population Action International, *Sustaining Water: Population and the Future of Renewable Water Supplies* [online], 1993. <www.cnie.org/pop/pai/h2o-toc.html>

17. Global Programme of Action for the Protection of the Marine Environment from Land-based Activities, [online], framework document for Strategic Action Plan. <www.gpa.unep.org/documents/ihe_cd/introduction.htm>

18. World Summit on Sustainable Development, *Summit Agreement on New Goal to Increase Access to Sanitation* [online]. <www.johannesburgsummit.org/html/whats_new/featurestory>

19. Rachel L. Swarns, "Broad Accord Reached at Global Environment Meeting," *New York Times*, September 4, 2002, Section A, p. 6.

20. National Science and Technology Council, Committee on Environment and Natural Resources, *An Integrated Assessment: Hypoxia in the Northern Gulf of Mexico*, May 2000.

21. P. Falkowski, et al., "The Global Carbon Cycle: A Test of Our Knowledge of the Earth as a System," *Science* 290(5490), pp. 291–296.

22. National Research Council, *Clean Coastal Waters: Understanding and Reducing the Effects of Nutrient Pollution*, Commission on Geosciences, Environment, and Resources, 2000.

23. National Research Council, *Clean Coastal Waters: Understanding and Reducing the Effects of Nutrient Pollution,* Commission on Geosciences, Environment and Resources, 2000.

24. Greg Bloom, "Tijuana's Ecoparque: Decentralized Water Treatment and Reuse," *Frontera NorteSur* [online], May 2001. <www.nmsu.edu/~frontera/may01/feat3.html>

25. H.G. Meyer, "Tijuana Gets Green with Park Fed Recycled Water: Ecoparque Faces Growth Questions," *San Diego Union-Tribune,* July 30, 2001, editorial page.

26. YourHomePlanet Project [online]. <www.yourhomeplanet.com/case_studies/ecohotels/europe/>

27. Coral Reef Alliance [online], <www.coralreefalliance.org/parks/guidelines.html>

28. B.R. Barber, *Jihad vs. McWorld: How Globalism and Tribalism are Reshaping the World,* Ballantine Books, 1996, pp. 268–288.

29. U.S. Environmental Protection Agency [online]. <www.epa.gov/air/aqtrnd01/acidrain.html>

30. Environmental Defense [online]. <www.environmentaldefense.org>

31. Partnership for Climate Action [online]. <www.pca-online.org>

32. *Solutions,* Environmental Defense newsletter, V. 34(1), 2003, pp. 4–5.

33. CNN Interactive, "Millions Left Without Power in West," *U.S. News Story Page* [online], August 10, 1996; CNN Interactive, "Domino Effect" Zapped Power in West," *Sci-Tech Story Page* [online], August 11, 1996. <www.cnn.com>

34. California Energy Commission, *California 2002–2012 Electricity Outlook Report* [online]. <www.energy.ca.gov/reports/2002-06-10_700-01-004F.PDF>

35. Nancy Vogel, "Davis Signs Bill Boosting Clean Energy," *Los Angeles Times,* September 13, 2002, p. B-10.

36. R. Pelc and R.M. Fujita, "Renewable Energy and the Ocean," *Marine Policy* 26(4), pp. 471–479.

Chapter 4. Coral Reefs: The Ocean's Sensitive Child

1. J. Whitfield, "Sewage Casts Pox on Reefs," *Nature,* June 18, 2002.

2. Irish Family Planning Association, *Women and Children First: the ICPD Programme of Action is Working* [online].

<www.ifpa.ie/campaigns/wcf/success.html>

3. World Resources Institute, Sustainable Development Information Service: Global Trends. <www.wri.org/wri/trends/popgrow.html>

4. Clive Wilkinson, *Status of Coral Reefs of the World: 1998*, Global Coral Reef Monitoring Network, 1998. Available from the Australian Institute of Marine Science [online]. <www.aims.gov.au/pages/research/coral-bleaching/scr1998/scr-00.htm>

5. Shifting Baselines website, <www.shiftingbaselines.org>

6. Jeremy Jackson, et al., "Historical Overfishing and the Recent Collapse of Coastal Ecosystems," *Science* 293(5530), pp. 629–634.

7. Ingrid Holmes, "Snail Toxin Could Ease Chronic Pain," *Nature*, July 19, 2002.

8. Andrew Pollack, "Biological Products Raise Genetic Ownership Issues," *New York Times*, November 26, 1999, Section A, p. 1.

9. National Institute of Biodiversity of Costa Rica (INBio) [online]. <www.inbio.ac.cr/en/pdb/prosp.html>

10. Judy Foreman, "Drug Hunters Can't See Rainforest for the Medicines," *Boston Globe* [online], March 27, 2001. <www.boston.com/globe/columns/foreman/archive/032701.htm>

11. Christopher Locke, "Forest Pharmers go Bioprospecting," *Red Herring Magazine* [online], April 12, 2001. <www.redherring.com/mag/issue95/1750018975.html>

12. Industry Intelligence, *Bioprospecting: Raiding Nature's Pharmacy* [online], September 20, 2001. <www.inpharm.com/intelligence/ims031001.html>

13. Judy Foreman, "Drug Hunters Can't See Rainforest for the Medicines," *Boston Globe*, March 27, 2001 [online], <www.boston.com/globe/columns/foreman/archive/032701.htm>

14. Judy Foreman, "Drug Hunters Can't See Rainforest for the Medicines," *Boston Globe* [online], March 27, 2001. <www.boston.com/globe/columns/foreman/archive/032701.htm>

15. Executive Order No. 247, President Fidel Ramos of the Republic of the Philippines [online]. <www.chmbio.org.ph/eo247.html>

16. Andrew Pollack, "Biological Products Raise Genetic Ownership Issues," *New York Times*, November 26, 1999, p. C-1.

17. R.V. Salm, S.E. Smith, and G. Llewellyn, "Mitigating the Impact of Coral Bleaching Through Marine Protected Area Design," pp.

81–88 in Schuttenberg, H.Z. (ed.), *Coral Bleaching: Causes, Consequences and Response*, Ninth International Coral Reef Symposium, 2001. Coastal Management Report No. 2230, Coastal Resources Center, University of Rhode Island.

18. R.V. Salm, S.E. Smith, and G. Llewellyn, "Mitigating the Impact of Coral Bleaching Through Marine Protected Area Design," pp. 81–88 in Schuttenberg, H.Z. (ed.), *Coral Bleaching: Causes, Consequences and Response*, Ninth International Coral Reef Symposium, 2001. Coastal Management Report No. 2230, Coastal Resources Center, University of Rhode Island.

19. Lester R. Brown, "Rising Sea Level Forcing Evacuation of Island Country," *Earth Policy Institute Eco-Economy Updates* [online], November 15, 2001–2.
<www.earth-policy.org/updates/update2.htm>

20. B. Heavner and S. Churchill, *Renewables Work: Job Growth from Renewable Energy Development in California*, CALPIRG Charitable Trust [online], 2002.
<www.calpirg.org/reports/renewableswork.pdf>

21. B. Heavner and S. Churchill, *Renewables Work: Job Growth from Renewable Energy Development in California*, CALPIRG Charitable Trust [online], 2002.
<www.calpirg.org/reports/renewableswork.pdf>

22. Dry Tortugas Ecological Reserve, Proposal B, Florida Keys National Marine Sanctuary, USA [online].
<www.panda.org/resources/publications/water/mpreserves/eco_drytort.htm>

23. National Research Council, "Consequences of Everglades Restoration for Florida Bay are Uncertain," National Research Council press release [online], August 8, 2002.
<www.nationalacademies.org/news.nsf>

24. *Life in Early Hawai'i: The Ahupua'a*, Kamehameha Schools Press, Third Edition, 1994. E.S. Craighill Handy and Elizabeth Green Handy, *Native Planters in Old Hawaii*, Bernice P. Bishop Museum Bulletin 233, Bishop Museum Press, Honolulu, Hawaii. Revised Edition, 1991.

25. Margaret Titcomb, *Native Use of Fish in Hawaii*, University of Hawaii Press, 1972.

26. David Malo, *Hawaiian Antiquities*, Bishop Museum Press, 1898.

27. Margaret Titcomb, *Native Use of Fish in Hawaii*, University of Hawaii Press, 1972.

28. David Starr Jordan and B.W. Evermann, *The Fishes and Fisheries of the Hawaiian Islands,* A Preliminary Report to the U.S. Commission for 1901, 1902.

Chapter 5. The Continental Shelf: The Ocean's Engine

1. National Marine Fisheries Service, *Status of Fisheries of the United States.* Report to Congress, 2000.

2. T.D. Marsh, M.W. Beck, and S.E. Reisewitz, *Leasing and Restoration of Submerged Lands: Strategies for Community-based, Watershed-scale Conservation.* The Nature Conservancy, Arlington, Virginia USA, 2002.

3. For a review, see National Academy of Sciences (National Research Council), *Sharing the Fish: Toward a National Policy on Individual Fishing Quotas,* National Academies Press, 1999.

Chapter 6. The Shape of the Sea

1. K.D. Hyrenbach, K.A. Forney, and P.K. Dayton, "Marine Protected Areas and Ocean Basin Management," *Aquatic Conservation: Marine and Freshwater Ecosystems* 10(6), pp. 437–458.

2. R.W. Owen, "Eddies of the California Current System: Physical and Ecological Characteristics," in D.M. Power (ed.), *California Islands: Proceedings of a Multidisciplinary Symposium,* Santa Barbara Museum of Natural History (1980), pp. 237–263.

3. K.D. Hyrenbach, K.A. Forney, and P.K. Dayton, "Marine Protected Areas and Ocean Basin Management," *Aquatic Conservation: Marine and Freshwater Ecosystems* 10(6), pp. 437–458.

4. United Nations Food and Agriculture Organization, *The State of World Fisheries and Aquaculture* [online]. <www.fao.org/DOCREP/003/>

5. H. Weimerskirch and R.P. Wilson, "Oceanic Respite for Wandering Albatrosses," *Nature* 406(6799), p. 955.

6. B.A. Block, H. Dewar, S.B. Blackwell, T.D. Williams, E.D. Prince, C.J. Farwell, A. Boustany, S.L.H. Teo, A. Seitz, A. Walli, and D. Fudge, "Migratory Movements, Depth Preferences, and Thermal Biology of Atlantic Bluefin Tuna," *Science* 293(5533), pp. 1310–1314.

7. Elizabeth A. Hayes, *A Review of the Southern Bluefin Tuna Fishery: Implications for Ecologically Sustainable Management* [online], TRAFFIC Oceania 1997. <www.traffic.org/factfile/tuna_summary.html>

8. Commission for the Conservation of Southern Bluefin Tuna [online]. <www.ccsbt.org/docs/management.html>

9. International Commission for the Conservation of Atlantic Tunas, Report 2000–2001 [online]. <www.iccat.es/documents/BET.pdf>

10. Robin Allen, *Review of the Status of Bigeye Tuna in the Eastern Pacific Ocean*, Inter-American Tropical Tuna Commission Scientific Working Group 2000 [online]. <www.iattc.org/PDF_Files>

11. National Research Council, *Effectiveness and Impact of Corporate Average Fuel Economy Standards*, National Academies Press, 2002.

12. Family Health International, *Behavior Change: A Summary of Four Major Theories* [online]. <www.fhi.org/en/aids/aidscap/aidspubs/behres/bcr4theo.html>

13. Dayton L. Alverson, M.H. Freeberg, and S.A. Murawski, *A Global Assessment of Fisheries Bycatch and Discards*, United Nations Food and Agriculture Organization Technical Paper 339, 1996.

14. D. Pauly, V. Christensen, J. Dalsgaard, R. Froese, F. Torres, Jr., "Fishing Down Marine Food Webs," *Science* 279(5352), pp. 860–863.

15. D. Pauly, V. Christensen, S. Guenette, T.J. Pitcher, U.R. Sumaila, C.J. Walters, R. Watson, and D. Zeller, "Towards Sustainability in World Fisheries," *Nature* 418(6898), pp. 689–695.

16. P. Weber, *Abandoned Seas: Reversing the Decline of the Oceans*, Worldwatch Paper (1993) 116, p. 14.

17. J.P. Barry, C.H. Baxter, R.D. Sagarin, and S.E. Gilman, "Climate-related, Long-term Faunal Changes in a California Rocky Intertidal Community," *Science* 267(5198), pp. 672–675.

18. D. Roemmich and J. McGowan, "Climatic Warming and the Decline of Zooplankton in the California Current," *Science* 267(5202), pp. 1324–1326.

19. United States National Assessment Synthesis Team, U.S. Global Change Research Program, *Climate Change Impacts on the United States: The Potential Consequences of Climate Variability and Change: Overview – Coastal Areas and Marine Resources* [online]. <www.usgcrp.gov/usgcrp/Library/nationalassessment/overview-coastal.htm>

20. National Aeronautic and Space Administration, Pacific Decadal Oscillation, Ocean Surface Topography from Space [online]. <http://topex-www.jpl.nasa.gov/science/pdo.html>

21. V.S. Kennedy, R.R. Twilley, J.A. Kleypas, J.H. Cowman, Jr., and S.R. Hare, *Coastal and Marine Ecosystems and Global Climate Change: Potential Effects on U.S. Resources*, Pew Center on Global Climate Change, 2002.

22. E. Buck, *Acoustic Thermometry of Ocean Climate: Marine Mammal Issues*, Congressional Research Service Report for Congress, 95-603 ENR, 1995.

23. E. Buck, *Acoustic Thermometry of Ocean Climate: Marine Mammal Issues*, Congressional Research Service Report for Congress, 95-603 ENR, 1995.

24. Ocean Research Foundation, *Acoustic Thermometry of Ocean Climate* [online], Spring 1998. <www.orf.org/PDFs/spring.pdf>

25. The formal name of the agreement is the United Nations Agreement for the Implementation of the Provisions of the United Nations Convention on the Law of the Sea of 10 December 1982 Relating to the Conservation and Management of Straddling Fish Stocks and Highly Migratory Fish Stocks [online]. <www.un.org/Depts/los/convention_agreements/convention_overview_fish_stocks.htm>

26. United Nations Food and Agriculture Organization Press Release 98/62, *FAO Calls For Strict Management Of Fishing Capacity — International Agreement Proposes Concrete Actions* [online], 1998. <www.fao.org/WAICENT/OIS/PRESS_NE/PRES-SENG/1998/pren9862.htm>

27. United Nations Food and Agriculture Organization Press Release 98/62, *FAO Calls For Strict Management Of Fishing Capacity - International Agreement Proposes Concrete Actions* [online], 1998. <www.fao.org/WAICENT/OIS/PRESS_NE/PRES-SENG/1998/pren9862.htm>

28. World Wildlife Fund, *Hard Facts, Hidden Problems: A Review of the Current Data on Fishing Subsidies*, WWF Technical Report [online], 2002. <www.panda.org/downloads/marine/Hard_Facts_Hidden_Problem_rev2.doc>

29. World Wildlife Fund, *Hard Facts, Hidden Problems: A Review of the Current Data on Fishing Subsidies*, WWF Technical Report [online], 2002. <www.panda.org/downloads/marine/Hard_Facts_Hidden_Problem_rev2.doc>

30. United Nations Food and Agriculture Organization (FAO). Report of the Consultation on the Management of Fishing

Capacity, Shark Fisheries and Incidental Catch of Seabirds in Longline Fisheries. Rome, Italy, 26–30 October 1998. *FAO Fisheries Report*, No. 593, Rome, FAO, 1998.

31. World Wildlife Fund, *Hard Facts, Hidden Problems: A Review of the Current Data on Fishing Subsidies*, WWF Technical Report, 2002, [online]. <www.panda.org/downloads/marine/Hard_Facts_Hidden_Proble m_rev2.doc>

32. E.F. Melvin, J. Parrish, K.S. Dietrich, and O.S. Hamel, *Solutions to Seabird Bycatch in Alaska's Demersal Longline Fishery*, U.S. National Marine Fisheries Service Report No. 99-AKR-023, 2001.

33. A.K. Kalmer, R.M. Fujita, and C.F. Wurster, *Seabird Bycatch in Longline Fisheries*. Background paper for the meeting of the World Conservation Union of the IUCN – the World Conservation Union – in Montreal, 14–23 October 1996. Available from Environmental Defense, 5655 College Avenue, Oakland California 94618 USA.

34. United Nations Law of the Sea Conference [online]. <www.un.org/Depts/los/fish_stocks_conference/fish_stocks_conf erence.htm>

35. Tony Bartelme, "Tragedy of the seas: Technology, Competition Swamp Fisheries," *Charleston Post and Courier* [online], June 23, 1996. <http://archives.charleston.net/fish/fish1.html>

36. From the Convention for the Conservation and Management of Highly Migratory Fish Stocks in the Western and Central Pacific Ocean: "all waters of the Pacific Ocean bounded to the south and to the east by a line drawn from the south coast of Australia due south along the 141° meridian of east longitude to its intersection with the 55° parallel of south latitude; thence due east along the 55° parallel of south latitude to its intersection with the 150° meridian of east longitude; thence due south along the 150° meridian of east longitude to its intersection with the 60° parallel of south latitude; thence due east along the 60° parallel of south latitude to its intersection with the 130° meridian of west longitude; thence due north along the 130° meridian of west longitude to its intersection with the 4° parallel of south latitude; thence due west along the 4° parallel of south latitude to its intersection with the 150° meridian of west longitude; thence due north along the 150° meridian of west longitude."

37. Convention for the Conservation and Management of Highly Migratory Fish Stocks in the Western and Central Pacific Ocean, Section 7, Article 22, [online].

· <www.ocean-affairs.com/pdf/text.pdf>

38. K. Miller, G. Munro, R. McKelvey, and P. Tyedmers, "Climate, Uncertainty, and the Pacific Salmon Treaty: Insights on the Harvest Management Game," IIFET 2000 Proceedings [online], 2000. <www.esig.ucar.edu/HP_miller/pubs/267.pdf>

39. D. Pauly, V. Christensen, S. Guénette, T.J. Pitcher, U.R. Sumaila, C.J. Walters, R. Watson and D. Zeller, "Towards Sustainability in World Fisheries," *Nature* 418(6898), pp. 689–695.

40. Dayton L. Alverson, M.H. Freeberg, and S.A. Murawski, *A Global Assessment of Fisheries Bycatch and Discards,* United Nations Food and Agriculture Organization Technical Paper 339, 1996.

41. National Marine Fisheries Service, *Reducing Dolphin Mortality in the ETP Tuna Purse Seine Fishery* [online]. <www.nmfs.noaa.ogov/prot_res/readingrm/tunadolphin/time-line.pdf>

42. S. Norris, "Thinking Like an Ocean," *Conservation in Practice* 3(4), pp. 16–17.

43. National Marine Fisheries Service. *Reducing Dolphin Mortality in the ETP Tuna Purse Seine Fishery* [online]. <www.nmfs.noaa.ogov/prot_res/readingrm/tunadolphin/time-line.pdf>

44. Interamerican Tropical Tuna Commission [online]. <www.iattc.org>

45. Dayton L. Alverson, M.H. Freeberg, and S.A. Murawski, *A Global Assessment of Fisheries Bycatch and Discards,* United Nations Food and Agriculture Organization Technical Paper 339, 1996.

46. S. Norris, "Thinking Like an Ocean," *Conservation in Practice* 3(4), p. 12.

47. Nina Young, *Protecting Dolphins and the Ocean Ecosystem,* Center for Marine Conservation Statement before the Subcommittee on Oceans and Fisheries, Senate Commerce, Science, and Transportation Committee [online], April 30, 1996. <www.environmentaldefense.org/documents>

48. Federal Register 64(88), pp. 24590–24592

49. Southwest Fisheries Center of the National Marine Fisheries Service, *Report to Congress,* 25 March 1999, U.S. National Oceanic and Atmospheric Administration, U.S. Department of Commerce.

50. Congressional Research Service, *Commercial Fisheries: Economic Aid and Capacity Reduction II,* CRS Report 97-441 ENR, 1997.

51. T. Day, *Oceans,* Facts on File, 1999.

52. National Wildlife Federation, *Endangered Sea Turtles are Affected by International Trade Disputes* [online].
    <www.nwf.org/trade/seaturtles.html>

53. B.R. Barber, *Jihad vs. McWorld,* Ballantine Books, 1996.

Chapter 7. The Deep Sea: In Over Our Heads?

1. H.V. Thurman, and A.P. Trujillo, *Essentials of Oceanography,* 6th Ed., Prentice Hall, 1999.

2. P. Herring, *The Biology of the Deep Ocean,* Oxford University Press, 2002.

3. B. Robison and J. Connor, *The Deep Sea,* Monterey Aquarium Press, 1999.

4. A.C. Duxbury, A.B. Duxbury, and K.A. Svedrup, *An Introduction to the World's Oceans,* 6th Ed., McGraw-Hill, 2000.

5. A.C. Duxbury, A.B. Duxbury, and K.A. Svedrup, *An Introduction to the World's Oceans,* 6th Ed., McGraw-Hill, 2000.

6. T. Day, *Oceans,* Facts on File, 1999.

7. H.V. Thurman and A.P. Trujillo, *Essentials of Oceanography,* 6th Ed., Prentice Hall, 1999.

8. A.C. Duxbury, A.B. Duxbury, and K.A. Svedrup, *An Introduction to the World's Oceans,* 6th Ed., McGraw-Hill, 2000.

9. K. Kaoma Mwenda, "Deep Sea-bed Mining Under Customary International Law," *Murdoch University Electronic Journal of Law* 7(2), June 2000.

10. Marjorie Ann Brown, *The Law of the Sea Convention and U.S. Policy.* Congressional Research Service Issue Brief for Congress IB95010 [online], 2001.
    <www.ncseonline.org/NLE/CRSreports/Marine/mar-16.cfm>

11. P. Herring, *The Biology of the Deep Ocean,* Oxford University Press, 2002.

12. J. Halfar and R.M. Fujita, "Precautionary Management of Deep Sea Mining," *Marine Policy* 26(2), pp. 103–106.

13. J. Halfar and R.M. Fujita, "Precautionary Management of Deep Sea Mining," *Marine Policy* 26(2), pp. 103–106.

14. A.C. Duxbury, A.B. Duxbury, and K.A. Svedrup, *An Introduction to the World's Oceans,* 6th Ed., McGraw-Hill, 2000.

15. J. Halfar and R.M. Fujita, "Precautionary Management of Deep Sea Mining," *Marine Policy* 26(2): 103–106.

16. P. Herring, *The Biology of the Deep Ocean*, Oxford University Press, 2002.

17. B. Gaylord, "Mining Undersea Gold: Companies are Preparing to Tackle Mining's Next Frontier — Mineral Rich Deposits on the Ocean Floor," *Far Eastern Economic Review*, June 22, 2000, page 42.

18. A.C. Duxbury, A.B. Duxbury, and K.A. Svedrup, *An Introduction to the World's Oceans*, 6th Ed., McGraw-Hill, 2000.

19. T. Day, *Oceans*, Facts on File, 1999.

20. T. Day, *Oceans*, Facts on File, 1999.

21. F. Pearce,, "Green Foundations," *New Scientist* 13 July 2002, pp. 39–40.

22. H.V. Thurman and A.P. Trujillo, *Essentials of Oceanography*, 6th Ed., Prentice Hall, 1999.

23. H.V. Thurman and A.P. Trujillo, *Essentials of Oceanography*, 6th Ed., Prentice Hall, 1999.

24. T. Day, *Oceans*, Facts on File, 1999.

25. World Wildlife Fund, *Hard Facts, Hidden Problems: A Review of the Current Data on Fishing Subsidies*, WWF Technical Report [online], 2002. <www.panda.org/downloads/marine/Hard_Facts_Hidden_Probl em_rev2.doc>

26. Transcript of the Report by Maurice F. Strong, Chairman of the Earth Council and Rio+5 Forum presented to the United Nations Commission on Sustainable Development Special Ministerial Session, April 8, 1997.

27. G. Porter and Janet Welsh Brown, *Global Environmental Politics*, 2nd Ed., Westview Press, 1996.

28. G. Porter and Janet Welsh Brown, *Global Environmental Politics*, 2nd Ed., Westview Press, 1996.

29. P.M. Morrisette, "The Evolution of Policy Responses to Stratospheric Ozone Depletion," *Natural Resources Journal* 29: 793–820.

30. G. Porter and Janet Welsh Brown, *Global Environmental Politics*, 2nd Ed., Westview Press, 1996.

31. G. Porter and Janet Welsh Brown, *Global Environmental Politics*,

2nd Ed., Westview Press, 1996.

32. H. French, *From Rio to Johannesburg and Beyond: Assessing the Summit*, Worldwatch Institute, World Summit Policy Brief number 12, 2002.

33. G. Porter and Janet Welsh Brown, *Global Environmental Politics*, 2nd Ed., Westview Press, 1996.

Chapter 8. Creating a New Ocean Ethic

1. J. Benyas, *Biomimicry: Innovation Inspired by Nature*, William Morrow, 1997.

2. Population Research Bureau *2002 World Population Datasheet* [online]. <www.prb.org>

3. R. Pelc and R.M. Fujita, "Renewable Energy and the Ocean," *Marine Policy* 26(4), pp. 471–479.

4. National Oceanic and Atmospheric Administration, National Marine Fisheries Service Office of Enforcement, *Vessel Monitoring Systems* [online]. <www.nmfs.noaa.gov/ole/vms.html>

5. Canada-South Pacific Ocean Development Program Press Release [online], March 13, 2001.
<www.c-spodp.org/Press percent20Releases/03_13_01.htm>

6. National Oceanic and Atmospheric Administration, National Marine Fisheries Service Office of Enforcement, *Vessel Monitoring Systems* [online]. <www.nmfs.noaa.gov/ole/vms.html>

7. European Space Agency, "TESO: Helping to Safeguard the Environment," *European Space Agency News* [online], 8 April 2002. <www.esa.int/export/esaCP/ESA34FUTYWC_index_0.html>

8. Dow Chemical Company vs. U.S. (106 S. Ct. 1819).

9. J.A. Schumpeter, *Capitalism, Socialism and Democracy*, Harper, 1975 [original pub. 1942], pp. 82–85.

10. Malcolm Gladwell, *The Tipping Point: How Little Things Can Make a Big Difference*, Little, Brown, 2000. See also C. Haney, W.C. Banks, and P.G. Zimbardo, "Interpersonal Dynamics in a Simulated Prison," *International Journal of Criminology and Penology* 1, pp. 69–97.

11. Deborah Du Nann Winter, "Some Big Ideas for Some Big Problems," *American Psychologist* 55(5), pp. 516–522.

12. Malcolm Gladwell, *The Tipping Point: How Little Things Can Make a Big Difference*, Little, Brown, 2000.

13. E.O. Wilson, *The Future of Life*, Alfred A. Knopf, 2002, p. 156.

14. E.O. Wilson, *The Future of Life*, Alfred A. Knopf, 2002, p. 156.

15. Cited in S. Sivaraksa, "True Development," in A.H. Badiner, ed., *Dharma Gaia*, Parallax Press, 1990, p. 177.

16. Cited in J. Hayward, "Ecology and the Experience of Sacredness," in A.H. Badiner, ed., *Dharma Gaia*, Parallax Press, 1990, p. 64.

17. Cited in J. Macy, "The Greening of the Self," in A.H. Badiner, ed., *Dharma Gaia*, Parallax Press, 1990, p. 62.

18. Alice Calaprice, *The Expanded Quotable Einstein*, Princeton University Press, 2000, p. 267.

19. S. Begley, "Your Brain or Religion? Mystic Visions or Brain Circuits at Work?," *Newsweek*, May 7, 2001, p. 50.

20. S. Begley, "Your Brain or Religion? Mystic Visions or Brain Circuits at Work?," *Newsweek*, May 7, 2001, p. 50.

21. E.O. Wilson, *The Future of Life*, Alfred A. Knopf, 2002, p. 156.

CONTACTS AND RESOURCES

Organizations

Blue Ocean Institute
250 Lawrence Hill Road
Cold Spring Harbor, NY 11724
Phone: 1-877-BOI-SEAS
Email: info@blueoceaninstitute.org
Website: <www.blueoceaninstitute.org>

Bluewater Network
311 California, Suite 510
San Francisco, CA 94104
Phone: (415) 544-0790
Fax: (415) 544-0796
E-mail: blewater@bluewaternetwork.org
Website: <www.bluewaternetwork.org>

Center for Coastal Studies
Scripps Institution of Oceanography
University of California, San Diego
La Jolla, CA 92093-0209
Phone: (619) 534-4333
Fax: (619)534-0300
Website: <www-ccs.ucsd.edu>

Coral Reef Alliance
417 Montgomery Street, Suite 205
San Francisco, CA 94104
Phone: (415) 834-0900
1(888) CORAL-REEF
Fax: 415-834-0999
E-mail: info@coral.org
Website: <www.coralreefalliance.org>

Defenders of Wildlife
National Headquarters
1101 14th Street, NW, #1400
Washington, DC 20005
Phone: (202) 682-9400
E-mail: info@defenders.org
Website: <www.defenders.org>

Earthwatch Institute
3 Clock Tower Place, Suite 100
Box 75
Maynard, MA 01754
Phone: 1(800)-776-0188
Fax: (978) 461-2332
E-mail : info@earthwatch.org
Website: <www.earthwatch.org>

Environmental Defense
257 Park Avenue South
New York, NY 10010
Phone: (212) 505-2100
Fax: (212) 505-2375
Email: members@environmentaldefense.org
Website: <www.environmentaldefense.org>

Heal the Ocean
1129 State Street #26
Santa Barbara, CA 93101
Mail: P.O. Box 90106
Santa Barbara, CA 93190
Phone: (805)965-7570
Fax: (805) 962-0651
E-mail: info@healtheocean.org
Website: <www.healtheocean.org>

Marine Conservation Biology Institute (MCBI)
15805 NE 47th Court
Redmond, WA 98052
Phone: (425)883-8914
Fax: (425)883-3017
E-mail: mcbiweb@mcbi.org
Website: <www.mcbi.org>

National Marine Fisheries Service (NMFS)
NOAA Fisheries
1315 East West Highway, SSMC3
Silver Spring, MD 20910
Phone: (301) 713-2334
Fax: (301) 713-0596
Website: <www.nmfs.noaa.gov>

National Marine Sanctuaries
NOAA's National Marine Sanctuaries
1305 East-West Highway, 11th Floor
Silver Spring, MD 20910
Phone: (301) 713-3125
Fax: (301) 713-0404
E-mail: sanctuaries@noaa.gov
Website: <www.sanctuaries.noaa.gov>

National Oceanic and Atmospheric Administration (NOAA)
14th Street & Constitution Avenue, NW
Room 6217
Washington, DC 20230
Phone: (202) 482-6090
Fax: (202) 482-3154
E-mail: amswers@noaa.gov
Website: <www.noaa.gov>

National Sea Grant Program
Sea Grant National Media Relations Office
National Sea Grant College Program
1315 East-West Highway
SSMC3, #11460
Silver Spring, MD 20910
Phone: (301)713-2483
E-mail: Amy.Painter@noaa.gov
Website: <www.nsgo.seagrant.org>

Natural Resources Defense Council
40 West 20th Street
New York, NY 10011
Phone: (212) 727-2700
Fax: (212) 727-1773
E-mail: nrdcinfo@nrdc.org
Website: <www.nrdc.org>

The Ocean Conservancy
1725 DeSales Street NW, Suite 600
Washington, DC 20036
Phone: (202) 429-5609
Fax: (202) 872-0619
Website: <www.oceanconservancy.org>

Ocean Futures Society
325 Chapala Street
Santa Barbara, CA 93101
Phone: (805) 899-8899
E-mail: contact@oceanfutures.org
Website: <www.oceanfutures.org>

Ocean Wilderness Network
202 San Jose Avenue
Capitola, CA 95010
Phone: (831) 462-2550
Fax: (831) 462-2542
E-mail: info@oceanwildernessnetwork.org
Website: <www.oceanwildernessnetwork.org>

Oceana
2501 M Street NW, Suite 300
Washington, D.C. 20037-1311
Phone: (202) 833-3900
Fax: (202) 833-2070
E-mail: info@oceana.org
Website: <www.oceana.org>

REEF Environmental Education Foundation
P.O. Box 246
Key Largo, FL 33037
Phone: (305)852-0030
Fax: (305)852-0301
E-mail: reefhq@reef.org
Website: <www.reef.org>

Seafood Choices Alliance
1731 Connecticut Ave. NW, 4th Floor
Washington, DC 20009
Phone: 1 (866) 732-6673 (toll-free)
E-mail: info@seafoodchoices.com
Website: <www.seafoodchoices.com>
SeaWeb
1731 Connecticut Ave. NW, 4th Floor
Washington, DC 20009
Phone:(202) 483-9570
E-mail: seaweb@seaweb.org
Website: <www.seaweb.org>

Shifting Baselines.org
Website reviews current threats to the ocean, from coral reef death to
kelp forest overfishing to global fisheries depletion.
E-mail: info@shiftingbaslines.org
Website: <www.shiftingbaslines.org>

Surfrider Foundation USA
P.O. Box 6010
San Clemente, CA 92674-6010
Phone: (949) 492-8170
Fax: (949) 492-8142
E-mail: info@surfrider.org
Website: <www.surfrider.org>

Woods Hole Oceanographic Institute
93 Water Street, MS #16
Woods Hole, MA 02543
Phone: (508) 289-2252
E-mail: information@whoi.edu
Website: <www.whoi.edu/home>

World Wildlife Fund
1250 24th St. NW
Washington, DC 20037
Phone: 202-243-4800
E-mail: PIResponse@wwfns.org
Website: <www.worldwildlife.org>

Books

Blue Frontier: Saving America's Living Seas
by David Helvarg, Owl Books, 2002

Eye of the Albatross: Views of the Endangered Sea
by Carl Safina, Henry Holt & Company, Inc., 2002
Oceans 2020: Science, Trends, and the Challenge of Sustainability
by J.G. Field, G. Hempel, and C.P. Summerhayes, Island Press, 2002

Oceans End: Travels through Endangered Seas
by Colin Woodard, Basic Books, 2001

Seafood Lover's Almanac
Edited by Mercedes Lee. Contributors: Suzanne Iudicello and Carl
Safina, Audobon's Living Oceans, 2000

Sea Change: A Message of the Oceans
by Sylvia A. Earle, Fawcett Books, 1996

*Song for the Blue Ocean: Encounters Along the World's Coasts and
Beneath the Seas* by Carl Safina, Owl Books, 1999

Videos/DVDs

The Blue Planet: Seas of Life (Parts 1–4) (video/DVD)
David Attenborough, BBC Videos, 392 minutes, 2002.

Empty Oceans, Empty Nets (video)
Director Steve Cowan, produced by Habitat Media, 55 minutes,
2002. Originally shown on PBS.

Keepers of the Coast (video)
Michael Graber, Diana Schulz, Michael Graber Productions, 31 minutes, 1996.

The Living Sea (video/DVD)
Greg MacGillivraym, Image Entertainment, 39 minutes, 2000.

Silent Sentinels (video)
Richard Smith, Australian Broadcasting Corporation, 57 minutes,
1999.

INDEX

ABOUT THE AUTHOR

ROD FUJITA is a Senior Scientist at Environmental Defense in Oakland, California. He obtained his doctorate in marine ecology in 1985 from the Boston University Marine Program at the Marine Biological Laboratory in Woods Hole, Massachusetts, one of the world's premier marine research centers.

Dr. Fujita joined Environmental Defense's staff in 1988 where he has worked on a wide variety of issues, including acid rain, ozone depletion, global climate change, and protecting marine ecosystems. He was an advisor to the Intergovernmental Panel on Climate Change (IPCC) and to nongovernmental organizations in efforts leading up to the signing of the Framework Convention on Climate Change at the Earth Summit in Rio de Janeiro, and helped to develop the award winning Environmental Defense-American Museum of Natural History exhibition *Global Warming: Understanding the Forecast*, which toured the U.S.

Dr. Fujita's focus is on understanding and protecting the ocean. As a member of Environmental Defense's multidisciplinary Oceans Program team, Fujita leads efforts to create sustainable fisheries along the Pacific coast of the U.S. He is currently working to stop overfishing, to transform failing fisheries into profitable ones, and to create networks of marine reserves that protect marine biodiversity and ecosystem health. He has played a lead role in establishing the Florida Keys National Marine Sanctuary, has worked to establish one of the world's first science-based networks of marine reserves around California's Channel Islands, and has helped develop the Monterey Bay Aquarium's exhibition *Fishing for Solutions*. He also lectures widely, and is the author of numerous peer-reviewed publications, reports, and popular articles.

An appointee to many state and federal commissions and review panels, he was recently appointed to the National Marine Protected Areas Advisory Committee. In 2000, Dr. Fujita was awarded a Pew Fellowship in Marine Conservation to explore emerging issues in marine conservation, and to write *Heal the Ocean*.

PHOTO BY JOYCE SELKOW

If you have enjoyed *Heal The Ocean*,
you might also enjoy other

BOOKS TO BUILD A NEW SOCIETY

Our books provide positive solutions for people who want to
make a difference. We specialize in:

Sustainable Living • Ecological Design and Planning
Natural Building & Appropriate Technology • New Forestry
Environment and Justice • Conscientious Commerce
Progressive Leadership • Resistance and Community • Nonviolence
Educational and Parenting Resources

New Society Publishers

ENVIRONMENTAL BENEFITS STATEMENT

New Society Publishers has chosen to produce this book on Enviro recycled
paper made with 100% post consumer waste, processed chlorine free, and
old growth free.

For every 5,000 books printed, New Society saves the following resources:[1]

30	Trees
2,728	Pounds of Solid Waste
3,002	Gallons of Water
3,916	Kilowatt Hours of Electricity
4,960	Pounds of Greenhouse Gases
21	Pounds of HAPs, VOCs, and AOX Combined
8	Cubic Yards of Landfill Space

[1]Environmental benefits are calculated based on research done by the Environmental Defense Fund and
other members of the Paper Task Force who study the environmental impacts of the paper industry.
For more information on this environmental benefits statement, or to inquire about environmentally
friendly papers, please contact New Leaf Paper – info@newleafpaper.com Tel: 888 • 989 • 5323.

For a full list of NSP's titles, please call **1-800-567-6772** *or check out our web site at:*

www.newsociety.com

NEW SOCIETY PUBLISHERS

4563   50